Marx on Campus

Historical Materialism Book Series

The Historical Materialism Book Series is a major publishing initiative of the radical left. The capitalist crisis of the twenty-first century has been met by a resurgence of interest in critical Marxist theory. At the same time, the publishing institutions committed to Marxism have contracted markedly since the high point of the 1970s. The Historical Materialism Book Series is dedicated to addressing this situation by making available important works of Marxist theory. The aim of the series is to publish important theoretical contributions as the basis for vigorous intellectual debate and exchange on the left.

The peer-reviewed series publishes original monographs, translated texts, and reprints of classics across the bounds of academic disciplinary agendas and across the divisions of the left. The series is particularly concerned to encourage the internationalization of Marxist debate and aims to translate significant studies from beyond the English-speaking world.

For a full list of titles in the Historical Materialism Book Series available in paperback from Haymarket Books, visit:
https://www.haymarketbooks.org/series_collections/1-historical-materialism

Marx on Campus

A Short History of the Marburg School

Lothar Peter

Translated by
Loren Balhorn

Haymarket Books
Chicago, IL

First published in 2019 by Brill Academic Publishers, The Netherlands
© 2019 Koninklijke Brill NV, Leiden, The Netherlands

Published in paperback in 2020 by
Haymarket Books
P.O. Box 180165
Chicago, IL 60618
773-583-7884
www.haymarketbooks.org

ISBN: 978-1-64259-336-5

Distributed to the trade in the US through Consortium Book Sales and
Distribution (www.cbsd.com) and internationally through Ingram
Publisher Services International (www.ingramcontent.com).

This book was published with the generous support of Lannan
Foundation and Wallace Action Fund.

Special discounts are available for bulk purchases by organizations and
institutions. Please call 773-583-7884 or email info@haymarketbooks.org
for more information.

Cover design by Jamie Kerry and Ragina Johnson.

Printed in the United States.

10 9 8 7 6 5 4 3 2 1

Library of Congress Cataloging-in-Publication data is available.

In memory of Wolfgang Abendroth, Werner Hofmann, and Heinz Maus

Contents

Preface

The English-language publication of *Marx on Campus* gives me the opportunity to revise the book's preface. The original German edition has been met with a remarkable reception since first appearing in 2014, as reflected in the ongoing series of reviews in publications such as *Blätter für deutsche und internationale Politik*, *Das Argument*, and others up to and including the *Frankfurter Allgemeine Zeitung*.[1] I also held quite a few lectures on the topic and received countless letters and emails from people who were personally involved with the Marburg School at some point in their lives.

Marx on Campus clearly satisfied an existing desire to learn more not only about the history of mainstream social science, but also about non-conformist, alternative, and specifically socialist and Marxist currents in the social sciences at German universities. This is true not only for Germany itself but also for readers outside of the country, who likely associate critical and Marxist theory from the German-speaking world with the Frankfurt School of Max Horkheimer, Theodor W. Adorno, and Jürgen Habermas. The Marburg School by contrast embodies a wholly different type of relationship between critical theory and political praxis. The Marburg intellectuals were stubbornly dedicated to grasping scientific analysis and critique as the precondition and means of practical change to exploitative and oppressive social relations, and to seeking out collective actors capable of effecting these changes. In doing so the protagonists and supporters of the Marburg School saw themselves as political actors in the movements and struggles of their time, staking out a position in the national academic field clearly distinct from competing intellectual currents and schools. The wide-ranging public attacks against them were rooted in the nature of things, so to speak, that is in the reality that academic scholarship is not just a privilege to be enjoyed from the ivory tower, but is rather inevitably implicated in the opposing interests and conflicts of the society in which it is conducted.

Although the Marburg School exerted considerable influence beyond the borders of the provincial university town of Marburg an der Lahn in the second half of the twentieth century, its existence has largely been forgotten – a victim, if you will, of discursive-historical amnesia. This slim volume seeks to remedy that circumstance by describing for the reader how the Marburg School helped to keep the critique of capitalism and society alive during a period in (West)

---

1 Weiß 2015; Sorg 2014; Jäger 2014.

German history when such critique earned its proponents more outrage, scorn, and rejection than it did reputation or public recognition. Through fortunate coincidence it just so happens that Wolfgang Abendroth's long out-of-print *A Short History of the European Working Class,* one of precious few Marburg School works available in English, is to be reissued this year by Verso Books.[2] I hope that my book, together with the reprinting of Abendroth's classic, will make a small contribution to introducing this particular school of thought to a new generation of Marxist thinkers.

I feel inextricably linked to this Marburg School and owe to it a great deal of crucial intellectual and political impulses and experiences. After all, I lived in Marburg for ten years and was involved in many of the current's discussions, conflicts, and political projects. For that reason I feel capable of giving an overview of its development, contributions, and limitations without collapsing into hagiography, but also without denying my own personal proximity to the subject at hand.

Numerous individuals whose scholarly activity was connected to the Marburg School in some way, many of whom still see themselves as its representatives, read the manuscript or at least parts of it before its publication. That said, not everyone who worked as a political scientist or sociologist at the University of Marburg and held left-wing, socialist, or Marxist (that is to say, historical materialist) views identifies with what I depict in this book as the 'Marburg School'. Indeed, the manuscript provoked quite mixed reactions ranging from harsh rejection to informative commentaries, useful tips and additions, all the way to friendly support for the project, albeit sometimes with critical objections here and there.

As the author, for me working on the text also represented the kind of dual self-reflection Pierre Bourdieu called for in social-scientific praxis. Accordingly, I attempted to remain critically aware of the connotations of the theorems and concepts I used as well as reflect on my own position in the academic field. That said, I do not wish to deny that I also wrote the book in order to give expression to the memories tying me to the fortunes of the Marburg School.

The list of those who supported my project would be too long if I were to name them all, but that does not make my gratitude any less sincere. I thank PapyRossa Verlag for its support and assistance in completing the book, and the Historical Materialism Book Series for making it accessible to a global readership. I would also like to extend my thanks to the Dr. Heinz-Jung-Stiftung in Frankfurt am Main and the Stiftung für Sozialgeschichte des 20. Jahrhunderts

---

2 Abendroth 2019.

in Bremen for their generous financial support. Last but not least I thank Ingar Solty for his new introduction to the English edition and Loren Balhorn for taking on the translation with skill and dedication.

Lothar Peter
Bremen, Germany
February 2019

Abbreviations

ADF	*Aktion Demokratischer Fortschritt*
	(Democratic Progress Action)
AgF	*Arbeitsgemeinschaft für gewerkschaftliche Fragen*
	(Working Group for Trade Union Questions)
APO	*Außerparlamentarische Opposition*
	(Extra-Parliamentary Opposition)
BDW	*Bund demokratischer Wissenschaftler*
BdWi	*Bund demokratischer Wissenschaftlerinnen*
	und Wissenschaftler
	(League of Democratic Scientists)
BRD	*Bundesrepublik Deutschland*
	(Federal Republic of Germany, West Germany)
CDU	Christian Democratic Union
CGIL	*Confederazione Generale Italiana dei Lavoro*
	(Italian General Confederation of Labour)
CPE	*Contrat première embauche*
	(First Employment Contract)
ČSSR	Czechoslovak Socialist Republic
DDR	*Deutsche Demokratische Republik*
	(German Democratic Republic, East Germany)
DFG	*Deutsche Forschungsgemeinschaft*
	(German Research Foundation)
DGB	*Deutscher Gewerkschaftsbund*
	(German Trade Union Confederation)
DGS	*Deutsche Gesellschaft für Soziologie*
	(German Sociological Association)
DKP	*Deutsche Kommunistische Partei*
	(German Communist Party)
DVWP	*Deutsche Vereinigung für Politische Wissenschaft*
	(German Political Science Association)
EU	European Union
ELAS	*Ellinikós Laikós Apelevtherotikós Strató*
	(Greek People's Liberation Army)
FDGB	*Freier Deutscher Gewerkschaftsbund*
	(Free German Trade Union Federation)
FDP	*Freie Demokratische Partei*
	(Free Democratic Party)

GDR	German Democratic Republic
GEW	*Gewerkschaft Erziehung und Wissenschaft*
	(Education and Science Workers' Union)
GO	*Gewerkschaftliche Orientierung*
	(Trade-union orientation)
HBV	*Handel, Banken, Versicherungen*
	(Trade, Banks, and Insurances)
IG	*Industriegewerkschaft*
	(Industrial Union)
IMEMO	*Institut Mirovoj Ekonomiki i Mezhdunarodnyh Otnoshenij*
	(Institute of World Economy and International Relations)
IMSF	*Institut für Marxistische Studien und Forschungen*
	(Institute for Marxist Study and Research)
IPW	*Institut für internationale Politik und Wirtschaft*
	(Institute for International Politics and Economy)
KPD	*Kommunistische Partei Deutschlands*
	(Communist Party of Germany)
KPD/AO	*Kommunistische Partei Deutschlands/Aufbauorganisation*
KPO	*Kommunistische Partei – Opposition*
KZfSS	*Kölner Zeitschrift für Soziologie und Sozialpsychologie*
MAK	*Marxistischer Arbeitskreis*
	(Marxist Working Circle)
MSB	*Marxistischer Studentenbund (Spartakus)*
	(Marxist Student League)
NATO	North Atlantic Treaty Organisation
NPD	*Nationaldemokratische Partei Deutschlands*
	(National Democratic Party of Germany)
NS	National Socialism
NSDAP	*Nationalsozialistische Deutsche Arbeiterpartei*
	(National Socialist German Workers' Party)
PCF	*Parti Communiste Français*
	(Communist Party of France)
PDS	Party of Democratic Socialism
PSU	*Parti Socialiste Unifié*
	(Unified Socialist Party)
RGO	*Revolutionäre Gewerkschaftsopposition*
	(Revolutionary Trade Union Opposition)
SAPD	*Sozialistische Arbeiterpartei Deutschlands*
	(Socialist Workers' Party of Germany)
SBZ	*Sowjetische Besatzungszone*
	(Soviet Occupation Zone)

SDS   *Sozialistischer Deutscher Studentenbund*
      (Socialist German Student League)
SED   *Sozialistische Einheitspartei Deutschlands*
      (Socialist Unity Party of Germany)
SHB   *Sozialistischer Hochschulbund*
      (Socialist University League)
SOFI *Soziologisches Forschungsinstitut*
      (Sociological Research Institute)
SPD   *Sozialdemokratische Partei Deutschlands*
      (Social Democratic Party of Germany)
USSR Union of Soviet Socialist Republics
USA   United States of America
WDR   *Westdeutscher Rundfunk*
WTR   *Wissenschaftlich-technische Revolution*
      (Scientific-technical revolution)

Introduction

Ingar Solty

I appreciate being asked to write an introduction to Lothar Peter's history of the Marburg School, giving me the opportunity, as one of its last students, to sketch out some of its historical contexts, political developments, and scholarly influences. Many of these aspects feature in Peter's book, others I have decided to add. I do this not least in the interests of situating the Marburg School in national and international debates, and providing readers less familiar with German history useful background information.

The German intellectual current broadly described as the 'Frankfurt School' represents a global phenomenon even today, credited with a seemingly endless number of positive and negative contributions ranging from the de-Nazification of West Germany[1] to the creation of a body of political and philosophical literature decried as 'Cultural Marxism' seeking to surreptitiously undermine God, family, nation, and the very fabric of society itself.

Nothing of the sort can be said for the Marburg School. Seven decades after its formation, the ideas and political approaches characterising this current are still in need of an introduction to global debates on post-war Marxist and neo-Marxist thought. To the extent that the term rings any bells, it is probably among scholars in the social sciences and humanities familiar with the first philosophical and political movement associated with the label: neo-Kantianism. Emerging out of debates around the agrarian question and revisionism inside German Social Democracy following its re-legalisation in 1890, this current strove towards a philosophical amalgamation of Kantian thought with socialist ideas to create an ethical socialism for the petite bourgeoisie and the rising new class of intellectuals.[2]

The Marburg School's rather understated reputation is particularly confounding given the extent of its impact – and makes the fact that this volume is the first comprehensive history all the more remarkable. One could argue that the Marburg School altogether had as many if not more students and followers in West Germany than the Frankfurt School, and exerted at least as much if not more and deeper influence on the West German Left and West German society in general. It could also be argued that over the decades the students of the

---

1 Wiggershaus 1995.
2 Lehmann 1970.

Marburg School stayed truer to their current's core epistemological and praxis-political principles than could be said for the remains of the Frankfurt School and its devolution from the Marxist Workweeks to the increasingly conservative post-war thought of Max Horkheimer and Theodor Adorno, not to mention its further development into Jürgen Habermas's linguistic turn and the neo-idealism of Axel Honneth's philosophy of recognition and 'socialism'.[3]

Should some kind of eco-socialist transformation ever take place in Germany, historians and political scientists will likely find themselves writing tomes on the formal and informal networks formed by Marburg School pupils and their impact on politics. Stories both real and imagined would surface, written along similar lines and research frameworks as when political scientists reconstructed the formal and informal networks of the neoliberals and the Mont Pelerin Society or Straussians inside the neoconservative or 'Leo-conservative' George W. Bush administration.[4] Given all that, what exactly is the 'Marburg School' and why should anyone care about it beyond a general interest in the history of West German social science?

If it were really always the case that, as Karl Marx once put it, the 'dominant ideas of the ruling class are, in any age, the ruling ideas', then the Marburg School could never have existed. For the Marburg School was in fact part of a wider set of Marxist-oriented clusters of social scientists who much to the chagrin of ruling authorities managed to establish themselves in the Federal Republic of Germany.

The anti-Hitler coalition fell apart not long after the country's liberation from fascism and the signing of the Potsdam Agreement, giving way to the Cold War and a bipolar world order led by an imperialist United States in the West and the Soviet Union heading up the states of the Eastern Bloc. By 1947 it became increasingly clear that German unification was not a realistic prospect. All attempts to retain a unified, neutral, demilitarised country in the heart of Europe failed or were thwarted and by 1949 two German states existed. This border between East and West was not just the 'inner German' border conservative historians like to call it today, but in fact a border between two independent states backed by two increasingly antagonistic economic, political, and military blocs led by two nuclear superpowers threatening one another with mutual annihilation. Within a few years West Germany became the front line in the Cold War as the rivalry between the capitalist West and Eastern 'actually existing socialism' redrew the Central European map.

---

3   See Demirović 1999; Habermas 1984; Honneth 2017.
4   See Walpen 2004 and Nordmann 2005; Drury 1999; Drury 2005; Henning 2006.

As the United States declined a return to its pre-war isolationist policies and, fearing a relapse into the Great Depression, established itself as an imperial power in Central Europe,[5] the internal political configuration of West Germany became increasingly dependent on external dynamics – not least because the total surrender of Nazi Germany had also meant the effective end of the country's sovereignty. The immediate post-war period saw the rise of substantial anti-capitalist sentiment across Western Europe. Communists had played the dominant role in the national liberation and partisan movements in France and Italy, and now turned their respective parties into immensely influential political forces. The Italian Communist Party, for example, grew from 15,000 to 1.7 million members in one year (1944) and reached two million two years later.[6] These sorts of attitudes were even common in West Germany, which had just emerged from twelve years of barbaric Nazi rule and a genocidal war of annihilation in the Soviet Union. The experience of capitalist crisis marked by hyper-inflation, mass unemployment, and war had widely discredited the capitalist economic system in the public eye. This was reflected in the new state constitution of Hessia adopted in December 1946 foreseeing the kinds of socialisation and nationalisation that had also been mainstream political demands in the aftermath of World War I. Even the conservative Christian Democratic Union (CDU) had to account for the strong socialist sentiment among the German population, and stated in their first party programme, the 1947 Ahlen Programme, that 'capitalism has not been beneficial to the German people'. Regardless of discrepancies between constitutional rights and reality, as a consequence of this popular anti-capitalism progressive constitutions with basic social and democratic rights were drafted in Italy, France, and West Germany,[7] while East Germany received a socialist constitution including not only far-reaching social and economic rights, but also full emancipation and equal rights for women.[8]

The Cold War did away with much of this political climate. Resulting from a mixture of consent and force,[9] the reconstruction of the capitalist economic order and property relations exhibited a dual continuity with fascism itself. Firstly, the economic system and property relations that gave rise to Nazism

---

5 See Deppe, Salomon and Solty 2011; Panitch and Gindin 2012.
6 Magri 2011.
7 One of Wolfgang Abendroth's key legacies is his argument that the West German constitution did not prescribe a capitalist economic order and property relations but that specifically Article 14 allowed for a constitutional path to socialism: see Abendroth 1975.
8 Canfora 2006, pp. 174–97.
9 See Schmidt 1970; Schmidt and Fichter 1971; Huster et al. 1972.

in the first place remained intact. As Daniela Dahn argues, 'the demands of the Social Democratic Party in the West' including land reform and socialisation were ironically only realised in the Communist East.[10] Secondly, the continuity between Nazi Germany and post-war West Germany also included far-reaching continuity of economic, political, military, and cultural elites.[11] While the original Morgenthau Plan actually envisaged a deindustrialised and demilitarised German state, the US now relied on the old capitalist elites and repressive state apparatuses to remilitarise West Germany and integrate it into the emerging NATO defence framework. By the early 1950s most of the Nazi war economy's capitalist managers sentenced to lengthy prison terms at the Nuremberg Trials were released and returned to their old positions (expressed by the phrase 'Hitler ging – sie blieben').[12] Some corporations like IG Farben, which had partly operated the Auschwitz death camps and produced the Zyklon B gas used in the gas chambers, were actually larger and more powerful than before the war.[13] The presence of personnel from Nazi Germany in the old Federal Republic was widespread across the secret services (from the 'Organisation Gehlen' to the Federal Intelligence Service and the 'Federal Office for the Protection of the Constitution'), the military (from the old *Wehrmacht*, which was depicted as 'clean' and not implicated in the Holocaust, to the new federal army), the judicial system, the political system, and higher education.

The consequence was that the US military administration never implemented the comprehensive plan for democratising German higher education exiled Frankfurt School theorist Franz Neumann had developed on its behalf, with the sole exception of the Berlin city-state and the political science department of the Free University which developed a strong critical tradition encompassing figures like Elmar Altvater.[14] In West German higher education, by contrast, leading fascist intellectuals and proponents of the 'conservative revolution' from the Weimar and Nazi eras like Hans Freyer, author of the 1931 book *Revolution von rechts*,[15] Ernst Forsthoff, author of the 1933 book *Der totale Staat*,[16] and the aspiring Nazi state theorist Helmut Schelsky retained their positions as

10   Dahn 2010.
11   With regard to the cultural sphere, see for example the Federal Republic's striking difference between post-fascist and post-Communist transition in Solty 2015.
12   See Köhler 1996.
13   Köhler 1989.
14   Bebnowski 2018.
15   Freyer 1931.
16   Ernst Forsthoff was initially ousted from his position as a professor, but the Cold War restoration enabled him to return to academia as a professor in Heidelberg in 1952. In the mid-1950s he instigated the famous 'Forsthoff-Abendroth controversy', challenging Abendroth and his argument for a constitutional path to socialism in West Germany.

important social scientists. The isolation imposed on the 'Third Reich's crown legal theorist' Carl Schmitt was an exception, not the rule, and even he continued to exert influence on West German intellectual life.[17] The founder of the Marburg School, Wolfgang Abendroth, used to say that all appointments of leading constitutional judges in West Germany 'took place on a couch in Plettenberg', Schmitt's hometown in the provincial Sauerland to which he returned after the war.

The situation for left-leaning intellectuals and activists could not have been more different. From 1950 onwards, the conservative West German government under Chancellor Konrad Adenauer persecuted tens of thousands of socialists and Communists under the *Adenauer Erlass*, another legislative instalment in the storied German tradition of blacklisting leftists (Carlsbad Decrees of 1819–48, the *Bundesreaktionsbeschluss* and the Cologne Communist Trials of 1851–63, the Anti-Socialist Laws of 1878–90, and the Nazis' Civil Service Law of 1933–45). The new law excluded Communists and even alleged Communists from public service, and in 1956 the weakened Communist Party (KPD) that received 5.7 percent (1.36 million votes) in 1949 and 2.2 percent (607,860 votes) in 1953 was banned. The other, much larger party of the working class, the Social Democratic Party (SPD), adopted a new programme at its Bad Godesberg congress in 1959 shifting their political and ideological orientation away from Marxism and functioning as what Otto Kirchheimer called a 'catch-all party', rather than a class-based workers' party.[18] A new German Communist Party (DKP) was only permitted to form in 1968. Although the DKP was feared by the political establishment to the point of triggering new blacklists, wielded significant influence in the intellectual sphere, cultural scene, and the trade unions, and was the driving force behind many larger social movements such as the 1980s peace movement that mobilised hundreds of thousands, this new Communist Party was dependent on East German state funds and remained a marginal force. It never commanded more than slightly over two percent of the vote in state elections nor secured political representation beyond municipal assemblies. The de-escalation of political hostility towards the Communists that began in 1968 ended when the SPD and FDP coalition government instituted new blacklists against the revitalised Left known as the *Radikalen-Erlass*, lasting from 1972–9 on the federal level and prolonged at the state level until 1991.

Social Democracy's rightward pivot in the early 1970s drove many left-wing scholars and activists into an economic, social, and political Cold War abyss

---

17   Söllner 1992.
18   Kirchheimer 1966.

characterised by blacklisting, financial bankruptcy, and even imprisonment. This social stigmatisation had a tremendous impact on Marxist theory in the country, for, as Perry Anderson argued in his classic *Considerations on Western Marxism*,[19] Western Marxist theory tended to flourish particularly in those countries where leftists could rely on strong Communist parties as sources of intellectual inspiration, stable employment, and more during anti-Communist purges or politically motivated discrimination in the academy. In West Germany these conditions were lacking.

Under these circumstances the Marburg School's very existence is a historical anomaly. This impression is reinforced when one takes geographical circumstances into account, which could hardly have been less favourable for left-wing scholarship. After all, the Marburg School developed in the traditional university town of Marburg (50,000 residents with another 30,000 in the surrounding villages and towns, nearly 20,000 of them students) located in the geographical heart of Hessia, facing the financial centre Frankfurt am Main to the south and the traditionally Social Democratic, working-class arms manufacturing city of Kassel to the north.

As Lothar Peter describes in detail, the Marburg School's founders were political scientist and legal theorist Wolfgang Abendroth and sociologists Werner Hofmann and Heinz Maus. Under their influence a large segment of the student body grew increasingly left-wing, leading the conservative press to dub Marburg a 'German Communist Party cadre school'. Beyond the difficult conditions caused by the Cold War, the city's ability to attract young radicals even years after the Marburg School's institutional demise is particularly surprising given that it was traditionally a deeply conservative university town. Among German universities older institutions tend to be more right-wing, tied to the existence of all-male student fraternities known as *Burschenschaften* or *Korporationen*. Founded in the early 1800s by students enthused by the idea of a democratic nation-state, after the defeat of the 1848 Revolution, the absorption of the liberal bourgeoisie by the Bismarckian conservative state, and the founding of the German Empire not through democratic revolution from below but Bismarck's imperialist wars from above (1866–71) the fraternities' democratic nationalism gave way to a reactionary, anti-democratic, ultra-nationalist ideology promoting monarchism, colonialism, militarism, anti-socialism, and patriarchy.[20]

19   Anderson 1989.
20   See Machtan and Milles 1980, and on the conservative turn of the liberal bourgeoisie Kofler 1984, pp. 20–30.

While less than two percent of students belong to *Burschenschaften* today, their members constituted the majority in some cities for decades. The fraternities were particularly right-wing in Marburg, an old university town with hardly any industry and little to no industrial working class, going so far as to participate in political assassinations during the interwar period. When a united general strike of Communists and Social Democrats defeated the proto-fascist Kapp Putsch in 1920 and a 'Second Revolution' briefly appeared to be at stake,[21] *Burschenschaft* students from the 'Studentenkorps Marburg' founded on the initiative of the German Army in Kassel went to Thuringia to fight 'Bolshevism' and massacred 15 workers. The ensuing trial held in front of a military instead of a civil court ended in exonerations for all 14 students, demonstrating the state and legal system's support for the far-right. It was so scandalous that the famous left-wing publicist and lawyer Kurt Tucholsky wrote several poems and texts about the incident.[22] Thus, Abendroth, Maus, and Hofmann could hardly have expected to find fertile ground for their critical scholarship when they began teaching in Marburg.

Lothar Peter's telling of the improbable history of the Marburg School is also ground-breaking with regard to the German body of literature, and represents the first of its kind. Previous scholars have restricted the Marburg School to Wolfgang Abendroth, which is why it is sometimes also referred to as the 'Abendroth School'.[23] In these historiographies the Marburg School ends with his retirement in 1972 or his death in 1985 at the latest. Yet this neglects two things: firstly, the relevance of Hofmann and Maus, and secondly the development of the Abendroth School into an actual Marburg School stretching across disciplines, generations, and today cities and even countries. Lothar Peter has thankfully begun to fill the need for a history of the various developmental stages, continuities, and breaks within this particular understanding of Marxist scholarship.[24]

The Marburg School was – and one could argue, remains – a specific current in German Marxism. Marxism became the dominant framework for higher education in East Germany, where its narrow conceptualisation as 'Marxism-Leninism' led to vulgarisation in particular fields. This was particularly true of philosophy, although some East German philosophers like Wolfgang Heise conducted ground-breaking work. In other fields a final verdict concerning the quality, rigour, and lasting value of Marxist research remains up for debate.

21   See Weipert 2015 and Schütrumpf, Solty and Sonnenberg 2018.
22   On the murders in Thuringia see also the major study by Dietrich Heither (a disciple of Kühnl and Deppe) and Adelheid Schulze, Heither and Schulze 2015.
23   See Abendroth-Gruppe 2006.
24   See also Lothar Peter's argument in favour of this terminology (Peter 2019).

Some East German Marxism has been rehabilitated and its value acknowledged in some fields. This includes the Leipzig School of historians and their research on historical revolutions (Manfred Kossok, Walter Markov, Wolfgang Schröder, etc.), economic history (Jürgen Kuczynski's work, which also appeared in English), as well as geography, urban planning, and urban history (Lothar Kühne and others). A younger generation of scholars is beginning to question the Marxist-Leninist strawman that even Marxists in the West (especially from the 'Eurocommunist' tradition) long relied on to dismiss and ignore East German scholarship. A re-evaluation could potentially take place over the coming decades. West German philosopher and Free University of Berlin professor Wolfgang Fritz Haug, quite critical of state socialism in the 1980s and a supporter of Gorbachev,[25] has since integrated many East German scholars like Günther Mayer, Thomas Marxhausen, Wolfram Adolphi, Wolfgang Küttler, Lutz-Dieter Behrendt, and others into his gargantuan *Historical-Critical Dictionary of Marxism*.

Marxism was much more difficult to uphold in West Germany, but several Marxist schools and networks nevertheless developed over the years. Identifying their differences can help to excavate the Marburg School's particular contribution. Internationally, Frankfurt am Main is widely associated with capital 'C' Critical Theory and its post-war development as the Frankfurt School. Influenced by but independent from it, however, was the 'Capital Logic and State Derivation School' associated with Joachim Hirsch who taught political science in Frankfurt, and Elmar Altvater who became an internationally renowned figure at the Free University. The state derivation debate they instigated is one of the better-known German theoretical exchanges in the Anglophone world, as it also appeared prominently in the short-lived journal *Kapitalistate*.[26] As such, it was an important and genuinely West German contribution to Marxist state theory in the 1970s and featured alongside Claus Offe's contributions and Jürgen Habermas's *Legitimation Crisis*.[27]

Another network of left-wing scholarship existed in Bremen, where a Marxist and Marxian political economy tradition developed in the continuously SPD-governed city-state. Two of its leading figures were Rudolf Hickel and Jörg Huffschmid, who later co-founded the Memorandum Group as well as the 'Electoral Alternative for Work and Social Justice' (WASG), the West German political formation that developed out of the anti-Agenda 2010 and Hartz

25 See Haug 1985–7 and Haug 1989.
26 Clarke 1991.
27 For the Anglo-Saxon reception see Barrow 1993.

reforms protests in 2004 and merged with the Party of Democratic Socialism (PDS) to form Die Linke in 2007.[28] Although notable and internationally
renowned Marxists including the University of Tübingen's Ernst Bloch taught
at various West German universities, Frankfurt am Main, West Berlin, Bremen,
and Marburg represented the largest clusters of Marxist intellectuals in the
West.

The Marburg School may have begun with Abendroth's appointment in the
1950s, but it only became a full-blown 'school' through the Fordist era's mass
expansion of higher education. As a young boy in southern Hessia', Georg Fülberth once recalled, 'you could not cross the street without a Social Democrat
coming from the left and another coming from the right, taking you by the
hand, and saying: "You, kid, are going to go to university!"' The confluence
of a left-leaning SPD government in Hessia, the Cold War-induced need for
a better-educated working class following the 1957 'Sputnik Shock' and thus
more hiring in higher education, along with the existence of a leftist body of
Abendroth's assistants at that particular moment in time ensured that the student movement could install Frank Deppe as Abendroth's successor under the
slogan 'Marx an die Uni!', together with the Marxian historian Reinhard Kühnl,
Marxist political economist Georg Fülberth, and sociologist Dieter Boris. Of
course, given the Cold War situation the window of opportunity was short-
lived. As Lothar Peter shows, others from the Marburg School soon faced the
aforementioned West German anti-Communist purges. The new blacklists not
only disciplined the wider sphere of left-leaning intellectuals, but in Marburg
it concretely prevented the professorial appointment of Jürgen Harrer, against
whom Hessian Minister of Education Hans Krollmann (SPD) intervened directly and politically, as well as Wolfgang Hecker who was blacklisted for four
years because of his membership in the DKP. Moreover, the blacklists hindered
numerous Marxist scholars like USSR expert Gert Meyer, sociologist Rainer
Rilling, or the brilliant intellectual Reinhard Opitz whose PhD defence in 1973
fell right at the beginning of the purges.

But what was so specific about the Marburg brand of Marxist scholarship
and left-wing politics? Frank Deppe and others were activists in SDS. The Marburg SDSers were regarded as 'traditionalists' opposed to the 'New Left' anti-
authoritarian groups in Heidelberg, Munich (around Dieter Kunzelmann and
the later right-winger Frank Böckelmann), or Berlin (around the former East
German theology student Rudi Dutschke and future far-right intellectual Bernd
Rabehl). Dutschke and the anti-authoritarian wing of SDS tended towards

---

28   See Solty 2008 and Solty 2019.

Frankfurt School interpretations of post-war capitalism. They assumed the working class to be socially and culturally integrated into what they falsely conceived as 'late capitalism', were therefore critical of mass consumption and the 'culture industry', and saw revolution developing in and coming from the 'Third World' – perhaps even against the First World. They sympathised with the Vietnamese liberation struggle and increasingly with the Chinese Cultural Revolution. This New Left adhered to Theodor W. Adorno and Max Horkheimer's culture industry theory, Herbert Marcuse's marginal group strategy developed in *One-Dimensional Man*, and a kind of neo-anarchistic distrust of all existing institutions that would later become associated with Foucauldian thinking.

The 'traditionalist' epithet, on the other hand, meant strategic orientation towards the workers' movement and a more or less friendly stance towards the Soviet Union and socialist construction in East Germany. Unlike the school of Marxism developing around Wolfgang Fritz Haug and the long-standing periodical *Das Argument*, the Marburg School never really had a defined literary canon. Instead, the Marburg School was held together by a general posture or *Haltung*. This *Haltung* was and remains that *one must always pursue left-wing strategies on the left wing of the actually existing workers' movement*. In juxtaposition to the New Left, this entailed a rejection of bogus 'late capitalism' theories, the culturalisation of Marxism connected with it, and ultimately the strategic prioritisation of class struggle at home over mere support for anti-imperialism abroad.

With this general understanding, the Marburg School proved to be closer to the reality of Fordist capitalism than the various neo-Marxisms and radical left theories of the post-war era. While the anti-authoritarians and the New Left considered the working classes to be fully integrated into capitalism (based on concepts like 'false consciousness' and 'the formed society') and were flabbergasted when they rose up in May 1968 in Paris or conducted the wildcat strikes of 1967–8 in West Germany, the representatives of the Marburg School were not nearly as surprised. While they criticised the conservative aspects of West German co-determination as a particular version of corporatism in ways quite similar to Leo Panitch across the Atlantic,[29] they also realised that it represented an achievement of the workers' movement. In other words, by conceptualising the state as a contested terrain and not merely a sphere of capitalism's reproduction as the Frankfurt School and French Structuralism from Althusser to Foucault did, it could be reflected as a natural and merely temporary histor-

---

29   Deppe et al. 1969; Panitch 1976.

INTRODUCTION   11

ical compromise in a generally 'antagonistic society'.[30] The Marburg School was thus, to use the terminology of John Sanbonmatsu's knowledge-sociological history of poststructuralism, essentially Gramscian and 'counter-hegemonic', while much of the New Left expressed and maintained a Foucauldian 'anti-hegemonic' stance.[31]

Their traditionalism was not merely the result of theoretical considerations, however, but also reflected different experiences. It is striking that the Red Army Faction and other more eccentric expressions of the politics of 1968 were recruited from university towns with highly conservative faculties, most notably Heidelberg. The conservative nature of these universities – the fact that leftist students found an entirely unsupportive environment for critical thinking – reinforced Frankfurt School and Foucauldian notions that universities were strictly repressive institutions which could only be destroyed through 'revolution' from the outside rather than transformed from within.

The Marburg School's traditionalism also entailed a lack of the New Left's particular brand of elitism. The shift of many anti-authoritarian SDS members to highly authoritarian Maoist sects, the so-called *K-Gruppen*,[32] might puzzle some and appear as abrupt shifts in politics and personalities. However, the New Left was always characterised by a strong elitist undercurrent vis-à-vis the 'integrated' masses and the rest of society. This elitism conceptualised the masses as integrated through consumerism, sexually repressed, and potentially fascist[33] – a notion underscored by the rabid anti-Communist attacks and violence against left-wing students. The anti-authoritarian wing of SDS misinterpreted the 1968 rebellion as a world revolutionary situation. Due to its flawed state theory and reproductionist thinking, it also misinterpreted the state's backlash coupled with the rise of the neo-Nazi National Democratic Party (NPD) as a return of fascism potentially giving the Left a chance to make up for the failure of 1933. Needless to say, the short-lived nature of the rebellion generated intense disappointment among many revolutionary students. Ironically, many of them were positively surprised by the working-class strike wave, and idealised their newfound revolutionary subject so much that they began to regard the defeat of the alleged 'world revolution' as resulting from a lack of organic connection to the working class. The sexual

---

30   Abendroth 1972a.
31   Sanbonmatsu 2004.
32   On the history of one of the largest *K-Gruppen* that partly dissolved into the Green Party in 1979–80, the Kommunistische Bund, see Steffen 2002, a Marburg School dissertation supervised by Georg Fülberth.
33   This was largely due to the influence of Wilhelm Reich's Marxian psychoanalytic writings and *The Mass Psychology of Fascism* (Reich 1980) in particular.

revolution vanguardism of yesterday now morphed into a new Maoist/Stalinist working-class party vanguardism. Some of the 'revolutionaries', especially the Maoists, sought to undo the distinction between manual and mental labour by becoming workers themselves. Oftentimes they found out the hard and disillusioning way that factory workers were not eagerly waiting to be educated about their objective interests, let alone the need to engage in anti-imperialist activism.[34] Only a few of the most dedicated lasted very long.

The Marburg School avoided most of these follies for a number of reasons. First of all, their relation to the existing working class was based not on theoretical considerations or a desperate search for a new revolutionary subject away from Foucauldian or Marcusian fringe-group strategies, but rather on a connection to the real-concrete history of the German workers' movement through Abendroth himself. This connection was also enabled by the unique structures of the Arbeitsgemeinschaft gewerkschaftliche Fragen (AgF), which since the 1950s has enabled students to co-teach worker education seminars alongside mostly IG Metall-affiliated metalworkers in the auto industry. As a result of this real experience and exposure to working-class life and struggles, the Marburg School tended to neither abhor nor idealise and romanticise the class but confront it as it was. This led Frank Deppe to declare in one of his most famous monographs that not 'unity' but in fact 'division' characterised the natural state of the working class.[35] In a manner similar to the British Marxist historians and E.P. Thompson's class theory and his critique of Althusser and French structural abstractionism,[36] class consciousness and class formation were never a given but something to be politically organised. The class did not exist unless it was 'made'. If Marxists were disappointed by the working class, then they had disappointed the working class. If the working class was not revolutionary and maybe even appeared reactionary at a given historical juncture, like the US workers' movement during the Vietnam War, then Marxists had failed politically.

Secondly, the Marburg School did not regard 1968 as a world-revolutionary movement because although strike levels rose significantly, the student and working-class movements clearly remained small minorities especially in West Germany.[37] Thirdly, for this reason the Marburg School traditionalists did not experience 1968 as a defeat. This was not so much because their hopes were

---

34   A wonderful cultural critique of this kind of *Haltung* can be found in the 1970 song 'Die Kunst, Andersmeinende für den Sozialismus zu gewinnen' by Communist singer-songwriter Dieter Süverkrüp.
35   Deppe 1981.
36   Thompson 2013 and Thompson 1978.
37   Gehrke and Horn 2018.

not as high as the anti-authoritarian SDS wing's (although this was also true), but because they experienced 1968 and its aftermath as a kind of victory. The three years of the social-liberal reformist coalition from its formation in 1969 to the anti-Communist blacklisting policies had witnessed a demo-cratisation of higher education. Feudalist, authoritarian university structures were replaced by student and professorial assistants' co-determination and the Marburg School managed to install Marxist scholarship in the political science and sociology departments. A year after Wolfgang Abendroth penned the introduction to Christian Riecher's Antonio Gramsci anthology, the first real mass publication initiating the West German Gramsci revival,[38] the Mar-burg School intellectuals expressed a kind of Gramscian understanding of the state and (counter-)hegemony and accepted the university as a contested ter-rain on which they were advancing. This also enabled them to identify the differences between a liberal and an authoritarian bourgeois state, while the anti-authoritarian wing suspected fascism around every corner. To the ultra-leftists, the Marburg orientation was of course always seen as 'reformist' – the *K-Gruppen* continued to attack the 'reformist German Communist Party' – and, due to its lack of a 'New Man'-style cultural revolutionism, was perceived as bor-ing, less hip, and even petty.[39]

Frank Deppe would later argue that the peculiar nature of 1968 in West German history had to do with the fact that Germany never experienced a successful social(ist) revolution. Therefore, all counter-revolutions entailed the revolutionaries either being exiled (after 1848 and 1933) or murdered (after 1918–19 and 1933). The peculiar nature of 1968 was that the subjective revolu-tionaries essentially remained stuck in non-revolutionary times and had to find new ways of remaining politically active after their perceived defeat.

A strongly anti-statist, anti-institutionalist, and ultra-leftist or neo-anarchist tendency remained a striking feature of the Marxism found at the Free Uni-versity of Berlin. While Dutschke regarded Haug as a traditionalist and pro-Soviet Marxist (in his diaries he refers to Haug as 'SED Haug' and quotes him as saying 'You guys want the revolution on both sides, I only want it on one'),[40] Wolf-Dieter Narr and Johannes Agnoli kept this strong ultra-leftist, anti-statist, neo-anarchist sentiment alive. Even among the more Marxist State Deriva-tion School scholars in Frankfurt like Joachim Hirsch, a particular anti-statist and anarchist element continues to exist even today, bringing his (subjectively

---

38   Gramsci 1967.
39   In the late 1990s an infamous graffiti in the toilets of the Philosophical Faculty in Marburg
        read: 'That wasn't socialism at all, that was *Spießerkram*'.
40   Dutschke 2003, p. 212.

more powerless) academic milieu into proximity with the undogmatic Left in
Frankfurt and the autonomous movement, and even leading some to harbour
secret sympathies for the Red Army Faction. Some of the Hirschians eventually
suffered under the ruthless persecution of alleged RAF supporters following
the 'German Autumn' in 1977. Following Marx's and Bebel's original critique,
Marburg School traditionalism strongly disapproved of this so-called 'urban-
guerrilla warfare' as 'individual terror'. This did not prevent some of them from
expressing general human kindness and solidarity with RAF political prisoners
after the group dissolved on 20 April 1998. Georg Fülberth became a frequent
visitor of Christian Klar from the second RAF generation while he was still
imprisoned and denied release.[41]

The Marburg School's consolidation as an important force in radical socialist politics was of course contested. Lothar Peter's book chronicles the vicious
attacks the Marburg School faced, particularly in the wake of a co-authored,
politically motivated comparative analysis of West and East Germany that was
not a highpoint of Marburg School scholarship or intellectual rigour, along with
another co-authored critical history of the German trade unions.[42] These difficulties were exacerbated by the end of the short period of new Marxist hiring in
the early 1970s. The philosopher Hans Heinz Holz was appointed to a professorship in Marburg as one of the last Marxists after a long and hard battle in 1971,
but much to the Marburg School's dismay decided to move to the University of
Groningen in 1978, where much later he would train Die Linke politician Sahra
Wagenknecht. Philosophy was lost.

The Marburg School was by no means homogenous. Its general 'traditionalist' orientation may have unified its protagonists, but theoretical and analytical
differences existed – not least between departments. Dieter Boris developed
a notably Third Worldist approach and helped introduce dependency and
world systems theory to Marburg. Meanwhile, the strategic disaster of the
aforementioned volume comparing East and West Germany spurred divisions
between Frank Deppe and Georg Fülberth in particular.[43] Deppe oriented himself towards Western Marxist debates and Antonio Gramsci's work, whereas

---

41   Klar spent more than 26 years in prison and was not paroled until 19 December 2008, find-
      ing employment as an intern at the Berlin Ensemble and later as a technical assistant in
      the office of Die Linke MP Diether Dehm.
42   Jung et al. 1971; Deppe, Fülberth and Harrer 1977.
43   Together Abendroth, Deppe, Fülberth, and Dieter Boris also collaborated closely with
      the Frankfurt-based Institut für Marxistische Studien und Forschungen (IMSF) founded
      in 1968 with close ties to the DKP. Its directors were Heinz Jung and key party theorist
      Josef Schleifstein. The institute produced seminal works and empirical studies on West
      German class structure, state monopoly capitalism, the changing composition and con-

Fülberth initially engaged heavily in university politics and then countered
Gramscianism and the critique of economism and mechanistic materialism
with an attempt to strengthen the critique of political economy itself. For that
purpose, he founded the Forschungsgruppe Politische Ökonomie and maintained that focus throughout the next decades, producing widely read canon-
ical texts on Marxist political economy. Deppe, however, considered Gramsci
to be an integral part of productive Marxist thought. While not departing from
Marxism and the Marxist classics, he learned Italian and delved deeply into
Gramsci's political and state theory to produce a major study on Machiavelli in
1987.[44]

As a student of the Marburg School himself, it is to Lothar Peter's credit
that he does not exclude some of the School's weaknesses, deficiencies, and
even lacunae – for instance in the fields of ecology and feminism[45] – as well as
some of its strategic mistakes and internal divisions. His book is far from hagi-
ographic, but rather an excellent study tying together post-war history, political economy, sociology of knowledge, and theories of the intellectual (which
he himself excelled in).[46] Peter also shows how the Marburg School reorganised itself after the decline and fall of actually existing socialism, evaluating its
demise and failures in numerous monographs and theoretical writings.

---

sciousness of the working class the state and development of the workers' movement
(including strike analyses), and co-organised conferences and congresses with the IMEMO
in Moscow and IPW in Berlin. IMSF staff included Marburg School scholars like Kurt
Steinhaus, author of a seminal dissertation on pre-colonial development obstacles in the
Ottoman Empire, André Leisewitz, Eberhard Dähne, and Klaus Pickshaus. The Bremen
offspring of the Marburg School Lothar Peter and Hellmuth Lange, were also close IMSF
collaborators. The so-called 'moderniser' wing of the DKP was recruited largely from the
IMSF in the mid- to late 1980s, and it was from those circles in 1990–1 that the influential
journal Z. Zeitschrift Marxistische Erneuerung (Journal of Marxist Renewal) was formed,
which some jokingly call the Zeitschrift Marburger Erneuerung. See also Deppe 2018.

44   Deppe 1987.
45   This has clearly been an undertheorised and under-researched weak spot of the Marburg
School. The connection to Ingrid Kurz-Scherf, who ran the Gender Studies wing of the
political science department and was also a trade-union researcher, became too weak over
time and suggests missed opportunities. However, with regard to the theorisation of natural social relations and social reproduction it should be noted that the early Marburg
School exile of Karl Hermann Tjaden and Margarete Tjaden-Steinhauer to the University
of Kassel played a crucial role in bringing ecological and feminist debates into an explicitly
Marxist political economy framework with their development of the concept of *Senken-
belastung* and their historical studies on human civilisational history including family
relations. See Lambrecht, Tjaden and Tjaden-Steinhauer 1998 and Tjaden-Steinhauer and
Tjaden 2001.
46   See for example Peter 2012.

In what remains, some of the potential theses stated at the beginning will at least be hinted at. The Marburg School professors are obviously less internationally known than Adorno, Horkheimer, or Marcuse, but the same is true in Germany. This seems to be due to a number of reasons: firstly, they were never exiled and thus never played a role in the American and British university systems (writing in the lingua franca of global scholarship); secondly, as uncompromising Marxists they could not play a comparable role on public television, radio, etc.; and thirdly their strategic and situation-oriented thinking made it more difficult to produce the kind of classic academic works with a vaguely left-wing bent the Frankfurt School excelled in.

Yet even under the conditions of the Cold War and despite the dominance of anti-Communism, the Marburg School proved quite influential with regard to the formation of West German common sense. Reinhard Kühnl's books on the relationship between fascism and liberalism as two kinds of political systems in bourgeois society, on the history of German fascism, and on theories of fascism became bestsellers. His 1971 *Formen bürgerlicher Herrschaft. Liberalismus, Faschismus* sold more than a quarter-million copies by 1990.[47] *Der deutsche Faschismus in Quellen und Dokumenten* went through numerous editions.[48] Through these books Kühnl's work played a significant role training *Gymnasium* teachers in West Germany. Tens of thousands were influenced by his critical understanding of German fascism and educated hundreds of thousands of *Gymnasium* students in that vein. *Formen bürgerlicher Herrschaft*, for example, was so common that classroom sets of around 40 copies could even be found at the deeply conservative Protestant school I attended in a provincial Westphalian town.[49] One could go so far as to argue that Kühnl's impact laid the groundwork for the Left's victory in the *Historikerstreit* of the mid-1980s.[50]

Frank Deppe exerted a remarkable influence on the West German workers' movement, particularly IG Metall, the largest German trade union with 2.3 million members today and 3.6 million at its highpoint in 1991. Deppe became the single most important intellectual for the left wing of IG Metall including board members like Horst Schmitthenner and Klaus Pickshaus, and remains so even

---

47   Kühnl 1971.
48   Kühnl 1975.
49   Kühnl's books were published by Rowohlt. Many others were published by Pahl-Rugenstein Verlag in Cologne. The Marburg School also had its own publishing house, VAG (Verlag Arbeiterbewegung und Gesellschaftswissenschaften), where Gerd Hardach published more than 100 volumes – many of which were Marburg School dissertations.
50   See Kühnl 1987.

after his 2006 retirement. Hans-Jürgen Urban, one of his disciples and closest friends, later became a leading member of the IG Metall executive board.

Georg Fülberth also impacted civil society in ways uncommon for university professors. Beyond his far-reaching scholarly works on the political economy of capitalism and socialism,[51] he is renowned as one of Germany's wittiest, most lucid, and humorous left-wing journalistic writers. He also played a key role in debates on the history of both German states and why state socialism collapsed.[52] His many publications enjoyed a wide audience beyond narrow left-wing academic and political circles. Furthermore, his impact on local politics as a Communist Party activist, municipal representative, and long-standing local historian made him one of the most well-known and respected figures in the city. This was reflected in a *Frankfurter Rundschau* article on three things tourists had to see in Marburg: the town's historic castle, the medieval Elisabeth Church, and Georg Fülberth.

In short, the Marburg School's influence was widespread against all odds. In some ways it could be seen as a kind of 'Masonic Marxism', the impact of which is felt in more subtle ways than is usually the case with narrowly university-oriented and less strategic thinkers in higher education.

Nevertheless, the Marburg School failed to continue its existence at the University of Marburg itself. The dismantling of the very institution that put the city on the scholarly map in the first place was a scandalous affair. Reinhard Kühnl's and Georg Fülberth's positions were initially supposed to be combined and devoted to research on political extremism. More than a decade after the end of the Cold War that gave birth to this very unscientific doctrine, their Marxian research on fascism, German history, and the fundamental critique of 'totalitarianism' theory was to be replaced by totalitarianism theory itself.[53] Ultimately, the position was never filled. When Frank Deppe retired two years later his research was supposed to be renewed. But when Andreas Bieler from Nottingham University, the department's first choice, did not accept his nomination, the generally hostile administration used this convenient fact to cancel Deppe's succession entirely. Diether Plehwe, who was second in line, moved to the prestigious Berlin Social Science Center (WZB).

Still, Marxist scholarship has not vanished from Marburg entirely. As Lothar Peter shows in his final chapter, the junior professorship of Deppe's former assistant Hans-Juergen Bieling was later renewed and filled by the Poulantzian state theorist and EU scholar John Kannankulam. Although Kannankulam

51   Fülberth 2005; Fülberth 2018; Fülberth 2010.
52   Fülberth 1982; Fülberth 1999a; Fülberth 2007; Fülberth 1991; Fülberth 1993; Fülberth 1994.
53   Wippermann 2009, pp. 14–24.

helps to keep Marxist research alive in Marburg, his theoretical background is clearly the state theory developed by Joachim Hirsch in Frankfurt.[54]

The institutional demise of the Marburg School does not mean that the Marburg School died. Today the school and its general theoretical and practical *Haltung* continues to exist outside its place of origin. The new Marburg, at least when it comes to higher education, is most certainly the empire of Klaus Dörre at the sociology department in Jena. Here, Deppe's former assistant continues all the relevant fields of his research – from the analysis of global capitalism and its contradictions (including Dörre's new take on the *Landnahme* theorem) to the analysis of working-class reformation and working-class consciousness, and trade union revitalisation strategy. With Hans-Jürgen Urban as a guest professor, the Marburg School is now strongly embedded at Jena.

Hans-Juergen Bieling's appointment as Professor of International Relations at the University of Tübingen where he now runs West Germany's leading international relations journal *Zeitschrift für Internationale Beziehungen*, Kühnl disciple Gudrun Hentges's appointment as Christoph Butterwegge's successor at the University of Cologne, and the appointment of Bieling's assistant Stefanie Wöhl at the Technical University in Vienna have prolonged the Marburg School into the future. Other tenure-track positions are also likely, including David Salomon, currently a visiting professor at the University of Hildesheim, Patrick Eser at the University of Kassel, Amy Holmes at the American University in Cairo, Anne Tittor at the University of Kassel, and Stefan Schmalz at the University of Jena. The list grows even longer if one includes the disciples of Kurt Lenk at the University of Aachen, who alongside Karl Hermann Tjaden became one of the earliest Marburg-related 'offspring' professors outside of the city, or Lothar Peter and his students.

In short, the Marburg School today is one in diaspora. It joins in a pluralist fashion the remaining and emerging islands of Marxist scholarship in the German-speaking countries, which include the University of Salzburg (Christian Zeller and Stefanie Hürtgen), the University of Kassel (Christoph Scherrer, Sonja Buckel, and Alexander Gallas), the University of Vienna (Ulrich Brand),

---

54   Many would say that the cancellation of its Marxist tradition has been to the detriment of the university itself, as today it has grown somewhat irrelevant. Once a national phenomenon and a magnet for radicals from all over the world, the Bologna Process and the cultivation of so-called 'elite' universities relegated it to one of Hessia's less important campuses, overtaken by Frankfurt am Main and Kassel. Unfortunately, the Marburg professors were not disproportionately or overwhelmingly successful in positioning their disciples as professors at other universities, let alone creating new Marxist hubs and clusters of Marxists elsewhere.

the University of Basel (Oliver Nachtwey), the Hochschule für Wirtschaft und Recht in Berlin (Markus Wissen), and the Rosa-Luxemburg-Stiftung's Institute for Critical Social Analysis, the largest cluster of Marxist research in the German-speaking world today (Mario Candeias, Michael Brie, Alex Demirovic, Thomas Sablowski, Katharina Pühl, Ingar Solty, Judith Dellheim, Horst Kahrs, Lutz Brangsch, and many others).

The general praxis orientation of Marburg School disciples has actually deepened, as the newest (or last) generation of Marburg School intellectuals apply their *Haltung* to new fields of class struggle. Many have become labour leaders and intellectuals, such as Urban (board member and co-chair of IG Metall), Thorsten Schulten (chief economist of the WSI Archive at the trade unions' Hans-Böckler-Stiftung), Martin Beckmann (Ver.di department of politics and planning), Melanie Wehrheim (Ver.di director of professional policy), Ingo Schäfer (DGB executive board), or labour activists like Conny Weißbach, Rosa Schwenger, and Fabian Rehm (all Ver.di organisers), while others built the Institute for Critical Social Analysis (Rainer Rilling), or joined it as faculty (Ingar Solty) and permanent collaborators (Axel Gehring). Some have become Die Linke leaders and intellectuals, joining the Linke-led government in Thuringia (Paul Wellsow, Volker Hinck) under Minister President Bodo Ramelow (a former Marburg trade-unionist himself), becoming Die Linke's co-chair and parliamentary group leader in Hessia (Jan Schalauske), or joining the research department of Die Linke's federal parliamentary group (former Kühnl assistant Gert Wiegel). Others became high-profile labour journalists (Johannes Schulten, Guido Speckmann, and Stefan Schoppengerd), publish Marxist books (Jürgen Harrer of PapyRossa Verlag) or journals (André Leisewitz of Z.), are influential political activists and intellectuals in Armenia (Vahram Soghomonyan), or professors around the globe – most notably in the Republic of Korea.

The disappearance of Marxism from the University of Marburg is just one reminder that the period of academic Marxism the Fordist mass expansion of higher education facilitated represented a historical anomaly. Universities are generally designed to train capitalist society's political elite and not the revolutionaries seeking to overthrow it. Georg Fülberth once made this case in his piece 'Marxismus Emeritus' on the retirement of the 1960s and 1970s Marxist professors, published in the national weekly *Die Zeit*.[55] As Frank Deppe's close friend and collaborator Leo Panitch likes to say: if Lenin and Luxemburg had been university professors, maybe the October Revolution would never have

---

55 Fülberth 1999b.

happened. Deppe underscored the significance of this particular moment in history that brought the Marburg School into being in his own writing on the relevance of the 1968 movement.[56]

And yet neither has the struggle over the university as a contested terrain ended, nor can the possibility of a new mass uprising against capitalism be ruled out entirely. The new social movements and the New Left faced the dilemma of ascending at the precise moment when neoliberalism pushed the workers' movement onto a historic defensive, what Frank Deppe calls that movement's 'Great Transformation'.[57] When elements of 1968 rose to political power as part of the coalition government between Social Democrats and Greens they were only able to implement reforms that did not oppose the interests of capital. Rather than the socialisation of all socially reproductive labour in a high-paying public sector, symbolic representation measures and quotas on the boards of private, for-profit corporations were all that could be achieved. Nothing remained of the 1968ers' position that ecological sustainability was impossible in a capitalist society forced to keep growing at its own peril. Instead, market-based 'solutions' and consumer sovereignty were proposed while production and property relations remained untouched. The lesson to be learned from this experience is that any progress not only in the sphere of production but also that of reproduction requires power resources rooted in the capital/labour antagonism where capital is most vulnerable. Thus, the Marburg School *Haltung* – the notion that wherever you are, in or outside the university, strategy must be developed with and on the left wing of the workers' movement – remains key to making any progress towards the transformation of an unsustainable status quo possible once again.

---

56   Deppe 1977, p. 8.
57   Deppe 2012a.

CHAPTER 1

Abendroth School or Marburg School?

1 What Constitutes a School of Thought?

Schools of thought often play an important role in the academic and social rel‑
evance of individual disciplines, as they possess a potential for socialisation
emerging from the institutionalised, formal or informal long-term interaction
between multiple actors and are capable of developing a higher level of pro‑
ductivity and efficacy than the sum of isolated, individual activities could.[1]
But what actually constitutes an intellectual current or school of thought? The
following characteristics make up the primary distinction between them and
other organisational forms of intellectual labour.

Schools of thought generally owe their existence to the exceptional work
of (sometimes charismatic) individuals who create a new scholarly paradigm,
represent a new way of thinking, or develop new, ground-breaking research
methods. The specific character of a school, however, can only emerge when
the activity of these individual personalities leads further actors to identify
with them and interact with them over the long term, thereby forming an iden‑
tity as an 'epistemic community'.[2] This interaction context of the 'epistemic
community' condenses into institutional stability, is often geographically tied
to specific locations, and includes long-term activities such as publishing journ‑
als or organising conferences. The protagonists of a given school not only
identify with the school's paradigm in their own work but also actively rep‑
resent it in the public sphere. When all or at least most of these characteristics
coincide, we can speak of a school of thought.

---

1   See Peter 2001, pp. 9–64. On the topic of sociological schools see, among others, Lepenies 1981.
2   On the concept of the 'epistemic community' see Holzner and Marx 1979. The authors define
    an 'epistemic community' as follows: 'The term *epistemic community* thus designates those
    knowledge-oriented work communities in which cultural standards and social arrangements
    interpenetrate around a primary commitment to epistemic criteria in knowledge production
    and application. In these terms, science is not the only epistemic community ... The establish‑
    ment of a common frame of reference with shared epistemic criteria provides all members
    of such a community access to a consensually validated perspective for the construction of
    reality. The perspective required by the epistemic community must also be integrated into
    a sense of personal identity; this may vary from complete personal transformation through
    conversion to the establishment of a segmental role of identity, which the individual adopts
    in the capacity of professional worker' (p. 109). Hans Manfred Bock also uses the term 'epi‑
    stemic community' in Bock 2007.

The social sciences are rife with distinct schools of thought formed along these lines. Some of the most well-known include the Durkheimian school, the Annales school in French historiography, the Chicago school in American sociology, the Freiburg school in German political science, or the Frankfurt and Cologne schools in German sociology. The Marburg School, on the other hand, is rarely mentioned – and when it is then often in reference to a different Marburg school, namely the philosophical 'Marburg school' of Neo-Kantianism (Hermann Cohen, Paul Natorp, and others) in the late nineteenth and early twentieth centuries.[3] Political impulses also emanated from this school: the philosophy of Hermann Cohen in particular proved inspiring for the wing of German Social Democracy that we know today as 'revisionism'. The Marburg Neo-Kantians' version of an 'ethical socialism' provided the revisionists with a philosophical justification equally incompatible with both materialist rationalisations as well as a revolutionary orientation for the workers' movement.[4] That said, Marburg Neo-Kantianism was by no means 'unpolitical'. The Prussian government noted with suspicion that Cohen and Natorp had served as electors (a function of the Prussian three-class franchise) for the left-liberal candidate, professor of international law Walther Schücking, and were equally displeased with the great deal of importance the professors attached to the 'social question'. Yet the problems confronting the Marburg Neo-Kantians were largely restricted to the internal dimensions of academia, which is hardly surprising given that their underlying philosophical understanding refrained from any pretensions to immediate political engagement.

This philosophical self-sufficiency did not prevent attacks and slanders against it from emerging, however. Cohen for example faced discrimination in internal university proceedings such as tenure hearings, in which more or less openly anti-Semitic sentiments often came to the fore.[5] While Cohen on the one hand sympathised with Social Democracy's right wing and defended himself against anti-Semitic machinations, on the other hand he, like the majority of what Fritz K. Ringer once called the 'German mandarins', joined in the jubilant war celebrations in 1914. The Neo-Kantian Marburg school's reputation and public influence began to decline with the founding of the Weimar Republic, and exhibits no relationship or continuity with the other Marburg school that

3   On Marburg school philosophy see Holzhey 1994. For the standard reference work on the history of political philosophy in Germany from Hegel to Troeltsch and Simmel also detailing the 'ethical socialism' of the Neo-Kantian Marburg school and Hermann Cohen in particular, see Lübbe 1974.
4   See Sieg 1994, esp. pp. 225–34.
5   See Sieg 1994, pp. 471–81.

is the main focus of the present text: the left-wing 'Marburg School' in German social science, beginning in 1950 with Wolfgang Abendroth's appointment to a full professorship as the newly-created chair of *Wissenschaftliche Politik* (scientific politics)[6] at the Philipps University of Marburg, and ending in the early 2000s.

As is documented in the following, this Marburg School exhibits all of the aforementioned characteristics of a social-scientific school of thought. Whether we should speak of a 'Marburg School' or perhaps rather an 'Abendroth School', however, remains a controversial question. Speaking in the latter's favour is the overriding significance of Abendroth's charismatic personality marked by impeccable personal integrity, trustworthiness, and courage, his many years spent working in Marburg, and, as hinted at above, the simple fact that the 'Marburg School' label is already claimed by the Neo-Kantian philosophical tradition.[7]

2   Why the 'Marburg School'?

This volume will nevertheless favour the label 'Marburg School' to denote the development of social sciences in Marburg after 1950. Why? The decisive factor is simply that although Wolfgang Abendroth was undeniably the school's leading figure, sociologist Werner Hofmann left a similarly powerful impression on Marburg social science (albeit not entirely shorn of patriarchal-authoritarian characteristics) despite only spending several years there. Moreover, we cannot neglect the oft-overlooked contributions of Max Horkheimer's former assistant Heinz Maus who came to Marburg as a professor of sociology in 1960. This constellation of academic personnel would soon find illustrative expression in the metaphor of the 'Marburg Triumvirate'.[8] The notion of a 'Marburg School' is further corroborated by the fact that the scholarly-political orientation this 'Triumvirate' embodied would not cease with Werner Hofmann's early death in 1969, Abendroth's retirement in 1972, or that of Maus in 1977, but would instead be carried on by a younger generation of Marburg political scientists and sociologists for another three decades.

Yet the question as to whether the left-wing social-scientific 'Marburg School' fulfils the criteria of a new scholarly paradigm or a new epistemolo-

---

6   Rupp 2001.
7   On scholars arguing for the notion of a 'Marburg School' see Kammler 2001, Jung 1994, Abendroth-Gruppe 2006.
8   Schäfer 2004.

gical current as emphasised above demands an answer. Should we choose to respond in the affirmative, then it still requires further explanation insofar as this school's scholarly production was less a truly original paradigmatic creation so much as a reconstruction, update, and application of an already existing theory of history and society which despite its world-historical significance was nevertheless largely shunned in West Germany, hounded from 'collective memory' (Maurice Halbwachs) and intellectually marginalised: Marxism.[9] Paradoxically, the contrast between Marburg's status as a provincial university town with a well-known Nazi past on one hand and the universalistic tendency of socialist discourses on the other fostered rather than hindered the growth of the Marburg School as an intellectual 'sociotope' (Georg Fülberth), which later would even have the side-effect of electing multiple Communists to the Marburg municipal assembly.

How did it come to pass that this sociotope managed to emerge in Marburg of all places, that this small city with its medieval town centre would become a major bastion of academic and political Marxism in West Germany?[10] All facets of city life in Marburg, counting roughly 50,000 inhabitants in 1960, had been profoundly shaped by the university since the nineteenth century – its institutions, its personnel, and more than anything its primary clientele, the students. During the 1960s they dominated city life and the cultural scene in their thousands. The impulses and actions emanating from the university influenced the town and the local population to a disproportionate extent and more intensively than in West Germany's major cities, where universities also played a significant role but were forced to compete for influence with other large institutions such as corporations, government ministries, sports clubs, or major political organisations and trade unions. Founded in 1527, the Philipps University of Marburg looks back on a proud tradition replete with illustrious names like Hermann Cohen, Paul Natorp, Ernst Robert Curtius, Rudolf Bultmann, and Martin Heidegger, and maintained uncontested cultural hegemony in the city further reinforced rather than curtailed by the pharmaceutical factory founded by Nobel Prize winner Emil von Behring in the neighbouring town of Marbach (incorporated in 1974).[11]

---

9   No West German university professors in the 1950s or early 1960s adopted a Marxist theoretical orientation other than Abendroth, Maus, Hofmann, and the representatives of the Frankfurt School. One Marxist of the previous generation, Leo Kofler (1907–95), served as a substitute professor for Urs Jaeggi in Berlin in 1972, and only received the title of honorary professor permitting him to teach at the Ruhr University in Bochum in 1975.

10   See, more recently, Rosa-Luxemburg-Club Marburg 2013.

11   Rosa-Luxemburg-Club Marburg 2013, p. 117 ff.

These conditions explain why academia and academics themselves could influence the urban public in a more immediate way than was possible in the West German metropolises. Moreover, given that multiple renowned professors like Abendroth, Hofmann, and Maus represented a shared scholarly and political orientation that distinguished itself sharply from the dominant teaching methods and theories not only in Marburg but across the country, it should come as little surprise that they made waves not only within the university but throughout the entire city (and beyond).

The school's growth was further facilitated by a specific cultural-political circumstance which until then had remained an unquestioned fact of city life not yet challenged by fundamental critique: namely, the constant and demonstrative presence of student fraternities (*Korporationen*) in the university town. These fraternities preferred such idyllic provincial town milieus, as urban centres carried the risk of being marginalised as backwards and laughable. For the students of the Marxists Abendroth, Hoffman, and Maus on the other hand, the symbolic world of the fraternities – with their mixture of patriarchal authoritarianism, reactionary ideology often bleeding into fascistic overtones, and bourgeois elitist social habitus – served as a catalyst for the development of radically oppositional thinking and corresponding political activity. In this way, the left-wing professors' socially critical message contributed to an ideological polarisation among the Marburg student population.

A further moment for the extraordinary resonance of Abendroth, Hofmann, and Maus's teachings were the favourable spatial and temporal conditions of social interaction and communication at the time. Neither long journeys nor inconvenient appointments were needed for students to discuss what they learned from the Marxist professors and, in turn, draw weighty practical conclusions together – regardless of how justified or misguided individual actions may have been. The rapidly growing milieu of leftward-moving students under the influence of Marxist theory were accessible to one another at practically all times, thereby realising in their own way what Niklas Luhmann would have called 'interaction systems with face-to-face contact'.[12] Similar was true for the communicative networks of the Marburg School's academic staff: meetings were possible virtually anytime and anywhere one desired in the university cafeteria, private apartments, pubs, or classrooms. All of this was in turn 'overdetermined' by the emergence of the student and protest movement beginning in the mid-1960s, which swept up even the hitherto tame and sleepy town of Marburg.

---

12   See Luhmann 1995, p. 193 ff.

Thus, that Abendroth and later Maus and Hofmann – despite the intellectually suffocating hegemony of theoretical and methodological positions like the
dogma of totalitarianism, formal concepts of democracy, structural functionalism, convergence theory, and anthropologising approaches to social theory
dominant at the time – nevertheless made Marxist theory the Archimedean
point of their work and attempted to apply it to the analysis of contemporary
social processes and structures represents an innovative contribution as such,
approaching the status and function of a new paradigm. In this sense, then, it
is indeed justified to refer to the existence of a 'Marburg School' in the social
sciences.

At first glance, it may appear sensible to describe the left-wing Marburg
School as a school of *Gesellschaftswissenschaft* (science of society). This designation would in fact also correspond to the self-understanding of its protagonists. Why does this volume neglect to do so, instead favouring the label of a
'social-scientific school'?

The term 'society' was highly popular in debates between left-wing social
scientists at the time. It was intended to serve as a categorical counterweight
to the spectrum of approaches which pursued, for example, an analysis of
partial aspects of social behaviour and activity (behaviourism, role theory),
worked with cultural-anthropological hypotheses (Arnold Gehlen), or counterposed labour and interaction (Jürgen Habermas). At the same time, 'society'
also sought to express that the complexity and contradictoriness of concrete
economic, political, and cultural processes could be expressed in a totalising
systematic concept, which in turn implied that these processes were linked
to one another by internal laws obscured by 'bourgeois science' in order to
remove social reality from the possibility of practical and political change.
The concept of 'society' was to help overcome the extensive differentiation
and self-sufficiency of separate disciplines like political science, sociology, and
history as well as recognise and practice interdisciplinarity as an integrative
principle of research in order to accurately grasp the object of study's alleged
unity. This also included some understandings of the concept emerging from
Marxist theory which ascribed an oversimplified, 'form-determining' function
over individual phenomena to economic relations. These sought to explain all
empirically observable problems with recourse to (capitalist) society's 'laws of
motion', which – although this is true not only of the Marburg School – produced in its more dogmatic variants a scholastic construct known as 'derivative
Marxism' (*Ableitungsmarxismus*).

The centrality of 'society' as a concept was reflected in the self-description
of *Fachbereich* 03 at the University of Marburg, which emerged out of the
erstwhile philosophy department in 1971 and comprised the subjects of polit-

ical science, sociology, pedagogy, and philosophy. The department dubbed itself a department of *Gesellschaftswissenschaften*, 'the sciences of society', and merged the subjects of sociology and political science into a common 'unified programme of study'. But because discussion around the rationale behind this ambitious self-description soon fizzled out (as a knowledgeable participant in the departmental restructuring process retrospectively observed),[13] the following depiction of the Marburg School will deploy the less exacting designation of 'social-scientific'. This corresponds to a rather pragmatic approach to academic work, keenly aware of the discernible limits to the capacity of the disciplines making up the Marburg School. The various deficits, mistakes, one-sided interpretations, and abstractifications it contained were by no means a 'monopoly' of the Marburg School, but rather accompany and affect – albeit in constantly shifting forms and with varying intentions – the social sciences to this day.

Like other intellectual currents, the Marburg School underwent multiple phases in its development.[14] Four general phases can be distinguished: first, a phase of emergence and consolidation (from the early 1950s to the mid-1960s); second, a phase dominated by the Marburg Triumvirate between 1966 and 1972; third, a phase marked by the continuation of a Marxist orientation by the post-Abendroth generation from the mid-1970s to the 'epochal rupture' in 1990; and, ultimately, the fourth phase beginning with the state-socialist system's collapse and Germany's 'reunification' until the first years of the new millennium. These different phases cannot be understood in terms of academic debates alone, but call for social and political contextualisation – not least because the protagonists of the Marburg School themselves not only interpreted the concrete social relations of their time but also explicitly sought to change them through their scholarly praxis. Thus, the Marburg School's intellectual and scientific development cannot be adequately reconstructed or understood without taking political and social processes and events into account.

In the meantime a plethora of oftentimes extensive and meticulous biographical studies of Abendroth, detailed accounts of his political contributions to the history of the Federal Republic, and bibliographical surveys of his oeuvre have appeared.[15] His significance has been illuminated in intel-

---

13   Correspondence between Rainer Rilling and the author, 5 April 2013.

14   Lutz Raphael identifies four generations of the French historiographical 'Annales School', see Raphael 1997.

15   Of significance are two comprehensive monographs on the life and work of Wolfgang Abendroth: Diers 2006 and Heigl 2008. Diverse, informative writing on Abendroth's life and work can also be found in Balzer, Bock and Schöler 2001. Michael Buckmiller's editorial efforts compiling the collected works of Wolfgang Abendroth in recent years is also of

lectual-sociological terms, while the Marburg School itself has been explored both institutional-historically and comparatively. Yet almost all of the existing studies end with Abendroth's departure from university life. By introducing a third and a fourth phase, this volume contradicts the both erroneous as well as occasionally intentional suggestion that the Marburg School ended with Abendroth's retirement. In order to push against this notion and also because the Marburg School until the early 1970s has already been studied from various angles over the years, this book consciously devotes more attention to the third and fourth phases than has for whatever reason been the case in the existing literature. In this sense, the following depiction diverges from the common understanding of the Marburg School primarily in two aspects: firstly, it explicitly incorporates sociology, and secondly does not view the Marburg School as ending with Abendroth's retirement.

---

major significance. Four volumes have been issued by the Hanover publishing house he founded, Offizin-Verlag, thus far. The fourth volume contains Abendroth's texts from 1964 to 1966.

CHAPTER 2

First Phase: Gradual Formation, 1950 to the Mid-1960s

1   Social and Political Context

The first phase of the Marburg School developed in the context of the recon-struction, stabilisation, and expansion of capitalist relations of property and production in West Germany, which had initially persisted in a latent form post-1945.[1] The 1948 currency reform, however, represented a measure not only signi-fying a major rupture in terms of monetary policy but also laying the economic foundations for what soon led to the political division of Germany into two independent states, albeit controlled by the respective occupying powers: the Federal Republic of Germany and the German Democratic Republic (GDR). The Federal Republic's integration into the Western sphere of influence, expressed economically by its membership in the European Coal and Steel Community (a common market for coal, iron, and steel and the predecessor to today's European Union), and militarily in its joining NATO in 1955 negated all pro-spects for the development of an independent Federal Republic outside the influence of the Western great powers. Domestically, this corresponded not only to a nearly seamless reintegration of countless former Nazis into business, politics, the courts, and academia, but also to massive repression of opposi-tional political forces. Mass movements for democratising the economy (co-determination in the steel industry in 1951, the industrial relations law in 1952) were redirected and the broad popular opposition to remilitarisation neut-ralised, while more fundamental political opposition was forcibly repressed, such as the banning of the Communist Party (KPD). The transformation of the Social Democratic Party (SPD) from a workers' party into a cross-class 'people's party' (symbolised by the Godesberg Programme in 1959) deactivated the par-liament as a potential forum for the articulation of social and political altern-atives. As the newfound dynamism of West German capitalism introduced by the so-called 'Miracle on the Rhine' or *Wirtschaftswunder* brought with it a

---

1   The following sections on the social and political development of the Federal Republic are based on, among others, Fülberth 2012, Recker 2009, Wirsching 2006, Görtemaker 1999, Schildt and Siegfried 2009.

reduction in unemployment and rising living standards for the wage-earning
population and the GDR exhibited little attraction as an alternative system,
socialist thought and activity in West Germany was reduced to a shrinking
minority of workers, trade union functionaries, left-wing Social Democrats, left-
socialists, underground Communists, and a handful of intellectuals.

It is unsurprising that anti-Communism managed to rise to the level of
quasi-state doctrine under such conditions, placing even slightly divergent
political opinions and activity under the general suspicion of being associated with Communism. The mutually reinforcing dynamic of the 'social market
economy', rising living standards, Western integration, and ideological demonisation of all principally critical political aspirations facilitated a cross-party
system consensus accompanied by a crippling, only rarely disturbed intellectual and cultural 'graveyard quiet'. Yet the first signs of major turbulence in
the capitalist process of accumulation would bring movement into these social
relations, which had appeared forever insulated against economic dislocations
and social inequalities. This development in turn brings us to several of the
problems which repeatedly confronted the founders of the Marburg School,
first and foremost Wolfgang Abendroth.

2   Wolfgang Abendroth (1906–85)

Wolfgang Abendroth was born the son of a middle school teacher in Elberfeld
near the German city of Wuppertal in 1906.[2] He spent his school years in Frankfurt am Main where he became active in left-wing youth organisations at a very
young age. His criticisms of the KPD leadership's ultra-left orientation led to his
expulsion from the party in 1928, which he first joined in the early 1920s. He subsequently joined the Communist Party (Opposition), or KPO, which called for a
united front policy between the rival currents of the workers' movement. After
studying law he worked as a junior lawyer without giving up his political activity, but could not finish his dissertation on industrial relations law following
the Nazi rise to power in 1933. Despite the serious risks it entailed, Abendroth
returned to Germany from Bern after completing a doctorate in international
law in order to immediately resume illegal resistance work. He was arrested
by the Gestapo in 1937 and sentenced to four years in prison, but held fast to

---

2 A lively impression of Abendroth's personal development can be found in the conversations
   conducted with Barbara Dietrich and Joachim Perels, see Dietrich and Perels 1976; see also
   the highly detailed Diers 2006.

his political convictions. He was conscripted into the infamous prisoner bat-
talion (or 'probationary brigade' in Nazi terminology) '999' and sent to Greece
in 1943, where he soon managed to defect to the partisans of the Greek People's
Liberation Army (Ellinikós Laikós Apelevtherotikós St07ató, or ELAS). After the
war, Abendroth was interned by the British in Egypt. Following his release he
worked in the legal apparatus of the Soviet occupation zone, where he was
appointed to an extraordinary professorship of international law at the University of Leipzig and a professorship of public law at the University of Jena in
the same year. Due to his ongoing membership in the SPD – illegal following
the founding of the Socialist Unity Party (SED) – and his cooperation with its
office for eastern affairs, he was forced to flee to the West in late 1948.

A professorship at the Hochschule für Arbeit, Politik und Wirtschaft in Wil-
helmshaven was followed by an appointment in Marburg in 1950. Such a development would have been impossible without the attitudes of leading Social
Democratic politicians in 'Red Hessia' at the time, still significantly influenced
by the experience of fascism. Yet the SPD's self-understanding would soon shift,
and roughly ten years later Abendroth was expelled from the party along with
several others for continuing to support the left-wing student organisation,
the Sozialistischer Deutscher Studentenbund or SDS, which had already been
expelled in 1961.[3]

Beyond the specifics of what he said in lectures, seminars, or public debates – which he did while conveying absolute credence – eluding the magnet-
ism of his personal presence proved difficult. Although sometimes articulating
himself in adventurously long sentences, he never lost his train of thought.
His manner of speaking was lively, even passionate, and filled with a seemingly inexhaustible *élan vital*. Although biographically rooted in Frankfurt's
cultural milieu, his speech was shorn of any trace of the local dialect. Always
friendly and never patronising, he engaged those he encountered who did not
necessarily consider themselves his friends with a carefree openness. Having
experienced political repression, brutal mistreatment, years in prison and war,
fear seemed to be an unknown feeling to him.[4] Yet despite his accommodating
behaviour, interaction with others was always guided by that which he considered academically and politically relevant. He proved incapable of feeling
hate at a time when the reinstatement of former Nazis as professors after 1945,
even in law departments, provided him with more than ample justification.[5]

---

3 On the history of SDS see, among others, Fichter and Lönnendonker 2007.
4 Although he rarely spoke about it in public, he left no doubt as to the physical and psycholo-
   gical torture visited upon him.
5 Abendroth discusses this in, for example, Dietrich and Perels 1976, p. 212, as well as in a tele-

He was generous in his relationships with his staff and students, attentive and free of any professorial arrogance. In political engagements he was militant and decisive.

A major portion of Abendroth's life as an academic and political personality is thanks to his wife, Lisa. While the spouses of Werner Hofmann and Heinz Maus disappeared behind the thick curtain of traditional gender roles and remained practically invisible to the public eye, Lisa Abendroth found herself confronted with the problem of having to shelve her own scholarly and political ambitions in order to support Wolfgang in a self-sacrificing manner, without which he would have been unable to produce the output that characterises his legacy today. This presented Lisa Abendroth with an existential dilemma that she never managed to resolve, although she would have liked to work as a historian. Nevertheless, as Heiner Halberstadt wrote following her death in 2012 she never felt co-opted by Wolfgang Abendroth, as she 'was always able to align her own thinking, actions, and feelings with his in the broad outlines and moments'.[6] She completed her own doctorate supervised by the historian Wilhelm Mommsen, the father of historians Hans and Wolfgang Mommsen, shortly before the war's end in 1945, but was later so preoccupied with caring for her family and supporting her husband that no time was left for her own academic work. She nevertheless managed, where possible, to participate in seminars, discussions, and 'editorial and conceptual' preparation of Abendroth's publications.[7] Later, following his retirement, she took on volunteer positions in the SPD and was noted for numerous impressive speeches, before leaving the party in 2002 in protest against Gerhard Schröder's looming 'Agenda 2010' austerity policies.

Abendroth, who in political terms was practically 'socialised' into the left wing of the German workers' movement, saw his views confirmed by the development of the Federal Republic in the aspects considered relevant to the Marburg School's understanding, as well as challenged to present a radical intellectual and political competing vision without negating the necessity of practical-political compromises and partial solutions to specific problems.

The reconstruction of the old relations of power and property – entailing the de facto rehabilitation and reinstatement of large groups of Nazi-era business, state, and cultural elites across West Germany – prompted renewed considerations regarding the relationship between capitalism, fascism, and democracy,

---

vision programme aired by Westdeutscher Rundfunk in 1987 titled *Ein deutsches Schicksal: Wolfgang Abendroth* (Westdeutscher Rundfunk 2012).

6   Halberstadt 2012, p. 55.
7   See Deppe 2012b, p. 52.

while the drifting apart of concentrated economic power and political democracy motivated Abendroth to work out the necessary prerequisites for a 'social
democracy'. He saw in Social Democracy's accommodation of capitalism a
primary reason behind the crisis of the West German workers' movement – in
his eyes the only collective actor capable of carrying out fundamental reforms
and a transformation of capitalism. Marxist theory represented for him the
only convincing foundation for a scientifically plausible and politically effective analysis of modern capitalism along with its politically, legally, and culturally reproducing and legitimising institutions and actors.

Abendroth taught and wrote books and articles about the aforementioned
topics, some of which were greeted with a broad reception or inspired related
research. The critical reappraisal of fascism, for example, left an impression in
a collected volume edited by Abendroth on theories of fascism, in which the
interconnections between the economic and political interests of the ruling
social classes and fascist movements were the overriding focus.[8]

A solicitor and expert in international law by training, Abendroth's interpretation of the West German constitution or Basic Law as well as his conception
of democracy came into conflict with the dominant approach to constitutional
law as exemplified by Ernst Forsthoff, author of the 1933 volume on the 'total
state'.[9] While Forsthoff drew on a formally liberal conception of the state of law
after 1945 and rejected the concept of a 'social state of law' as a legally imper-
missible category, Abendroth by contrast identified both the constitutional
possibility and politically necessity of practically implementing in political
terms normative determinations such as those found in Paragraphs 14, 15 and 20
of the Basic Law with the help of a democratically legitimated state. As Joachim
Perels aptly put it, this aim was diametrically opposed to the understanding
of state and society prevalent in the thinking of figures like Forsthoff.[10] While
Forsthoff viewed the state as independent of society, which he saw as self-
regulating and sought to shield from all possible state intervention, Abendroth
saw in the Basic Law the constitutional legitimacy for a state-mediated configuration and reconfiguration of society. In doing so, Abendroth looked to the
Weimar-era constitution, and referred theoretically to the Austrian professor of
constitutional law Hermann Heller, who taught in Frankfurt until 1933 and in
the late 1920s called for the 'law-ification of the economy'[11] and an expansion of
the welfare state as a counterweight to the political dominance of the proper-

---

8   Abendroth 1967.
9   On Abendroth's conception of the social state and democracy see Abendroth 1972 f.
10   Perels 2006.
11   See Perels 2006, p. 103.

tied classes and the looming toppling of parliament by reactionary and fascist forces. Abendroth wrote of the 'logical relationship between social statehood, democracy, and constitutionality' in 1954, stating: 'The decisive moment in the thought of social statehood in relation to the legal foundation of the Basic Law thus consists of the fact that the belief in the immanent righteousness of the existing economic and social order is subsumed and that, for this reason, the economic and social order is subjected to shaping by the state organs in which the democratic self-determination of the people is represented'.[12]

Abendroth harboured no doubts that the central political actor in developing a social state and a democratic economy as well as a potential socialist transformation could only be the working class. It represented the wage-earning masses in political and trade union terms – that is to say, the majority of the population which was on the one hand still most immediately subjected to the coercions and risks of the capitalist economy despite rising living standards, but on the other also occupied a key position as the collective producer of society's wealth within the process of material reproduction and was thus to be understood as the decisive force of social and political change.[13]

Alongside other articles and essays, Abendroth fleshed out this conception in his *A Short History of the European Working Class*, originally published in German by Suhrkamp Verlag in 1965, and in English in 1972 by New Left Books and Monthly Review Press.[14] This study was guided by two fundamental ideas: the first consisted of a normative connection between socialism and democracy, while the second was motivated not least by his own biographical experiences, namely the need for the political unity of the workers' movement and more specifically its Social Democratic and Communist wings. Methodologically, 'social history' was oriented (albeit not explicitly) around pioneering works like Arthur Rosenberg's reflections on *Democracy and Socialism*[15] in the sense that they did not limit themselves to the usual intellectual history or that of events and organisations, but rather incorporated aspects of economic development and social change and thereby anticipated, at least to some extent, elements of historiographical methodologies later developed more systematically by the 'Bielefeld School' around historians Hans-Ulrich Wehler and Jürgen Kocka.[16] The ultimate ambitions of Abendroth and the Bielefeld School, however, would

---

12   Abendroth 1972f, p. 114. On Abendroth's views concerning the state of law and the social state see, more recently, Fischer-Lescano, Perels and Scholle 2012.

13   Abendroth 1972e.

14   Abendroth 1968a; Abendroth 2019.

15   Rosenberg 1939.

16   See Hitzer and Welskopp 2010.

diverge significantly. While Abendroth stood for a socialist perspective in the European workers' movement, the representatives of the Bielefeld School were more associated with a social-democratic modernisation paradigm.

Neither at this time nor later in his career would Abendroth compile a more comprehensive theory of the political or political science as such. Although he possessed all of the necessary prerequisites to execute such a project – a profound base of knowledge, extraordinary analytical capabilities, and argumentative rigour – he neglected to produce a broader, systematic theoretical treatise precisely because he consistently prioritised the practical-political relevance of his work over foundational research. Consequently, his reflections on this point tend to be rather modest. Nevertheless, he succeeded in launching an *Einführung in die politische Wissenschaft* (Introduction to Political Science)[17] that quickly became a standard reference work in the discipline, probably not least because its Marxian-inspired but not exclusively Marxist character offered a contrasting programme to mainstream political science at the time. Multiple authors from the circle of Marburg staff and graduate students contributed to the introductory volume. In his opening chapter on 'Subject Matter and Method of Political Science', Jörg Kammler[18] drew a sharp distinction between the function of a domination-critical conception of the discipline and the political-ethical orientation of the then-hegemonic 'Freiburg School', describing it as follows:

> Proceeding from the *historical* and *social* character of the political, it conceives political praxis as a specific praxis, and institutions of domination as institutions of a given society. Political domination becomes comprehensible to it in the political organisation of a concrete historical society. As its recourse to society forbids us from abstractly fixing political structures and processes in any given sphere of the political, it thus requires incorporating the process of economic reproduction and the social struc-

---

17   Abendroth and Lenk 1968.
18   Born in 1940, Jörg Kammler was Abendroth's assistant from 1965–7. He completed his doctorate in 1972 with an outstandingly researched dissertation on the political theory of Georg Lukács that is still worth reading today (Kammler 1974). Initially a lecturer, he later became a professor of political science at the Gesamthochschule Kassel (now the University of Kassel) from 1974–95. His fields of expertise include research on fascism and resistance. Jörg spent years dealing with the life of his father, Hans Kammler, a high-ranking ss officer who occupied executive positions in the Nazi terror apparatus and worked on the V2 missile project towards the end of the war. This biographical background was also a major impetus behind Jörg Kammler's interest in researching the anti-Nazi resistance. Jörg Kammler died on 27 August 2013.

ture emerging from it as the basis of the distribution of political and social power, along with the praxis of individuals or social groups referring to this distribution of power, into the critical analysis of political science.[19]

In doing so, he drew on a short but precedent-setting text by Abendroth in which he described political science as 'political sociology'. Rather than ascribing to the state and its institutions an independent existence *sui generis* and restricting analysis to the immanent functioning thereof, political sociology was obliged to explore the relationship between the political as such and the structures of society. By not only making political praxis its object of study but also regularly influencing this praxis, however, political sociology itself fulfilled an eminently practical-political function:

> Political sociology is – whether it seeks to be or not – related to praxis. Not only because political *praxis* constitutes its *subject matter*, even when conducting ideology-critical analysis of political theories or developing a political theory of its own. It is also related because political sociology, by analysing political praxis or working out a political theory itself, serves and changes political praxis.[20]

Reflections such as the one cited above point to an essential facet of Abendroth's personality: namely, his public engagement as a Marxist intellectual. As Hans Manfred Bock accurately notes, his continuous activity as a political scientist and constitutional lawyer as well as his function as a pioneering thinker of the left-wing trade union and social-democratic spectrum in the 1950s consolidated his status as an intellectual 'who was connected to a not-negligible degree of public influence and initiative'.[21] This status would continue into the early 1960s, before Abendroth became an intellectual protagonist of the renaissance of Marxism and the student movement in the Federal Republic in 1968. Frank Deppe saw in Abendroth not only an 'organic intellectual of the workers' movement' but more than anything the '*type of the intervening, socialist intellectual*'.[22] Jürgen Habermas's formulation that Abendroth had been a 'partisan professor in the country of followers' provides an adequately appreciative and memorable characterisation.[23] Nor should we forget the fact – character-

---

19   Kammler 1968, p. 16.
20   Abendroth 1972g, p. 11.
21   Bock 2001b, p. 227.
22   Deppe 2006a, p. 48.
23   Habermas 1966.

istic of West Germany's dull and authoritarian intellectual atmosphere before 1968 – that due to Horkheimer's low opinion of him, Theodor Adorno did not dare allow the 'too left-wing'-appearing Habermas to complete his doctorate in Frankfurt, forcing him to relocate to Marburg where he finished *The Structural Transformation of the Public Sphere* under Abendroth's supervision in 1961.[24]

3   Students, Doctoral Candidates, Staff

Marxism did not emerge as the authoritative and identity-forming paradigm at the Marburg *Institut für wissenschaftliche Politik* (Institute for Scientific Politics) until the mid-1960s. Looking back on the aforementioned volume *Einführung*, one of its most important authors Jörg Kammler would conclude that the individual contributions were 'by no means ... consistently informed by a coherent Marxist vocabulary and form of analysis', noting that Abendroth's liberal stance permitted the volume 'to be composed in the spirit of a pluralistic left-wing opening towards a Marxist-oriented critique of democracy and capitalism'.[25]

Beyond the fact that a further political science professorship occupied by non-Marxists existed alongside Abendroth (initially by Erich Matthias,[26] an expert on party research particularly of the SPD and the Weimar Republic, and later by Ernst Otto Czempiel[27] who worked in the field of international relations) relativised a unified left-wing orientation of the institute at the faculty level, the circle of academic staff and graduate students around Abendroth was by no means homogenous either. They shared a respect and admiration, even veneration of Abendroth's political and moral authority, but nevertheless remained far from a stable 'epistemic community' at this point. The political spectrum within the group ranged from left-liberal to social-democratic and

---

24   Habermas 1991. He dedicated the book 'to Wolfgang Abendroth in gratitude'.

25   Kammler 2001, pp. 149–50.

26   Erich Matthias (1921–83) was a political scientist and contemporary historian. He worked as an extraordinary professor at the Institute for Political Science at the Philipps University in Marburg from 1961–5, before taking up a professorship at the University of Mannheim in 1965. Among other works, he became known academically for the volume co-edited with Rudolf Morsey *Das Ende der Parteien 1933* (Matthias and Morsey 1960).

27   Ernst Otto Czempiel (1927–2017) was professor of international politics at the Institute for Political Science from 1966–70. and later a professor at the University of Frankfurt. Czempiel is known for, among other things, various publications on security and peace policies. He co-founded the Hessische Stiftung für Friedens- und Konfliktforschung and remained a member of its board until 1996.

independent left-wing views all the way to left-socialist positions. More than a few of the students of the first generation who completed their doctorates under Abendroth or became assistants would go on to find academic success and receive professorships at other universities, including Werner Link, Kurt Kliem, Hans-Gerd Schumann, Kurt Lenk, Arno Klönne, Axel Azzola, and others.[28] Although Abendroth's assistant since 1961, Hanno Drechsler distinguished himself in his field with research on the so-called 'middle groups'[29] between the SPD and KPD but failed to enter academia.[30] Among this first generation of graduate students and assistants, Arno Klönne[31] probably came closest to embodying Abendroth's notion of cultivating Marxist theory as part of a practical-political agenda. Lenk, however, also belonged to the most prominent staff members influenced by Marxist theory, and would later become quite well-known as the author of several publications on the critique of conservative ideology, the 'conservative revolution', and right-wing extremism.

The topical focuses, level of participation in the internal affairs of the institute, and level of academic output in and around the Marburg School differed heavily. Several of the institute's many dissertations prove particularly notable, such as Karl Hermann (Kay) Tjaden's investigation of the KPO,[32] a split from

---

28   On the heterogeneity of the circle of students, doctoral candidates, and graduates around Abendroth see Bock 2001a.

29   Encouraged by Abendroth, this research on the 'middle groups' between SPD and KPD near the end of the Weimar Republic and the early Nazi period included the KPO, the 'Rote Kämpfer', the Internationaler Sozialistischer Kampfbund, the Sozialistische Arbeiterpartei Deutschlands (SAPD), and the 'Neu Beginnen' group.

30   After working as an administrator at the universities of Marburg and Giessen for several years, Hanno Drechsler (1931–2003) was elected mayor of Marburg for the SPD in 1970. He held this office until 1992.

31   Arno Klönne (1931–2015) was a member of SDS, studied sociology and political science, and completed his doctorate in 1955 under Abendroth with a dissertation on the Hitler Youth. He worked as, among others, a member of the academic staff at the Sozialforschungsstelle Münster and was appointed to a professorship at the University of Paderborn in 1978. Focuses of his academic work included studies of the German workers' movement as well as conservatism and right-wing extremism. Together with Dieter Claessens and Armin Tschoerpe he compiled a standard textbook on the *Sozialkunde der Bundesrepublik Deutschland* in several editions in 1965. Klönne was active in the cultural scene, the peace movement, and local politics.

32   Born in 1929, Kurt Lenk first studied under Adorno, Horkheimer, and Carlo Schmid in Frankfurt am Main. He finished his *Habilitation* in 1964 under Abendroth on the topic of 'Marx in the sociology of knowledge'. Serving on Marburg's academic council until 1966, he then taught at the University of Erlangen from 1966–72. Afterwards he was called to the Aachen Polytechnical University where he served as director of the university's political science institute until his retirement in 1994. Lenk is known for his numerous publications on ideology critique in Marx's work, conservativism, and the 'Conservative Revolution'.

the KPD near the end of the Weimar Republic, in which early signs of the extraordinary analytical and systematic rigour that would generally character-ise the author's later work can be seen. Similar is true for Hans Manfred Bock's profound investigation of German 'Syndicalism and Left Communism (1918–1925)', which arguably remains the uncontested standard reference work on the topic to this day.[33] Also worthy of mention is Frank Deppe's differentiated, rich in material, and analytically ambitious study of the relation between political theory and praxis in the life of Auguste Blanqui.[34]

Despite the sometimes highly divergent scholarly and political preferences of the actors involved, the elements of institutionalisation and cooperative relationships characteristic of intellectual schools of thought gradually began to form. The journal *Marburger Abhandlungen zur politischen Wissenschaft*, published by Verlag Anton Hain in Meisenheim am Glan, was launched in 1964 on Abendroth's initiative. Collaborative publications such as the *Einführung* or the establishment of a graduate seminar in which a 'grey hierarchy' of prot-agonists, the fight for symbolic capital, and academic interaction overlapped helped to form the contours of the school.

An informal group of sociologists and political scientists began to emerge in the shadows of regular institute life with its day-to-day routines during this period, which initially included several students and began to move in an expli-citly Marxist direction. This group included Karl Hermann (Kay) Tjaden, Mar-garete (Annegret) Tjaden-Steinhauer, Rüdiger Griepenburg, Frank Deppe, Kurt Steinhaus, Georg Fülberth, Dieter Boris, Jürgen Harrer, Helge Knüppel, Gert Meyer, Eberhard Dähne, Lothar Peter, and others.[35] They were all active or

---

When Abendroth died in 1985, Lenk wrote an obituary in the *Kölner Zeitschrift für Soziolo-gie und Sozialpsychologie* ending with the words: 'The reach of his activities as a scholar and *homo politicus* cannot yet be measured today. A generous, personal as well as mod-est and helpful teacher and educator, his critical social-scientific impulses live on with his friends and students', see Lenk 1985.

33   Bock 1969. Born in 1940, Bock taught at the Institut d'Allemand at the University of Paris III from 1969–71, where he was appointed *professeur associé*. He was then appoin-ted to the Gesamthochschule Kassel in 1972 to a professorship of political sociology in the political science department. Alongside his teaching responsibilities and extensive com-parative studies largely in the field of German-French cultural relations, he also took on guest professorships in Paris and the US and remained active for decades as an author and co-editor of the journal *Lendemains. Études comparées sur la France/Vergleichende Frankreichforschung*. Bock has made several competent contributions to the intellectual sociology of the Marburg School. In 2006 he was awarded the high French cultural award, the *Chevalier de l'Ordre des Palmes Académiques*.

34   Deppe 1968. The dissertation was later published in book form, see Deppe 1970.

35   Other names from the aforementioned group will be referred to later on in some way or

formerly active members of SDS. In an informal festschrift published only in manuscript form to mark Wolfgang Abendroth's 60th birthday, over half of the contributors were SDS members or had been members during their university studies.

another. Born in 1941, Helge Knüppel completed her dissertation about Greek political history under Abendroth. She was later employed in the Hamburg social administration. Kurt Steinhaus (1938–1991), a leading member of SDS, was a sociologist and political scientist. After his dissertation under Abendroth on the 'sociology of the Turkish revolution', published by the Europäischer Verlagsanstalt in Frankfurt am Main in 1969, he worked at the IMSF in Frankfurt before becoming a staffer at the DKP party executive in Düsseldorf. Eberhard Dähne (1938–2010) was a sociologist. He was the national chair of SDS in 1961–2. He worked as an assistant at the Sociological Seminar of the Phillips University of Marburg from 1963–7. As a co-founder of the 'Institute for Social-Scientific Research' in Marburg, he conducted studies of empirical social research before completing his own sociological dissertation about the tertiary sector supervised by Heinz Maus in 1972. In 1973 he became a research fellow at the IMSF, where he worked until 1989. He first represented the DKP as a city councillor from 1972–9 and later the PDS as an independent in the Frankfurt am Main city council.

CHAPTER 3

Second Phase: Emergence of an 'Epistemic Community', Mid-1960s to Early 1970s

1   Social and Political Context

The social and political landscape of the Federal Republic began to change considerably in the mid-1960s. West Germany found itself confronted with an unexpected economic recession for the first time in its history, leading to an (albeit brief) decline in the gross national product and a sudden tripling of unemployment to one half million. The first 'grand coalition' between the Christian Democrats (CDU) and the SPD, formed in December 1966 and comprising former Nazi Party member Kurt Georg Kiesinger as chancellor and once-exiled resistance fighter Willy Brandt as vice-chancellor and foreign minister, was tasked with conducting efficient crisis management by updating elements of Keynesian economic policy and deploying nevertheless largely defensive state intervention. The 'Law on Promoting the Stability and Growth of the Economy' and another on Medium-Term Financial Planning' were created by the federal government as instruments for interventionist and corrective measures targeting the economic conjuncture. The framework of this approach was provided by the so-called 'magic square' and 'global steering' policies, which would allegedly strike a balance between growth, price stability, full employment, and foreign trade balances.

Things would also begin to shift in foreign policy terms, namely in relations with the Eastern European state-socialist bloc and the GDR in particular following decades of ossification under the Cold War banner. This move would eventually lead to the foreign policy strategy of 'change through rapprochement' between the two German states later pursued by Chancellor Willy Brandt's social-liberal coalition. The grand coalition also facilitated the establishment of a long-controversial measure which had thus far consistently failed to secure a parliamentary majority: the passing of the so-called 'Emergency Acts' (*Notstandsgesetze*). The SPD's participation in the governing coalition removed it as a factor of resistance to the Emergency Acts, which was instead carried by a broad extra-parliamentary protest movement known as the *Außerparlamentarische Opposition* (APO). The movement found its primary base among some sections of the trade unions, specifically IG Metall, protesting students, and critical intellectuals. This deeper confrontation between opposing conceptions of the Federal Republic's future social and political character found its most acute expression in the conflicts provoked by the Emergency Acts. The struggle against the law coincided with the 1968 student movement, which reached its first initial highpoint in the anti-Springer campaign and actions against the Springer media empire following the attempted assassination of Rudi Dutschke. The war in Vietnam, anti-colonial liberation movements, and the emergence of neo-fascist forces such as the National Democratic Party (NPD) had a particularly intense mobilising effect on the young oppositional intelligentsia.

A renewal of labour struggles would also occur in parallel to other Western European countries, albeit markedly behind the extent and depth of strikes and other actions conducted by blue- and white-collar workers in France, Italy, and Great Britain.[1] Nevertheless, events like the spontaneous 'September strikes' in 1969 facilitated an at least partial leftward shift within the trade unions, expressed in among other things increased strike levels particularly in IG Metall.[2] That the ideological straightjacket of the Adenauer era with its authoritarian conformism and government policy of suppressing the country's Nazi past was beginning to unravel was evidenced by the founding (or 're-constitution') of the German Communist Party (DKP) in 1968, which took the place of the still-illegal KPD and sought to attract sections of the soon-to-collapse student movement and groups of left-wing intelligentsia. This party would go on to play a not-negligible role in the later history of the Marburg School.

It is always the case when seemingly unshakable social and political relations surprisingly begin to shift that the work and activity of cultural producers, avant-gardism, and innovative aesthetic processes will be involved – whether by seismographically anticipating the coming changes, radically questioning the status quo, or pushing forward new developments. This was also true of the cultural scene in the Federal Republic at the time, as pop art and neo-Dadaism began to emerge in the visual arts, particularly in the provocative art of Joseph Beuys, 'New German Cinema' directors like Ulrich Schamoni, Rainer Werner Fassbinder, and Volker Schlöndorff challenged audiences, and dramas like Rolf Hochhuth's *The Deputy* or Peter Weiss's *The Investigation* about the Auschwitz trials dragged the country's long-repressed and whitewashed Nazi past onto the theatre stage.[3]

---

1   See Albers, Goldschmidt and Oehlke 1971.
2   On this see Schumann, Gerlach, Gschlössl and Millhofer 1971; IMSF 1969.
3   Hochhuth 2006; Weiss 2010.

Mutually reinforcing each other to some extent, these and other moments fostered a political climate which both made evident the urgent need for reforms as well as led to the formation of a constellation of forces that would enable a new social-liberal governing coalition in 1969. Under the banner of new Chancellor Willy Brandt's ambitious slogan to 'dare more democracy', the government introduced a series of reforms (criminal and family law, industrial relations, university reforms, etc.) which, although not constituting a 're-founding of the Federal Republic' (Manfred Görtemaker) as such, certainly opened up possibilities beyond mere technocratic adjustments, along with a paradigm shift in foreign policy known as *Ostpolitik*.

2 Werner Hofmann (1922–69)

The process of the left-wing Marburg School's emergence received a forceful innovative thrust in the form of Werner Hofmann's appointment to a second professorship of sociology. Despite Heinz Maus's sociology professorship, the Marburg School was primarily represented by Wolfgang Abendroth and his group of staff and students until the mid-1960s. Werner Hofmann's appointment in 1966 brought with it perhaps not a one-sided shift, but certainly a noticeable reduction in the imbalance between the two disciplines. Maus had both remained consistently loyal to Abendroth as well as supported Werner Hofmann long before his appointment in years prior.[4] That said, he never managed – whether due to his systematic approach to his work, a certain predilection for a bohemian lifestyle, or whatever else – to establish himself alongside Abendroth and impute sociology with its own distinct contours. Hofmann's appointment changed this state of affairs.

Werner Hofmann was born into a bourgeois family in 1922 in Meiningen, Thuringia.[5] His mother was Catholic, his father, the director of a bank, Jewish. He was forced to spend several months in a forced labour camp in Jena due to his 'half-Jewish' ancestry in 1944–5. Following the war, his political convictions initially drove him to Leipzig in East Germany, but he fled to the West with his family in 1951 citing the lack of attention given to his academic work and significant material hardship. He completed his doctorate in Munich under the supervision of Adolf Weber in 1953 on the topic of national account systems, before receiving an assistantship from Hans Raupach at the Hochschule für Sozialwissenschaften (known as the Hochschule für Arbeit, Politik

---

4   Preface to Hofmann 1962.
5   On the following see Hofmann-Göttig 1999 (son of Werner Hofmann).

und Wirtschaft until 1956) in Wilhemshaven where he completed his *Habilitation* under Raupach with a study of *Die Arbeitsverfassung der Sowjetunion* (The Employment Regime of the Soviet Union) in 1958.[6] Hofmann moved to the University of Göttingen in the early 1960s, where he became an extraordinary professor and was awarded a *Venia legend* in the discipline of sociology. His appointment in Marburg, vocally supported by Abendroth and Maus, would follow in 1966.

Like Abendroth, Hofmann was rhetorically well-versed. His lectures were delivered practically fit to print, and he always spoke with steadfast conviction. Similar to Abendroth, most people who encountered him felt that his personality and intellectual partisanship were identical. In contrast to many social scientists of his time, Hofmann never gave the impression of standing 'beside himself' or that one was only communicating with a 'second nature'. As decisively as he spoke, equally constricting was his authoritative, perhaps even authoritarian attitude, often accompanied with a cutting tone that left not only his students but sometimes his colleagues cold as well. Anyone working with him had to either cultivate a thick skin or possess the necessary self-confidence to take Hofmann's categorical judgements, imperative commands, and blunt reactions in stride. That said, he was always willing to take a minute for clever ideas, interesting information, and reasonable objections – even when they came from his students.[7] Hofmann was thirsty for knowledge and possessed a keen intellectual sensitivity for new developments. His habitus as a tenured professor made it difficult for him to deal with the rebellious students and their unconventional ways of behaving. Even SDS members felt provoked into launching polemical attacks, although here the fixation on Hofmann's imposing personality also played a role.[8] None of this detracted from his individual stature in the eyes of the students, however, as evidenced by their shock and grief following his early death.

Whereas Abendroth called for an alternative to mainstream academia's conceptions of democracy and the social state, Hofmann for his part declared war on the dominant teachings of academic economics. He viewed the critique thereof as a crucial prerequisite for a socially critical sociology grounded in social economy. Hofmann had already made a name for himself with numer-

---

6   Hofmann 1956.

7   For example, he invited the author of this book – I was still a student in 1968 – to a personal meeting to discuss the situation in France characterised by student uprising and mass strikes. He had heard that I was studying the developments in the country at the time.

8   See the polemic between left-wing students and Werner Hofmann in the student newspaper *Marburger Blätter*, (2) 1969 and Hofmann's letter to the editor in (3) 1969.

ous monographs even before h:s Marburg appointment, containing both a historical-critical reception of classical economics[9] as well as a differentiated view of the Soviet Union shorn of clichés fixated on totalitarianism theory or terror. This was particularly true of his *Arbeitsverfassung*,[10] which was – in light of the ubiquitous ideological strength of anti-Communism across all social spheres at the time – both a personally courageous as well as intellectually praiseworthy accomplishment. In 1962 he would publish *Ideengeschichte der sozialen Bewegungen des 19. und 20. Jahrhunderts* (Intellectual History of the Social Movements of the Nineteenth and Twentieth Centuries), in a sense complementing Abendroth's *Short History of the European Working Class* which would appear several years later. An expanded sixth edition with contributions from Wolfgang Abendroth and Iring Fetscher appeared in 1979.[11]

As was true of Abendroth, Hofmann's work was driven not so much by academic ambition but rather was primarily devoted to demonstrating that capitalism was not an eternal, natural fact. A historical perspective on capitalism revealed a continuity and complexity between social movements, theories, and utopian models and experiments sharing a self-understanding as an alternative to capitalist domination and exploitation. Marxian theory may have occupied a central place in his *Ideengeschichte*, but other conceptions taken from the 'utopian socialists', Michael Bakunin's anarchism, Eduard Bernstein's revisionism, or even Vladimir Lenin and Antonio Gramsci could also be seen. The study explored new aspects in methodological terms in that it did not limit itself to descriptions immanent to theory, but rather consistently sought to explain discourses and theories in their respective contexts with recourse to real social, economic, and political developments. As the fourth edition proves, Hofmann also became aware that 'the centre of activity of the social movements' had begun to move 'out of its space of origin' into parts of the world hitherto detached from Western industrialism, whose populations had thus far been condemned to an existence as victims of the capitalist world market.[12] Hofmann assumed, however, that the social movements of the 'developmental space' – the 'Third World' – would prove unable to develop an independent economic model and instead take the path of 'accelerated catch-up industrialisation' by adapting Western 'economic thinking in the common good' to local conditions.[13]

---

9   Hofmann 1971d, Hofmann 1986, Hofmann 1971e.
10   Hofmann 1956.
11   Hofmann 1971c. The fourth printing appeared with the addendum 'assisted by Wolfgang Abendroth'.
12   Hofmann 1971c, p. 275.
13   Hofmann 1971c, p. 276.

Although deeply influenced by Marxism, Hofmann was not yet equipped with a systematic grounding in Marxist theory when he came to Marburg. Prior to his early death in 1969, his published works exhibited a variety of methodological aspects and substantive elements which cannot be traced back to Marxism as a closed theoretical system, as could be found in some social-scientific publications and disciplines in both the state-socialist countries (such as Erich Hahn's Marxist sociology in the GDR)[14] as well as capitalist Western Europe (the theory of state monopoly capitalism, or Ernest Mandel's analysis of capitalism).[15] To what extent the absence of a systemic theoretical unity in Hofmann's work should be considered detrimental is moot, but nevertheless did not stop him from producing a wide variety of noteworthy monographs and articles critical of capitalist society. Perhaps it was his certain lack of orthodoxy that allowed him to reach such an impressively large audience for academic standards, such as his *Grundelemente der Wirtschaftsgesellschaft* (Basic Elements of Economic Society), first published in 1969 and printing more than 170,000 copies by 1987.[16]

In this 'teachers' handbook', categories of critical-reformist bourgeois economics developed by figures like Otto von Zwiedineck-Südenhorst (1871–1957) or Hofmann's doctoral supervisor Adolf Weber (1876–1963) intermingle with the concept of 'social economy' in the sense of Max Weber, Werner Sombart, or Günter Schmölders, and primarily Karl Marx's political economy. It is little surprise that a host of conceptual ambiguities and theoretical weaknesses would find their way into an attempt at such a categorical synthesis. Thus, on the one hand Hofmann assumed that 'all economic production' rested 'on human labour, all material progress on additional labour',[17] yet on the other limited his reflections on pricing to the market sphere and thus excluded the relationship between production (and prices of production) and the market (and market prices) in need of actual analysis.[18] Unlike Marx, Hofmann neither dealt critically with nor adopted the valuation of labour power as a commodity as an axiom of his thinking.

It is for this reason that he viewed wage labour and capital less as a social relation so much as factors of an unmediated polarity in and through which both moments mutually reproduce each other – albeit antagonistically. Fur-

14   See Hahn 1968. Erich Hahn was one of the most influential philosophers and social scientists in the GDR.
15   See Boccara et al. 1971; Mandel 1968.
16   Hofmann 1969a.
17   Hofmann 1969a, p. 65.
18   See Hecker 1999, p. 116.

thermore, the problem of capitalist crises featured only rarely, and not as one of capitalism's structural problems. The development of a Marxist theory of political economy and society in Hofmann's work was not yet complete when *Grundelemente* was published.

A defining characteristic of Hofmann's contributions to the critique of economics as an academic discipline was his awareness of the historicity of its subject matter. He would criticise contemporary economics in the pages of the *Kölner Zeitschrift für Soziologie und Sozialpsychologie* in 1959 for its harmonising construction of a unified society, removed from all contradictions and steered by static behavioural laws.[19] In a lecture on the 'poverty of economics' later published in Wolfgang Abendroth's 60th birthday festschrift,[20] Hofmann described the transformation of classical economics into an 'ideological doctrine of justification' and identified five structural deficits in the 'new economic thinking': firstly, its neglect of labour's value-forming potential; secondly, its reduction of economic processes to microeconomic logics; thirdly, the de-socialisation of the economic; fourthly, an absolutisation of the individual type of the 'calculating entrepreneur'; and fifthly, a de-historicisation of its own economic perspective – what Pierre Bourdieu would later describe as 'scholastic epistemocentrism' in his critique of academia.[21]

Once in Marburg, Hofmann returned to topics he had already dealt with extensively in the past. One example is his study of Stalinism and anti-Communism, published by Suhrkamp in 1967 and already in its fifth printing by 1970.[22] Developed by Hofmann through a lively correspondence with Georg Lukács lasting several years, the study is remarkable in several aspects.[23] Most notably, it distinguished itself from practically all publications on the Soviet Union, Communism, and Stalinism in particular at the time which were pervaded by deep anti-Soviet and anti-Communist attitudes. Rather than seeking to understand the development, internal contradictions, and balance of forces through a Western lens fixated on Stalin's 'cult of personality' and a narrative of terroristic irrationality, Hofmann approached the difficult topic by seeking to explain the political deformations and repressive mechanisms of Soviet Russia through the contradictions between the backwardness of the country caused by premodern agriculture, illiteracy, and the crushing impact of the civil war and foreign military intervention on the one hand, and the gigantic targets

19   Hofmann 1959.
20   Hofmann 1971b.
21   Bourdieu 2000.
22   Hofmann 1969b.
23   See Lukács and Hofmann 1991.

set by the Soviet Communists (collectivisation of agriculture, industrialisation with simultaneous democratisation) on the other. He described this form of political rule emerging out of concrete historical restraints as an *Erziehungs-diktatur*, a dictatorial form of government seeking to raise the material and cultural level of the society it rules. Conceptually inspired by Max Weber, he investigated the Soviet type of bureaucracy and identified in the social character of power in the Soviet Union a 'specific opportunism of power on the general foundation of a proletarian society'.[24] He diagnosed a reification of Marxism into a 'closed philosophical system' lacking heuristic quality in Soviet theoretical debates, while the modification of the Soviet employment regime, democratisation measures, and the policy of 'peaceful coexistence' following Stalin's death gave him hope that Stalinism would be overcome in the long term and that implemented reforms would reactivate Soviet society's damaged, but not destroyed potential.

The last section of the book was devoted to the 'sociology of anti-Communism'. Hofmann criticised the Western reinterpretation of Marxism into a 'substitute religion', demonstrating how the Western debate had reduced the contradiction between social systems ultimately rooted in different relations of production into a contradiction between forms of political power. The projection of the 'social conflict' immanent to capitalism 'into the external space' corresponded to a ratcheting up of anti-Communism, the banning of the KPD, and a general militarisation of social life in the Federal Republic.[25] In retrospect, Hofmann can be criticised for underestimating the extent of terror and repression under Stalinism (perhaps due in part to the lack of available sources at the time) and for limiting his methodological approach to phenomena of the central institutions of power. With view to the period after Stalin's death in 1953, he neglected to explore whether the forms of political despotism and bureaucratic control that emerged during the Stalinist period lived on, and to what extent the reforms enacted on paper in fact counteracted them. Ultimately, he also overestimated the dynamism of the Soviet economy.[26]

Hofmann's collected volumes such as the 1968 *Universität, Ideologie, Gesellschaft* (University, Ideology, Society)[27] and *Abschied vom Bürgertum* (Farewell to the Bourgeoisie)[28] published posthumously in 1970 contained several sociological contributions in the stricter sense, dealing primarily with the crisis

---

24   Lukács and Hofmann 1991, p. 39.
25   Lukács and Hofmann 1991, p. 152.
26   See Hofmann's study along with the occasionally critical and thorough Meyer 1999.
27   Hofmann 1971f.
28   Hofmann 1970a.

of the universities and the modern self-understanding of the social sciences themselves. However, his transition from a 'doctrine of society' (*Gesellschafts-lehre*) largely inspired by economics to the discipline of sociology was expressed most poignantly in his studies on industrial sociology, which were also only published after his death.[29] Because macro-social priorities determined Hofmann's sociological thinking well into his time in Marburg, he never managed to conduct empirical research prior to his passing. As Maus also worked exclusively on theory, the socio-politically-guided macro-orientation and lack of empirical social research marks a professional deficit of Marburg sociology that limited its depth of focus in certain respects.

Like Abendroth, Hofmann also developed a public reputation as an engaging, rhetorically brilliant and convincing intellectual. In doing so he adhered to the vision of a publicly partisan scholarship aiming towards practical changes. He was active in the working group of the Kuratorium Notstand der Demokratie against the Emergency Acts, and in 1969 initiated the electoral alliance Aktion Demokratischer Fortschritt (ADF) in which the DKP also participated but failed with a depressing result in the 1969 federal elections.[30] Hofmann's most important and sustainable political achievement was arguably his contribution to the founding of the oppositional, left-wing Bund Demokratischer Wissenschaftler (BDW, later BdWi), which regenerated after a period of stagnation in 1972 and exists to this day.[31]

Although Hofmann evinced parallels to Abendroth in multiple respects, he embodied a different type of intellectual closer to the bourgeois-academic habitus of the 'German mandarins' illustrated so poignantly by Fritz K. Ringer at the beginning of the twentieth century.[32] Hofmann believed in the enlightening mission of the intellectual elite, essentially tasked with teaching the masses in a top-down manner. Exhibiting a degree of difference to Abendroth, he was by no means opposed to the trade unions but approached them from a certain distance and occasionally accused them of 'narrow-minded, unpolitical wage cretinism'.[33] He scorned the voluntarist actions of the student movement

29   Hofmann 1988.
30   Claas 1999.
31   See von Freyberg 1973.
32   This comparison is only valid to the extent that the 'mandarins' Ringer described viewed themselves as an intellectual elite, as was true of Hofmann to some degree despite his socialist self-understanding. Whereas Ringer's 'mandarins' expected acknowledgement from the ruling class and sought to maintain existing social relations, Hofmann embodied the exact opposite. See Ringer 1990.
33   Claas 1999, p. 228.

as 'petit bourgeois anarchism' and called on the students to enter into a 'process of self-education' through 'encounter' with the working population.[34]

Abendroth viewed things somewhat differently. His understanding of intellectuals' social-political function was closer to that of Antonio Gramsci's 'organic intellectual', which articulates its collective interests through the perspective of a specific social class. Although Abendroth was aware of the limits of their political possibilities, he saw the trade unions as an essential bearer of class interests. Like Hofmann, Abendroth also noted misguided perspectives in the student movement but responded to the rebellious students' occasionally bizarre practices and illusions in a relaxed manner, and defended the legitimate aspects of their protest rooted in their future as a wage-earning academic intelligentsia.

Hofmann and Abendroth would reach opposing conclusions with view to the so-called 'Prague Spring' in 1968 and the armed intervention by Warsaw Pact troops in the Czechoslovak Socialist Republic. While Abendroth derided the intervention as incompatible with socialist principles,[35] Hofmann defended it as an unavoidable measure to secure the foundations of socialism in the ČSSR against the risk of counterrevolution.[36]

3   Heinz Maus (1911–78)

Heinz Maus encountered difficulties establishing himself in the sociology department alongside Hofmann. Exhibiting scant ambitions in the years following his 1960 appointment, he faded into the background even more after Hofmann's arrival. But who was Heinz Maus?[37]

Born in Krefeld on the western bank of the Rhine in 1911 as the son of a master pastry chef, he completed apprenticeships as both a commercial merchant as well as a bookseller before moving to Frankfurt am Main to study sociology, philosophy, and economics. Max Horkheimer would become his most influential academic teacher, and Maus maintained his great indebtedness to him even later in life. He continued his studies in Bonn, Cologne, and

---

34   Hofmann 1971f, p. 48.
35   See Schöler 2001, p. 39. A bibliography of Abendroth's writings in this same volume contains a note that Abendroth, together with other members of the Sozialistischer Bund, composed a letter of protest addressed to 'West German Communists' against the invasion of the ČSSR on 22 August 1968 (see Balzer et al. 2001, p. 413).
36   Claas 1999, p. 228.
37   See in the following Schäfer 2006, esp. pp. 49–54. See also Greven and van de Moetter 1981.

Leipzig after 1933. He was arrested and accused of conspiring against the Nazis with the former editor of the national-revolutionary magazine *Der Widerstand* Ernst Niekisch during the latter's trial in 1937, but was in his own words 'gotten off the hook' by the Nazi-sympathising Leipzig sociology professor Hans Freyer.[38] Maus temporarily worked at the Oslo-based Institutt for Samfunnsforsking og Arbeidslære before completing his dissertation in Kiel in 1941 with a social-philosophical treatise on Schopenhauer shorn of any concessions to Nazi ideology. He served as a medic in the German Army from 1941–5 and was charged with 'the crime of treachery' in 1943, but only received a disciplinary action. After the war Maus spent two years in an assistant's position at the Humboldt University in East Berlin. Feeling intellectually restricted, however, he left the GDR and found a position with Max Horkheimer at the Institute for Social Research in 1951.[39] At the first German sociology congress following the war's end, Heinz Maus called as passionately as he did helplessly for German sociology to address its recent past.[40] A four-year stint in Frankfurt was followed by a lectureship at the Pädagogisches Institut in Weilburg (Hessia), before receiving his appointment to Marburg in 1960. Although he had contact with Abendroth and supported him and Hofmann in their resistance to the Emergency Acts, significant tensions would emerge between the two at the Sociological Seminar (later renamed the Institute for Sociology), most likely due to both the incompatibility of their personal characters as well as official 'incorrectness' and disciplinary misbehaviour on Maus's part.[41]

Maus made an academic name for himself with a series of book chapters and journal articles on topics of sociological history, French sociology, and cultural sociology, as well as through his role as co-editor of Luchterhand Verlag's *Soziologische Texte*, which featured sociological classics by authors such as Emile Durkheim, Karl Mannheim, Theodor Geiger, Georg Lukács, Lucien Goldmann, Eric Hobsbawm, Lewis A. Coser, C. Wright Mills, and countless others. Of lasting value was his chapter on the 'prehistory of empirical social research' in the *Handbuch der empirischen Sozialforschung* edited by René König, where Maus proved himself deeply knowledgeable of the material he worked on.[42] He reconstructed the complex development of empirical pro-

---

38   Schäfer 2006, p. 50.
39   See Demirović 1999, pp. 295–310.
40   See Schäfer 2006, p. 52. Maus himself published a report on 'Sociology in Germany, 1933 to 1945' in the 1959 volume of the *Kölner Zeitschrift für Soziologie und Sozialpsychologie* (Maus 1959).
41   Greven and van de Moetter 1981 p. 31.
42   See Maus 1973. Also of particular note is Maus 1956.

cedures, research and methodology, social statistics' struggle for academic recognition, as well as the interconnections between socio-political interventions, social critique, and empirical analysis, while his transnational perspective allowed him to take into account research conducted in Western Europe and the United States.[43]

Compared to Abendroth and Hofmann, Maus was not a particularly gifted speaker. His relatively small stature and somewhat rotund shape lent themselves well to the *bon vivant* lifestyle considered a typical cliché of his Rhenish background. He had a tendency to grow redundant when delivering lectures and seminars, regularly drifting off into a thicket of unexpected associations and mental leaps. Nevertheless, his intellectual foundation remained constant, and none ever doubted his links to the Frankfurt School and his teacher Horkheimer in particular, nor his loyalty to the political orientation of the Marburg School as laid out by Abendroth.[44] When relieved of institutional obligations in private, he proved himself to be a witty, culturally astute conversationalist open to avant-garde artistic currents.[45] Maus may have lacked the charisma of an Abendroth or a Hofmann, but it is hard to imagine the Marburg School without his specific contribution.

4   Abendroth, Hofmann, and Maus's Understanding of Marx and Marxism

4.1   *Wolfgang Abendroth*

Abendroth first came into contact with Marxist theory in his youth, discovering his interest in political education work as a member of the Free Socialist Youth and later as a member of the Communist Party's youth organisation. That said, beyond the *Communist Manifesto* his reading was largely limited to secondary literature.[46] For example, Abendroth read the theoretical publications of Dutch Left Communists Herman Gorter and Anton Pannekoek, one of the most esteemed authorities in radical left discourse of his time. He was evidently also familiar with Marx's position on the 1870–1 Franco-Prussian War, which he referred to in a 1929 article on the relationship between social-

---

43   A bibliography listing all of Maus's essential publications can be found in Kaestner 1984.

44   For example, he co-edited a volume of lectures on the Emergency Acts together with Werner Hofmann, see Hofmann and Maus 1967.

45   An informative overview of the many diverse aspects contained in Maus's sociological thought can be found in Salomon 2012.

46   See Diers 2006, p. 108.

ism and the nation.[47] A more intensive engagement with the original works of Marx and Engels would only begin relatively late in life, following the conclusion of World War II. Relevant publications on their theory would appear in the 1950s and 1960s, which however should not be understood as implying that Abendroth had not begun thinking in Marxist categories much earlier. By conducting a more thorough engagement with the writings of Marx and Engels, he both endowed his political positions with a theoretical foundation as well as affirmed the utility of their work as a theoretical compass for solving present and future social problems. In this sense, his interest was less of a purely academic nature than it was determined by the demands of left-wing political praxis, which was subjected to strict limits under the conditions of West German post-war restoration. At the time everything associated with Marxism, socialism, and Communism was placed under a hermeneutics of suspicion that it sought to undermine the economically prosperous and politically 'formed society' (Ludwig Erhard) through subversive means that was as primitive as it was efficient. Marxism's public image was shaped by authors like the autodidact Walter Theimer, the Jesuit writer Gustav A. Wetter, and the renegade Wolfgang Leonhard who left the GDR for Yugoslavia in 1949 after serving as a leading Communist functionary for some years.[48] Serious engagement with Marx and Engels was pushed to the academic fringes and mostly limited to questions like 'the young Marx's conception of man' or the popular topic of alienation, while political economy was derided as an ideological fossil.[49]

Abendroth rejected the notion of an opposition between the philosophical and the economic or the younger and older Marx. The all-round development of the individual was not only a topic of the young Marx in the *Economic and Philosophical Manuscripts of 1844* or the *German Ideology*, but rather was also addressed repeatedly by the 'mature Marx', as could be seen in the *Grundrisse* where Marx identified the decline in socially necessary labour time as the decisive prerequisite for developing subjectivity and individuality.[50] For Marx and Engels, labour constituted the historical moment facilitating both the unleashing of individual creative powers as well as their socialisation. The dynamic of the productive forces driven forward by labour Marx and Engels

---

47   Diers 2006, p. 265.
48   Theimer 1960; Wetter 1973; Leonhard 1979.
49   The Marxism studies published by the Studiengemeinschaft der evangelischen Akademie in Heidelberg were noteworthy for engaging with Marx without instrumentalising his work for purposes of ideological manipulation.
50   Abendroth 1985, p. 217.

recognised created the material foundation for a society free of coercion and crisis – that is to say, communism.

Abendroth referred heavily to Marx's reflections on the transformation of the modern production process, which in the course of scientification had fundamentally altered the role of humans in production. Namely, humans stepped out of the immediate production process in order to become its 'watchman' and 'regulator', as Abendroth quoted from a well-known passage in the *Grundrisse*.[51] In contrast to the growing tendency towards an abstractification of Marxist theory and the kind of 'seminar Marxism' growing increasingly prevalent since 1968 that pursued a categorical fetishisation of Marx divorced from empirical reality, Abendroth exclusively utilised Marx's theory to investigate contemporary social relations in terms of their political mutability. It is for this reason that he applied the analysis of the production process found in the *Grundrisse* to concrete instances of automation, which began restructuring the industrial landscape in the 1950s and provoked controversial debates within the workers' movement. Abendroth saw in the technological progress made possible by automation both enormous economic and social possibilities as well as glaring proof of the contradiction between forces and relations of production in 'late capitalism', which threatened to advance towards self-destruction:

> The contradiction between the forces of production developed by science and capitalist society's relations of production threatens, through the partialising and crippling of man and his further development based upon it, to end in a catastrophic regression of the historical process should it not be resolved by society establishing other relations of production which allow it to subject the forces of production to the conscious and collective decisions of all its individuals, making it useful for the free development of all its individuals.[52]

Yet unlike the apologists for technological progress within the social-democratic spectrum, Abendroth understood that the sublation of the contradiction between forces and relations of production (and with it the opening of a path towards communism) would not occur out of the technological dynamic automatically, but rather could only be historically realised 'in social struggle by those social classes which are most alienated under capitalist relations

---

51   Marx 1993, p. 705.
52   Abendroth 1985, p. 215f.

of production'.[53] Insisting on the necessity of class struggle corresponded to Abendroth's critical relativisaticn with view to the level of development in the Soviet Union and other stace-socialist countries which claimed to have already reached the stage of communism or at least be transitioning towards it. While Abendroth decried social deformations caused by Stalinism and 'partially bureaucratic forms of rule' in the Soviet Union on the one hand, he adhered to the validity of Marx and Engels's theory without consolidating it into a dogmatic system or mystifying it into an absolute holy writ on the other.[54]

Abendroth did not contribute any qualitatively novel moments to Marxist theory in the way that Horkheimer and Adorno's *Dialectic of Enlightenment*, E.P. Thompson's analysis of the making of the English working class,[55] or Louis Althusser's concept of 'ideological state apparatuses' did. Abendroth's relevance to Marxist theory lay rather in its operative dimension as well as in the defence of its capacity to grasp the present, emphatically rejecting the notion that Marxism had grown historically obsolete. Abendroth opposed the hypothesis – articulated in highly diverse variations – that concepts such as class and class struggle had been made irrelevant by changes to the social structure, rising mass consumption, state interventionism, and decommodification of labour power through the welfare state. When newer sociological theory postulated, for example, that the delegation of workplace discretion over the means of production from capital owners to a growing layer of managers undermined the foundations of Marxist theory, Abendroth countered that this development implied not the resolution of the contradiction between wage labour and capital, but merely its raising to a higher level:

> Nor does the argument that the rise of the managerial layer means property's relevance to the means of production has disappeared withstand closer inspection. That tendentially monopolistic capital takes on the form of capital joint-stock companies was already well-known to Marx and Engels ... The managers together with the owners of the majority of property titles thus constitute an inseparable unity: they represent and are co-opted by these interests, to the extent that they do not emerge from this layer or grow into it through the purchase of stock portfolios. The functional division emerging from the necessity of estab-

---

53   Abendroth 1985, p. 219.
54   Abendroth 1985, p. 221.
55   Thompson 2013.

lishing management is, in reality, not proof of the changing of our society's social structure ...[56]

Abendroth utilised Marxian theory primarily as a method that must be applied
to the analysis of empirical changes to capitalist society. In doing so he distinguished between two sides of the method: a structural side that grasps the general conditions of the relations of capitalist production and domination, and
a concrete side that analyses changing economic, social, and political forms.
Abendroth repeatedly sought to bring about that which he wrote concerning
the historical materialist method in general, as can be seen in his considerations on 'planning alternatives'.[57] Proceeding from the Marxian notion that
humans – unlike other living beings – can ideally anticipate the results of their
activity, Abendroth pointed out that planning also occurs in capitalism but
is reduced to the generation of profits and excludes the collective producers.
Over the course of capitalism's history, however, planning and regulating interventions into the arbitrariness and anarchy of capitalist competition had successfully been achieved, modifying the 'natural laws' of capitalist commodity
production in favour of the wage-earning producers – albeit without disabling
the profit principle as such.

With view to the situation in West German society, Abendroth searched
for possibilities to qualitatively expand planning processes in two moments.
The first moment comprised the specific character of West German capitalism,
which he described using the term 'organised capitalism' taken from Rudolf
Hilferding's famous studies on finance capital.[58] The second moment concerned the level of the forces of production, as the use of nuclear power and
growing automation of industrial production increasingly necessitated social
planning beyond the partial aims of the capitalist economy:

> With this, the overcoming of the contradictions between the *form of
> social planning* that organised capitalism has permitted and made neces-
> sary for exceptional situations and its *limits*, the restriction of planning
> agencies to the executive layers of organised capitalism and the restric-
> tion of the substance of planning to the securing of profit opportunities

---

56   Abendroth 1972e, p. 359 f.
57   Abendroth 1972c.
58   Rudolf Hilferding (1877–1941) used the term 'organised capitalism' in various essays and
     speeches after World War I, that is to say only after publishing *Finance Capital* in 1910,
     which was still based on a Marxist foundation. See esp. Hilferding 1982 as well as Deppe
     2003a.

for its economic entities, becomes the immediate necessity of the historical period in which we live ...[59]

Although Abendroth was aware that the principle of total social planning could
only be achieved politically – which for him meant through the struggle of
the workers' movement – he tended towards a certain optimism vis-à-vis the
productive forces from which Marx and Engels themselves were not entirely
free. Basing himself on lengthy quotations of the classics, Abendroth gave the
impression that the productive forces unleashed by the scientification of production only required their integration into the direction of a socialist planned
economy (albeit to be established politically) in order to unfold their socially
beneficial effects unhindered.[60] As the negation of liberal competition capitalism, 'organised capitalism' was the current confirmation of the Marxian
hypothesis that the conditions to solve all of humanity's problems were already
present. While Abendroth considered the term 'organised capitalism' adequate
to grasp the character of modern capitalism, he nevertheless distinguished
himself from the originator of this term in that he regarded the transformation
of organised capitalism into a socialist or rather communist society without
class struggle to be impossible. Class struggle was one of Marx and Engels's
categories which Abendroth reflected most deeply and sought to verify in a differentiated, strictly undogmatic fashion in the analysis of social and political
balances of forces, social-structural changes, and the mentality and forms of
consciousness in the present. As Abendroth thought primarily in political and
practical terms, he mostly acquired the theoretical elements and concepts of
Marx and Engels which had proven themselves analytically in light of reality as
it presented itself. Beyond the concepts of class and class struggle, this primarily entailed the function of the trade unions and the relationship between
democracy and socialism, along with reform and revolution.

Abendroth's understanding of Marx and Marxism can be summarised as
follows: Abendroth was well-acquainted with significant parts of Marx and
Engels's work and viewed it as a reliable foundation for his own endeavours.
He did not believe the essential aspects of this work to be in need of scientific
revision as far as its explanatory value with view to modern capitalist society
was concerned. Marxism's operative-political function was clearly at the heart
of this effort, in accordance with Abendroth's view that whether a scientific theory was correct or not could only be determined through practical application.

---

59   Abendroth 1972c, p. 481 f.
60   See Tjaden and Peter 2006.

Alongside the ideas of Marx and Engels, Abendroth also worked through concepts of Marxist discourse from the period after Marx and Engels, although these served primarily as affirmative illustration and corroboration of his own ideas. Further innovations and theoretical expansions of Marxism as developed (albeit often in controversial fashion worthy of critique) by figures like Rosa Luxemburg, Anton Pannekoek, Karl Korsch, Georg Lukács, Antonio Gramsci, Jean-Paul Sartre, and Herbert Marcuse all the way to Louis Althusser and Nicos Poulantzas were generally absent from Abendroth's work.[61] His creative contribution comprised more than anything a reality- and praxis-oriented heuristic application of Marxist theory to the concrete contradictions and social-political balance of forces of his time, along with the ability to identify the system of mediations between systemic-structural and concrete-historical social developments, and to process them for a socialist political praxis.

4.2   *Werner Hofmann*

Hoffman's path to Marxism was shaped by a critical interest in economics and what he perceived to be a yawning gulf between classical economics and the state of contemporary economic scholarship at the time. Hofmann systematically worked through the foundations of Marx's economic thought in his *Sozialökonomische Studientexte*.[62] In light of the dominant mechanisms of social-scientific discourse and economics in particular – caught between Germany's 'economic miracle', Western integration, and the Cold War – this was in itself an impressive and noteworthy undertaking. Hofmann began moving towards Marx and Marxism in his 1962 *Ideengeschichte der sozialen Bewegung* (Intellectual History of the Social Movement), extensively outlining central concepts of Marxian economics such as surplus value, capital, the rate of profit, accumulation, and crisis and applying them to an explanation of the ongoing 'changes to the economic society'. This work was continued and deepened in the *Sozialökonomische Studientexte*. Although Hofmann undeniably continued to see himself as a scholar of economics at this point, he recognised the wide-ranging social relevance of Marx's political economy through observing isolated economic phenomena. This was reflected in the pages of *Sozialökonomie*, which itself was reminiscent of Max Weber's unfinished project, *Basic Outlines of Social Economics*. Yet while Weber explicitly sought to integrate multiple disciplines into social economics, Hofmann was primarily concerned with explicating economics as a constitutive sphere for society as a whole. He saw Marx as having fulfilled this task in exemplary fashion:

---

61   On this, see Anderson 1989.
62   Hofmann 1971d; Hofmann 1986; Hofmann 1971e.

The founder of 'scientific socialism', Karl Marx (1818–1883), was the first to harmonise the theory of profit income, of *'surplus value'*, with the theory of the exchange of equivalents, and thereby overcome the hitherto antinomy of value and income theory ... The theory of value is the scientific foundation of the Marxian critique of capitalist society.[63]

Hofmann's depiction and critical appraisal of Marxian economic categories drew on a thorough reading of Marx's politico-economic writings. Such a deep engagement with Marx represented a rarity in scholarly economic discussions in the Federal Republic at the time, reflecting not only Hofmann's lack of intellectual prejudice but also – given the period's academically conservative atmosphere, often hostile to dissenting theoretical viewpoints – a degree of personal courage. Hofmann recognised that Marx was not only an outstanding theoretician of capitalism who had gone above and beyond the major figures of classical economics, but one who had also sought to present through his analysis the key to practically changing and overcoming it.

Hofmann's competent recapitulation of Marxian categories and the context thereof occurred alongside a critical comparison of non-Marxist literature on Marx. He criticised the contradiction in Marx alleged by Eugen von Böhm-Bawerk and others, who claimed that supporters of the Marxian theory of exploitation objectively reduced the value of commodities to the amount of labour time on the one hand while deriding the capitalists' appropriation of surplus value as 'unnatural' and 'unjust' on the other.[64] Hofmann countered this argument by emphasising that Marx viewed the production of surplus value as an immanent consequence of the capitalist production process, of the equivalent exchange of the labour commodity in return for wages and thus, in this sense, compatible with the law of value. Viewed from this angle, the exchange of equivalents and the production of surplus value were not a contradiction. Marx had thus formulated his critique on the economic level not morally, but analytically. Although Hofmann believed to have discovered several deficits in Marxian theory, such as in its conception of 'ground-rent',[65] he left no doubt as to his fundamental agreement with Marx's core arguments, particularly the impossibility of resolving the contradictions of capitalism within the capitalist system – not only in terms of the history of bourgeois society, but also with view to the future of modern 'market economy' capitalism. This was

63   Hofmann 1971d, p. 81 f.
64   Hofmann 1986, p. 135.
65   Hofmann 1986, p. 145 ff.

true, for example, of both Marx's prognosticated 'rising organic composition of capital' as well as the relation between 'absolute' and 'relative immiseration'.[66]

Hofmann turned to what Marx described as the 'laws of motion of the capitalist mode of production' in the third volume of the *Sozialökonomische Studientexte*.[67] Hofmann stressed Marx's bringing together of both 'material' reproduction as well as reproduction 'in terms of value' into a coherent relationship as a particularly valuable insight, which he did by describing them as a contradictory unity of systemic reproduction ('circulation') and systemic dynamic ('development').[68] Marx was able to do this because, among other reasons, he neglected to reduce the analysis of the social product in a certain period (gross social product) to consumer goods, but rather complemented them with the production of means of production as the essential 'department' driving forward the dynamic of capitalist development in the total process of material reproduction.

Despite his blatant affinity with Marx's thought, he rejected any sort of apologetic identification and repeatedly included critical remarks against various hypotheses of Marx in his depictions. Hofmann mentioned other critics to the extent that he agreed with their arguments and warned against the mechanical translation of Marxian 'accumulation schematics' into planning models,[69] while simultaneously integrating more general aspects of Marx related to the alienation of humans under capitalist conditions into his explication of economic categories. Referring to works by figures such as Erich Fromm, Heinrich Popitz, and Herbert Marcuse, he turned to the topic of alienation, the relevance of which as 'physical immiseration' he saw confirmed by studies such as those of the doyen of French industrial sociology Georges Friedmann or American sociologist David Riesman.[70]

Nor did Hofmann dodge the difficult topic of the 'dictatorship of the proletariat', which Marx and Engels had seen as an inevitable transitional stage towards a classless society at least in a certain state of the balance of political forces. Seeking to relativise the significance of the repressive functions of the dictatorship of the proletariat in the transition to socialism, Hofmann stressed that Marx and Engels had assumed the proletariat would constitute an overwhelming majority of society and the bourgeoisie only a minority. Hofmann

66   Hofmann 1986, p. 152 ff.
67   Hofmann 1971e, pp. 63–90.
68   Hofmann 1971e, p. 72.
69   Hofmann 1971e, p. 75.
70   Hofmann 1971c, p. 148.

was primarily concerned with placing this dictatorship's prospects, namely the 'withering away of the state' and the incorporation of state structures and functions into the immediate political self-determination of society, into the foreground as the actual essential problem.[71] In his view, the ambitious goal of party leaderships in countries like the Soviet Union to practically introduce the transition to communism would have to be measured against reality.

In his conceptual- and intellectual-historical reconstruction of Marxist theory, Hofmann was concerned with rendering the relevance of this theory of the present plausible and utilising its analytical potential to conduct research on modern capitalism. He probably came closest to this goal with his reflections on *Industriesoziologie für Arbeiter* (Industrial Sociology for Workers), although the book failed to reach his explicit aims.[72] Hofmann's industrial sociology did not limit itself to Marxist literature but nevertheless drew inspiration from Marx and Engels's theory in its decisive lines of argument, transmitting the methodological foundation and critical criterion against which he measured the concrete phenomena of modern industrial labour. In doing so, he analysed the Taylorist system of 'scientific management', 'psycho-technology', and the probing of worker productivity in the famous 'Hawthorne studies' as facets of capitalist rationalisation and subjective integration of the workforce into capital's logic of valorisation:

> The new requirement for which industrial sociology is to find a solution, however, can be summarised in one word: *'integration' of the workers into the dominant society* – that is to say, not only their actual, but even more so their *conscious and volitional integration* into the all-encompassing goal of capital valorisation, into capital's claim to society as a whole.[73]

With view to the processes of automation beginning to penetrate industrial production in the 1950s by increasingly transferring human control, regulation, and directional tasks onto electronic entities, Hofmann's analysis was guided largely by the Marxian theorem of the contradiction between forces and relations of production. Taking the state of non-Marxist research into account, he depicted the bursts of productivity unleashed by automation in terms of both their technical and economic side as well as the side relating to human labour.

---

71   Hofmann 1971c, p. 153.
72   Hofmann 1988.
73   Hofmann 1988, p. 40.

Focusing on the contradictory effects of automation under 'late capitalist' conditions, Hofmann demonstrated that the technically induced possibilities of
relieving human labour as well as rising productivity were increasingly irreconcilable with monopolistic property relations. 'Late capitalism' perverted what
could have been a blessing for humanity into new forms of workload, into the
risk of a 'setting free' of employment and into a driving force of the process of
capital concentration. In a classically Marxist line of argument, he interpreted
automation as a process which, historically, objectively called for casting off the
deforming and destructive chains of the relations of production:

> Thus, in the age of automation the forces of production continually testify
> against the relations of production of our late capitalist, monopolist
> world ... In this way it prevents the *setting free* of human powers from
> becoming human *liberation* and the forward progress of technology car-
> ries in its wake the social *progress* it so imperiously demands.[74]

Similar to Abendroth, Hofmann was on the one hand aware of the objective
possibilities of scientific-technical progress, while on the other harboured no
illusions concerning the difficult fact that its emancipatory effects could not
unfold without the political activity of the sole collective actor capable of succeeding in this enormous task: the working class.

Critique of capitalism and a certain enthusiasm vis-à-vis the productive
forces thus went hand-in-hand in Hofmann's career. In this sense, he was
indistinct from theories operating under Marxist auspices in the state-socialist
countries such as the 'theory of the scientific-technical revolution'.[75] Their
problem consisted primarily of their ascription of strictly emancipatory potential to the modern forces of production – namely the use of nuclear energy,
cybernetics, and automation – without acknowledging the entailed risks even
under non-capitalist social relations.

4.3   Heinz Maus

While Abendroth and Hofmann primarily applied Marx and Engels's theory
in terms of the perspective of social and political opportunities for intervening
into the logic of capitalist accumulation, Heinz Maus saw himself tasked with a
discursive-political defence of this theory against the phalanx of its opponents
and critics. In line with the intellectual style of the protagonists of 'critical the-

---

74   Hofmann 1988, p. 160.
75   See Kuzin et al. 1972. The team of authors responsible for the volume was of Soviet origin.

ory' expressed even in the way they constructed their sentences, Maus largely occupied himself (sometimes quite polemically) with the contemporary theoretical literature on Marx.

As early as 1952 while still serving as Horkheimer's assistant, Maus felt compelled to defend Marx's theory against the crass distortions he encountered in Walter Theimer's *Marxismus*, which was first published in 1950 and would go on to appear in numerous reprints.[76] Not without justification, Maus sneered at the simplistic reinterpretation of the dialectical method into a closed system of barren 'laws' as well as Theimer's assumption that the term 'dialectics' was etymologically derived from 'dialogue', but that history, in Theimer's words, rarely proceeded 'in the manner of a philosophical dialogue'.[77] By dismissing Hegel as an 'outdated philosopher' Theimer only demonstrated his own laughable ignorance, given that he was obviously unfamiliar with epochal works such as *The Science of Logic* or *The Phenomenology of the Spirit*. Maus mocked both Theimer's clichéd notion of dialectics as well as his utterly unfounded claim that Marx had been influenced by Auguste Comte and 'certainly learned a great deal from Comte', claiming that the 'fundamental principle of scientific socialism' was already 'contained in Comte's law of three stages'.[78] In response, Maus retorted that although Marx had read Comte, he despised what he called his 'shitty positivism'.[79]

Paradoxically, after declaring Marx (whose alleged mistakes he denounced) to be a student of Comte, Theimer then identified himself as a positivist, albeit only to use it as a weapon against Marx by identifying 'sceptical positivism' as the only legitimate methodology of scientific historical observation. Maus for his part dismissed this move with the succinct jab that Theimer's favoured brand of positivism could only be compatible with dominant relations to the extent that it provided them with acceptable empirical data. Should theory go beyond a mere collection of facts and begin to explain the interconnections between them, however, Theimer then declared theory to function as a 'stumbling block in critical times'.[80]

Alongside Theimer's hypothesis that history had disproven Marx's postulated anthropology of humanity's 'revolutionary essence' and his 'idealistic fun-

---

76   Maus 1981d.

77   Maus 1981d, p. 308.

78   Theimer, as quoted in Maus 1981d, p. 309. Maus highlighted tendencies that confused or combined positivism and historical materialist dialectics as early as 1952, see Maus 1981b.

79   Marx 1987, p. 292. For a highly differentiated discussion of Marx's relation to positivism, see the recent and worthwhile Marx biography (despite its debatable claim that Marx was essentially a man of the nineteenth century) Sperber 2013, esp. pp. 387–418.

80   Maus 1981d, p. 311.

damental assumption' that humans could become conscious of their interests, Maus also criticised his claim that the polarisation of the class structure as prophesised by Marx had failed to materialise. Here, Maus argued that Theimer was incapable of distinguishing between the ideology of a homogenous middle class and the real, accelerated loss of social independence through capital concentration.[81] Maus then turned somewhat abruptly away from the critical reading of Theimer's book to accuse both the 'socialist parties' in general as well as the Soviet Union in particular of a total break with Marxian theory, albeit without substantiating this serious accusation whatsoever. In this particular turn, Horkheimer and Adorno's aversions towards the countries of the socialist bloc and its understanding of Marxism can be seen.[82] Maus's assumption that Friedrich Engels's alleged popularisation of historical materialism had objectively facilitated revisionist and positivist tendencies (in the workers' movement) as well as dogmatisation is reminiscent of the positions of the Frankfurt School.[83] Maus expressed this scepticism vis-à-vis Engels five years later in the opening of a wide-ranging critical overview of recent publications on Marx and Marxism he regarded as important, when he was working as a lecturer of sociology at the Pädagogisches Institut in Weilburg, Hessia.[84]

In contrast to the sometimes caustic and scornful discussion of Theimer's work, Maus now adopted a soberer reviewing style clearly due to the quality of the authors in question. He began by mentioning the publications on Marx and Marxism emerging from circles around the two major German churches, specifically the Protestant Church, and conceded (despite many disagreements) that they unearthed important elements of Marx's work which otherwise would have most likely remained buried.[85] Although he criticised Paul Tillich's abstract-existentialist concept of alienation, he acknowledged that Til-

---

81   Maus 1981d, p. 313.
82   These aversions can be traced back to Horkheimer's construct of an 'authoritarian state' and an 'integral etatism' which he formulated during World War II, suggesting a structural identity between the fascist and Communist systems. On this see Wiggershaus 1995, p. 280 ff.
83   On Adorno's critical attitude towards Engels see, for example, Adorno 2004, p. 121, p. 249, p. 322. Adorno writes on p. 245 f.: 'In this entire antithetical construction, freedom and causality intersect. Kant's freedom, being the same as rational action, is also according to law, and free acts also "follow from rules." What has come out of this is the intolerable mortgage imposed on post-Kantian philosophy: that freedom without law is not freedom, that freedom exists only in identification with the law. Via the German idealists, this heritage has been passed on, with incalculably vast political consequences, to Friedrich Engels; it is the theoretical source of the false reconcilement'.
84   Maus 1981e.
85   Maus 1981e, p. 368.

lich raised a relevant question by asking who or what could function as the bearer of the struggle against alienation in the present. If Tillich had discovered a utopian moment in Marxism which however was disappointed by modern reality, then Maus countered with the argument that Marxism provided a convincing justification for the viability of utopia even under the conditions of modern society. Similar to Abendroth, he set himself apart from the conservative cultural pessimism that resonated among critical intellectuals of the period by stressing the enormous potential of modern technology to facilitate humanity's emancipation from social coercions. Here, Maus's proximity to interpretive patterns derived from theories of convergence and totalitarianism referred to above again become visible. While Abendroth and Hofmann insisted upon the qualitative difference between the state-socialist countries and capitalism despite their critical reservations regarding Stalinism and contemporary bureaucratic maldevelopments, Maus chose to equate East and West.[86]

Maus praised Heinrich Popitz's 'both interesting as well as intelligent book' on the critique of the present and the philosophy of history in the young Marx for its careful reconstruction of the concept of alienation in Hegel via Feuerbach up to Marx, but qualified his praise in that he correctly regarded Popitz's ascription to Marx of an inclination towards 'eschatology' and 'chiliasm' to be mistaken.[87] Maus also appreciated a contribution by Erwin Metzke, who delivered an unmistakable repudiation of attempts to disprove Marxian theory from the position of a 'vulgar materialism'.[88]

The most noteworthy of the other publications Maus took into account is Ralf Dahrendorf's dissertation on Marx,[89] which he regarded as intellectually brilliant. Its merits included Dahrendorf's methodological approach of conceptualising justice in Marx's work not as a social-ethical postulate but rather as deriving from his analysis of capitalist relations of production.[90] It was thus all the more astounding that even Dahrendorf divided Marx's work into a 'prophetic conception of history on the one hand, and social-scientific concepts on the other' in order to accept only the latter as relevant because empirically verifiable.[91] By doing so, however, Dahrendorf violated the 'living nerve of Marxian social theory' – the dialectic – by limiting critique to a sociology of

---

86   Maus 1981e, p. 369.
87   See Popitz 1953.
88   Maus 1981e, p. 375 f.
89   See Dahrendorf 1952.
90   Maus 1981e, p. 380 f.
91   Maus 1981e, p. 381.

empirical, factual research while simultaneously obscuring the 'dimension of the future' in socialist theory.

Like Abendroth and Hofmann, Maus saw in Marxian theory the still-valid and crucial theory for analysing modern 'late capitalism'. In doing so he occasionally differentiated between Marx and Engels, tending to view the latter's thought as afflicted with moments of dogmatisation. All three representatives of the Marburg School remained utterly convinced of the epistemological validity of the dialectical method and the central categories of Marx and Engels's work, which in Hofmann's case did not necessarily exclude critical deliberations concerning individual aspects of Marx's economic concepts. An obvious difference between Abendroth and Hofmann's understanding of Marxism on one hand and Maus's on the other consisted of their interpretation and evaluation of the history of the socialist states and their contemporary developmental deficits and political deformations. While Abendroth and Hofmann acknowledged deficits and contradictions they viewed them as theoretically and practically rectifiable, Maus – as a result of his intellectual influences from the Frankfurt School – alleged a systemic identity between social domination in East and West. For this reason it is worth taking a closer look into how the two left-wing schools of thought in Marburg and Frankfurt related to each other, given that both explicitly invoked the theory of historical materialism.

5   The Marburg and Frankfurt Schools: 'Social Critique' or 'Artistic Critique'?[92]

5.1   *Late Capitalism without Surplus Value and Classes?*
Although Maus explicitly viewed himself as a student of Max Horkheimer and parallels certainly existed between the Marburg Triumvirate and the representatives of the Frankfurt School (such as bitter experiences with fascism and a critical approach to capitalism), their relationship never went beyond sporadic contact. The respective intellectual cultures and approaches to scholarship were simply too divergent to facilitate a continual productive exchange, let alone collaborative projects.[93] Yet what, concretely, were the overlaps and divergences between the two schools?

---

92   The following section is largely identical to Peter 2007, originally published in *Das Argument*. On the concepts of 'social critique' and 'artistic critique' see p. 44 fn. 190.

93   On the comparison between the Frankfurt and Marburg Schools see Bock 2007 as well as Demirović 2006.

On the basis of three themes, this section illustrates how the key representatives of both intellectual schools analysed, interpreted, and evaluated the
topics and problems they considered relevant at the time. These are, firstly, the
problem of capitalism and class; secondly, their controversial assessments of
the 1968 student movement; and thirdly, the respective approaches to scholarship as practiced by each school. This comparison primarily references texts
produced in the 1950s, 1960s, and 1970s. Earlier major texts such as the contributions to political theory made by Friedrich Pollock, Otto Kirchheimer, or Franz
Neumann that had a major influence on the Institute for Social Research's
profile are only marginally accounted for. The same is true for both schools'
attitudes towards socialism and Communism.

That an engagement with capitalism constitutes a central task for socially
critical thought is fairly obvious, given that economic crises, social inequality,
violence, and alienation are all partially rooted in capitalist relations of production and appropriation. It is thus little surprise that the term 'capitalism'
played a significant, albeit sometimes quite distinctly interpreted role for both
the Frankfurt as well as Marburg Schools.

The Frankfurt thinkers approached the problem of capitalism largely by way
of theoretical reflection, conducted in the form of, among others, a reception
of Hegelian philosophy, Marxian analysis of capitalist commodity production
and its 'fetish character', along with an engagement with studies such as Georg
Lukács's *History and Class Consciousness*.[94] In doing so they became increasingly drawn to the question as to why capitalism, despite its immanent contradictions and oppressive relations, consistently managed to instrumentalise
the desires and consciousness of individuals in a way that conformed to the
system's needs. The Frankfurt School's scholarly interest was thus primarily directed not towards objective socio-economic processes and their corresponding
implications for the political balance of forces, changes to the form of the bourgeois state, and social and political conflicts, but rather the dimension of social
consciousness and the incorporation of subjectivity through the principle of
exchange value. At the same time, the Frankfurt School sought to integrate capitalism's modernising tendencies into its analysis of alienated desires and forms
of consciousness. Theodor W. Adorno, for example, claimed to bring concepts
derived from the analysis of capitalism down to a common denominator with
the competing concept of 'industrial society'.[95] This analytical move resulted
in the following assumption: society remained capitalist in terms of its rela-

---

94   See Jay 1973, p. 173 f. and p. 332, fn. 3.
95   In the following see Adorno 2003.

tions of production, yet in terms of its productive forces it could be considered an 'industrial society' to the extent that the rationality of industrial production permeates all areas of the economic process of reproduction. Although production continued to occur 'for the sake of profit', technological progress had made the 'doctrine of surplus value' obsolete. Because 'living labour', the actual source of surplus value, continued to shrink and even tended towards a threshold below which it would cease to play any role whatsoever, the Marxist theory of revolution had lost its plausibility. For if technological progress robbed the theory of surplus value of its foundation, then the working class would erode as well. Accordingly, it could no longer be regarded as a collective revolutionary subject and the notion of a 'class antagonism' in the sense of a social tension with the potential to blast apart the existing system also became obsolete.

These assumptions in Adorno's thought corresponded to a definitive dissolution of class consciousness in the highly industrialised countries of Western Europe and the United States.[96] Jürgen Habermas would later attempt to correct Adorno's rather metaphorical treatment of the categories of the Marxian labour theory of value and place it on a more solid foundation.[97] According to Habermas, the Marxian labour theory of value had lost its validity as a result of the scientification of the process of production. Capitalism's immanent crisis proneness had been effectively contained and neutralised by state intervention, class conflicts depoliticised by socio-political pacification and the institutionalisation of class compromises, while the economic contradictions of capitalist accumulation had shifted to the level of crises of political legitimation and moral motivation as a result. Consequently, hopes for a system-transcending role for the working class could no longer be upheld.[98]

To further bolster his hypothesis concerning the integration of the class antagonism, Adorno in turn reframed the dialectic of productive forces and relations of production by arguing that late capitalism had successfully established an absolute primacy of the relations of production, which pacified the explosive revolutionary potential of the productive forces. The 'predominance of the relations of production' had, according to Adorno, utterly usurped the productive forces and subjected both production and consumption to the logic of exchange value in equal measure, meaning that a system-transcending dynamic could no longer be expected from the productive forces.[99]

---

96   See Adorno 2003, p. 114 f.
97   See Habermas 1975, esp. pp. 50–60.
98   See Habermas 1975, p. 40.
99   Adorno 2003, p. 119 ff.

This particular reflection of Adorno's, however, was not entirely new. Herbert Marcuse had anticipated it in his *One-Dimensional Man* by equating the irrationality of modern rule with technical rationality as such: 'The most advanced areas of industrial society exhibit throughout these two features: a trend toward consummation of technological rationality, and intensive efforts to contain this trend within the established institutions. Here is the internal contradiction of this civilization: the irrational element in its rationality'.[100]

How did the representatives of the Marburg School respond to this interpretation of 'late capitalism' and its ruling function? Did they share the views of the Frankfurt scholars, or reject them? An answer to this question brings to light irreconcilable standpoints in the capitalism debate. Even Abendroth's approach to the problem diverged significantly from the theoretical-philosophical approach of the Frankfurt School. As an 'organic' and simultaneously critical and independent intellectual of the revolutionary workers' movement (as Frank Deppe once accurately described him) committed to the development of class consciousness among the workers and the political unity of the workers' movement, the young Abendroth's deliberations proceeded from the assumption that capitalism was a system based on exploitation.[101] An explicit engagement with the question of capitalism would only impose itself on Abendroth in the period after World War II when, in the context of the West German economic miracle and the discourse of a 'bourgeoisification of the working class', the alleged disappearance of capitalism along with its replacement by 'modern industrial society' became a widespread ideological stereotype. With view to the question of the existence or erosion of the working class and the possibility of restoring class consciousness, Abendroth stood for a contrary position to that of the Frankfurt School. Though he conceded that the material living standard of the wage-labouring masses had risen considerably and the majority of wage-earners had subjectively accepted status quo social relations for the time being, this did not negate the continued existence of capitalist class distinctions and contradictions as long as wage-earners were 'fundamentally subordinate to the decision-making power of capital in their work'.[102] Critical social theory – which, for Abendroth, meant if not exclusively then at least primarily Marxist theory – was still tasked with restoring class consciousness and contributing to the politicisation of the workers' movement, as much as it was currently dominated by illusions of social partnership and

100   Marcuse 2007, p. 19.
101   Deppe 2006a.
102   Abendroth 1972d, p. 25.

class harmony.[103] The French, Italian, Belgian, and other examples proved that
the absence of class consciousness in late capitalism was by no means a law
of nature, but rather could be corrected through socialist theory and praxis. In
this Abendroth concurred with Werner Hofmann, who for his part had initiated
a left-wing political education programme tailored to fit the specific interests
of wage-earners and designed to foster their process of becoming (class-)con-
scious.[104]

Abendroth and Hofmann opposed the Frankfurt School's views not only
with view to the existence and political significance of the class antagonism in
capitalism, but also in their assessment of the dialectic of forces and relations
of production. They contested the notion that modern capitalism had robbed
the productive forces of their emancipatory utility entirely and perverted them
to a mere means of securing domination. Where Adorno saw a total predominance of the relations of production in late capitalism, Abendroth drew on the
classical Marxist view that the forces of production unleashed by capitalism
itself had grown incompatible with the anarchy of capitalist competition.[105]
Not even the recently emerged 'organised capitalism', as Abendroth described
the contemporary stage of capitalist development with reference to Rudolf Hilferding, could successfully resolve this contradiction. Such a solution would
ultimately only be possible under the conditions of a socialist planned economy – a prospect that had ceased to appear purely utopian.

Werner Hofmann's studies on rationalisation and automation led him to
similar conclusions. Automation in society had opened up the historic possibility of releasing 'human labour energies for higher, more human general-
civilisational and cultural purposes', but the 'late capitalist, monopolist world'
blocked the practical social recognition of this chance.[106]

If one inquires as to what holds true today from both schools' controversial
findings concerning the theme of capitalism, class, and forces of production,
the following answer can be given: at first glance, a great deal appears to argue
against the Marburg School. An emphatic concept of the working class is no
longer popular and capitalism continues to exploit the so-called forces of production at will, while the overwhelming majority of individuals continue to
acquiesce to the imperatives of the dominant social relations without com-
plaining just as they did 50 years ago.

103   Abendroth 1972b, p. 460.
104   Hofmann 1988.
105   Abendroth 1972c, p. 465, p. 467, p. 475, p. 477.
106   Hofmann 1988, p. 159 f.

Upon closer inspection, however, a different picture emerges that in fact corroborates the views of the Marburg School in many essential aspects. The politicisation of the wage-earning population continues to be a decisive precondition for achieving social and democratic reforms, even if the working class once glorified by the Left as the so-called 'revolutionary subject' seems to have been worn out for good. Moreover, capitalism remains unable to resolve class antagonisms despite its immense material productivity, even if it exhibits a different social physiognomy than in the phase of Manchester or Taylorist capitalism. On the contrary: class divisions, social exclusion, and impoverishment are growing increasingly acute today and the contradictions between capitalist relations and forces of production persist, starkly and depressingly evidenced by mass unemployment and the environmental crisis.

Thus, the problem raised by Abendroth and Hofmann of rationally directing the forces of production in the interests of society remains current in both scholarly as well as political terms, even if in the future this directing would have to go beyond the immediate spheres of commodity and services production and incorporate the complexity of the human-nature relation.[107]

Does this mean the Frankfurt School's contributions to an analysis of capitalism should be written off as worthless? The Frankfurt School's critique of capitalism certainly does not consist of a coherent analysis of the socio-economic processes of socialisation in modern capitalism. Rather, it consists much more of well-differentiated insights into the relationships between capital's logic of economic valorisation and its symbolic violence, which instrumentalises, distorts, and reifies the subjectivity of individuals. The chapter on 'The Culture Industry' in *Dialectic of Enlightenment* makes terrifyingly clear how individuals' economic dependency on capital extends beyond the factory halls, department stores, and offices in the form of subjugation to the imperatives of cultural consumption and mass media, expressed laconically by Horkheimer and Adorno with the line: 'Amusement under late capitalism is the prolongation of work'.[108] Should the social, emotional, aesthetic, and erotic desires serviced by the 'culture industry' grow so falsified and deformed that individuals begin to identify with that which in truth dominates them, then capitalist rule no longer has anything to fear from the emancipatory potential of said desires. This critical message conveyed in *Dialectic of Enlightenment* is as valid today as it was the day it was written.

---

107   On this see several contributions by Karl Hermann Tjaden, esp. Tjaden 1990, pp. 113–216.
108   Horkheimer and Adorno 1997, p. 137.

5.2   *The 1968 Student Movement: Anxieties in Frankfurt, Realism in*
       Marburg

The representatives of both the Frankfurt as well as Marburg Schools are widely regarded as intellectual precursors and mentors to the student movement of 1968. Yet the relationship between these established academic proponents of socially critical thought and the rebellious students in Frankfurt would not be without conflict. In fact, it even led to intense clashes, such as when Adorno called the police on students occupying the Institute for Social Research in 1969.[109]

Jürgen Habermas had already emerged as a trenchant critic of the radical student movement and SDS in particular in 1967, applying the unfortunate label of 'left-wing fascism' to the students and distancing himself (sometimes quite polemically) from the movement.[110] Habermas interpreted the left-wing student movement as a socio-psychological phenomenon,[111] a knee-jerk response to the divergence between social wealth on the one hand and a rigid but 'increasingly fragile ideology of achievement', property fetishism, and status fixation in late capitalism on the other.[112] Not economic hardship and coercion but rather a rejection of consumerist and privatised depoliticisation were the actual sources of the student movement, whose provocative 'happening' tactics and rulebreaking, however, had morphed into 'ritualised forms of extortion'.[113] According to Habermas, the slogans and aims of the students rested on false premises that would necessarily lead to disastrous political consequences.

The radical student activists' dogmatic self-assuredness had, Habermas presumed, suggested to the rest of the students the existence of a state of fascist conditions and forced upon them a 'tactic of pseudo-revolution', which however was doomed to utter hopelessness. Rather than actions for their own sake and proclaiming a revolutionary crisis in the absence of any real foundation for such a diagnosis, the student movement ought to accept the necessity of a 'long-term educational strategy on a mass scale'.[114] Without such education, the student movement would inevitably isolate itself and ultimately end in a downright suicidal form of actionism.

---

109   See Kraushaar 1998, p. 557 f. Kraushaar cites a file entry from February 1969, the author of
      which he surmises to most likely be Theodor W. Adorno.
110   Habermas 1998.
111   In the following see Habermas 1968.
112   Habermas 1968, p. 9.
113   Habermas 1968, p. 7.
114   Habermas 1968, p. 14.

Herbert Marcuse took a contrary position to Habermas in the form of his so-called 'theory of marginal groups', initially limited to a few speculative impressions in the conclusion to *One-Dimensional Man*.[115] Proceeding from the notion of a social system that had successfully insulated itself against the eruption of internal contradictions through the pseudo-satisfaction of desires, consumerist integration, and 'repressive tolerance', Marcuse no longer believed (in line with Habermas) that the working class could be the source of a system-transcending movement in the sense of the traditional Marxist theory of revolution. Such a movement could only be expected from social groups which were not integrated into the 'totalitarian tendencies of the one-dimensional society', excluded from the integrative mechanism of the system and thus unaffected by said mechanism in terms of their consciousness.[116] Alongside the dropouts, unemployed, ethnic minorities, and civil rights activists he identified as the new revolutionary subject in *One-Dimensional Man*, elsewhere he would explicitly mention the students rejecting the late capitalist system.[117]

Although his hopes that the marginalised would constitute a new revolutionary subject were not based on convincing historical facts, Marcuse's marginal groups theory would soon become a guiding idea of the 'anti-authoritarian' students. Marcuse's emphatic embrace of the student protests was related to his specifically American background. The escalation of the Vietnam War, the social fragmentation of the US population, the unresolved race problem, and the actions of US imperialism formed a favourable substratum for student resistance on the campuses of American universities at a point in time when relatively little was occurring at German universities apart from several West Berlin-based initiatives around higher education policy.

The Marburg School's attitude to the students' demands and protests diverged starkly from both Habermas as well as Marcuse. Wolfgang Abendroth's response to Habermas's commentary positioned itself between 'democratic-liberal and revolutionary socialist critique', as reflected in the title of his contribution to the 1968 collected volume *Die Linke antwortet Habermas*. After Abendroth (who, as already mentioned, supervised Habermas's *Habilitation* in 1961 because Horkheimer was unwilling to habilitate him in Frankfurt for being 'too left-wing'!) rebuffed the invective of 'left-wing fascism' as a spontaneous verbal lapse while simultaneously relativising its importance, he primarily subjected Habermas's hypothesis, directed at the students, that the Marxian theory of value and with it the working class as a political subject had grown obsolete

---

115   Marcuse 2007, pp. 251–61.
116   Marcuse 2007, p. 260.
117   Marcuse 2014, p. 205.

to a rigorous critique.[118] Despite the enormous degree of technological progress, Abendroth substantiated, the apparatus of social production was still the
product of living labour and thus a materialisation of surplus value that capital
privately appropriated.[119] Although the students' glorification of the working
class was problematic and Habermas was correct in accusing the students of a
'tactic of pseudo-revolution', capital's need for academically trained workforces
evidenced common, overlapping interests between the students and the wage-
earning population. It was for this reason that Habermas's attempt to interpret
the student movement as a purely socio-psychological phenomenon fell short,
and his 'strategy of education on a mass scale' remained too abstract, for it
obscured the antagonism between material interests and capitulated to the
illusion that the political struggle against the ruling class could be reduced to
mere persuasion.[120]

Although Werner Hofmann's assessment of the student movement shared
several aspects of Habermas's aversion to the provocative tactics and omnipo-
tent fantasies of the 'anti-authoritarians', he did not fail to acknowledge the
structural sources of the protests, locating them in the 'actual core area of social
domination', namely in the contradictions of the capitalist relations of production.[121] Arguing that the conflict at the universities was thus a 'derivative
conflict', Hofmann advised the students to bring themselves into line with the
interests of the wage-earning workers, as they represented the collective bear-
ers of society and thus the actual object of social oppression. That said, this
depended upon the students becoming conscious of their own socially ambivalent position between academic training and dependent gainful employment rather than portraying themselves as the revolutionary avant-garde of the
working class.[122]

What comparative conclusions can be drawn from the Frankfurt and Marburg Schools' assessments of the student movement? The essentials of Habermas's and Marcuse's views were obviously incompatible, although some of
their considerations such as the improbability of a re-politicisation of the working class aligned. Habermas became so irritated by the actionistic appearance
and utopian excesses of the anti-authoritarian impulse that he lost sight of
the connections between student protests, the crisis of capitalist modernisation, and de-democratisation. Marcuse for his part absolutised social minor-

---

118   Abendroth 1968b.
119   Abendroth 1968b, p. 134.
120   Abendroth 1968b, p. 141.
121   See Hofmann 1971a, p. 47.
122   See Hofmann 1970b.

ities allegedly not yet ideologically integrated into the late capitalism system into an untouched, pure subject of the negation of domination shorn of all systemic constraints. He failed to grasp that oppression, social exclusion, and alienation – especially in the consciousness of marginalised layers of society – leave particularly deep scars, and by no means predestine them to become system-transcending actors. This could be seen in the outbursts of violence in the French *banlieues* in 2005 or the 2011 'riots' in England. Nor did he understand that the majority of the students remained trapped in a middle-class habitus that would not disappear spontaneously.[123]

By contrast, no substantial differences emerged between Hofmann and Abendroth although the contrast between their subjective and habitual reactions to the student movement could not be ignored. Rather, both tended to agree that the spectacular happenings and revolutionary romanticism were not the decisive factor as far as the student movement was concerned, but rather that their causes were rooted in the structural problems of the university system's adaptation to the needs of capitalist valorisation as well as a political and moral crisis of the Federal Republic following the Adenauer era. Hofmann and Abendroth attempted to derive a generalisable democratisation perspective out of the student movement, in which they viewed the wage-earning class and the workers' movement as the most important collective actor. This assessment stood in direct contrast to the Frankfurt School's position. It is worth mentioning that Adorno never expressed a more detailed opinion on the student movement.[124] His cultural habitus and distance to the depths of concrete political conflicts caused it to appear more uncanny in his eyes than as a relevant point of reference for socially critical thought.

5.3   *Understanding of Science*

The Frankfurt School's understanding of science centres around 'critical theory', famously founded by Max Horkheimer in his 1937 essay 'Traditional and Critical Theory' and subsequently elaborated and deepened by other representatives of the Frankfurt School in highly diverse fashion. If one seeks to briefly summarise the essential aspects of this understanding of science, we could say it consists of a consistent attempt to investigate the forms of thought and consciousness in which society is reflected and ideationally reproduced with view to their affirmative substance. In doing so, critical theory assumes the existence of a contradiction between the emancipatory possibilities of bourgeois society

---

123   See Peter 2006.
124   See Adorno's oral contributions in Kraushaar 1998.

on the one hand (particularly in its late capitalist form) and the actual relations of domination on the other, which is obscured by both the legitimising function of philosophical and social-scientific theories and methodologies as well as the consciousness of the masses identifying with said domination.

The critique of the traditional bourgeois concept of science of idealist and positivist provenance contained on the one hand a notion of social totality in which the particular is mediated through the general, while implying on the other the recognition of the material-economic grounding of all social processes. From this perspective, critical theory questioned scientific interpretations and assertions which in whichever way sought to do away with the context of socialisation of concrete social processes and actions in favour of isolated subjects, individual empirical facts, or idealist constructs. The Frankfurt School's critique of given theories and methodologies with which bourgeois-capitalist society seeks to reconcile its real contradictoriness corresponded to the development of an increasingly intensive engagement with the question as to why individuals paradoxically subjectively internalise and accept the social relations that oppress them. In working through this question, the Frankfurt School viewed itself as obliged to explain the ideological appearance behind the promises of progress, happiness, and freedom and develop an awareness of the fact that behind these promises' outward appearance lay a totality of domination.

The Frankfurt School's understanding of science based on critical theory made impressive contributions to the critique of both theory as well as methodology. These will be briefly illustrated here with recourse to two examples, namely Marcuse's essay on 'Industrialisation and Capitalism' in the work of Max Weber and Adorno's critique of methodology in empirical social research.[125]

Marcuse convincingly demonstrated that despite his sober analysis of the relationship between capitalist valorisation logic and bureaucratic rationality, Max Weber remained trapped in the 'equivalence of technical and capitalist reason'.[126] This equivalence prevented Weber from developing a concept of reason beyond modern capitalism and technology. Weber ruled out a social alternative to the systemic unity of capitalism and technical reason because he could only imagine socialism as an inevitable continuation of the bureaucratic apparatus brought forth by capitalism. As Marcuse explained, Max Weber predicted without illusions that the symbiosis of capitalism, technical reason, and

---

125   See Marcuse 1965 and Adorno 2000.
126   Marcuse 1965, p. 15.

bureaucratisation subjugated humanity to the domination of the system like the Fellahin of Ancient Egypt, but did not seek a way out of this catastrophic development in an historically possible emancipatory utilisation of technology, but rather in questionable hopes for a charismatic political saviour.[127]

As aptly as Marcuse demonstrated Max Weber's inability to distinguish between the capitalist exploitation of industry and technology and the possibility of an alternative social utilisation and direction of technical progress, it is difficult to comprehend why Marcuse (in *One-Dimensional Man*, for example) repeats precisely that which he correctly accused Max Weber of. His fascination with technical innovations being developed in the US was evidently so overwhelming that he was unable to recognise the antinomy of his own thought.

At the methodological level, the Frankfurt School's critique of Enlightenment discourse and its modern variants' affirmative faith in technology and progress simultaneously enabled a critique of the positivist approach to methodology that became established in Western Europe post-1945 under the influence of American social research.[28] Adorno's engagement with the methodologies of empirical social research did not restrict themselves to the epistemological dimensions of positivism and 'critical rationalism', but rather struck at the core of empirical social research, meaning that initially Adorno questioned the methodological fetishism dominant at his time, permeated as it was by instrumental reason that detached observed social phenomena from their social constitution and mediation in order to manipulate them as quasi-scientific objects.[129] The opinions and value judgements expressed by individuals are thus interpreted not as subjective expressions of social relations but rather regarded as immediately objective. But because, in Adorno's view, spontaneous subjective perception of society necessarily remains trapped in its ideological pretence, objective social relations cannot be inferred from the opinions and statements of individuals. This insight of Adorno tying the validity of empirical research to the coherence of socially critical theory also provides indispensable orientations for modern-day social science, insofar as sociology seeks to be more than the mere reproduction and justification of existing relations of domination.

Compared with the achievements of the Frankfurt School, Marburg's contributions to the field of theoretical and methodological social-scientific founda-

---

127   Marcuse 1965, p. 8f., p. 15.
128   On the influence of American social research on the development of social science in Germany post-1945 see Plé 1990.
129   Adorno 2000, p. 179.

tional research were without a doubt more modest. Abendroth only sporadically spoke out on epistemological and methodological problems and theories
of the social sciences, nor did he develop a political scientific theory either partially or as a whole. Nevertheless, Abendroth was by no means 'theory-less'.[130]
Rather, his thought drew on elements of historical materialism as worked out
in its foundations by Marx and Engels. Abendroth sought to apply these elements to the analysis of concrete social and political processes, institutions,
and movements without capitulating to the tendency towards dogmatism and
faith in so-called historical laws widespread in Marxist discourse at the time.
Theoretical and methodological questions interested Abendroth only with
respect to their explanatory value for the analysis of real social and political balances of forces in terms of the struggle for democracy and socialism. However,
this has also been portrayed as a deficiency in comparison to Adorno. Alex
Demirović, for example, contrasts the 'emphasis' of Adorno's theoretical work
to Abendroth's practical-political engagement: 'Engaged in day-to-day politics in a pronounced fashion, [Abendroth] clearly separated his own political-
theoretical position strongly from his academic work, which remained relatively shorn of theory and descriptive'.[131]

Whether dealing with Marx and Engels, Karl Kautsky, Rosa Luxemburg, Karl
Korsch, or Georg Lukács, Abendroth was consistently preoccupied with the
question as to what extent their thinking could be made fruitful for understanding the workers' movement and the political left. This practical accentuation of
his understanding of science can be explained in terms of a sociology of knowledge through Abendroth's life-long dedication to the workers' movement, into
which he was socialised and which he viewed as the only collective actor capable of applying scientific knowledge in political praxis with the prospect of
succeeding.[132] This close connection between scholarly activity, the needs of
the workers' movement, and the goal of a socialist transformation of 'late capitalism' set Abendroth apart from the representatives of the Frankfurt School,
whose work privileged a critique of both existing theories as well as the analysis
of objectified forms of individual consciousness.

Werner Hofmann's understanding of science and conception of the relationship between theory and praxis can be situated somewhere between Wolfgang

---

130   This can be seen in the brief but rich chapter summarising essential points of socially crit-
       ical thought in the political sciences found in Abendroth 1972a, pp. 9–13. The chapter is
       discussed more extensively in Tjaden and Peter 2006.
131   Demirović 1999, p. 478, fn. 413.
132   See Diers 2006. See also, for example, Abendroth 1976, p. 247 ff.

Abendroth and the Frankfurt School.[133] Hofmann shared with Abendroth social-scientific work's explicit relation to praxis, evident in his numerous contributions to a theoretical and methodological critique of the social sciences and contemporary economics specifically.[134] He accused the discipline of 'losing its knowledge concerning the central significance of productive, value-creating labour', of microeconomic reductionism, a fixation on *homo economicus*, as well as a de-historicisation of economic thought.[135] Similar was true of Heinz Maus, whose contact with the Frankfurt School was particularly intense before being appointed to Marburg following several detours, for whom the immanent technical critique and history of sociological theory took centre stage. Highly knowledgeable in the classics of French sociology, Heinz Maus sought to, among other things, update the contradictory theoretical relationship between sociological positivism (Comte, Durkheim) and socially critical sociology, as well as identify neo-positivism and neo-empiricism as technocratic knowledge to further social domination.[136] That said, Heinz Maus's activity – which grew increasingly scant by the mid-1960s – always remained overshadowed by that of Abendroth and Hofmann, whom he nevertheless often supported in relevant political initiatives such as those against the Emergency Acts.[137]

Critique of social domination and heteronomy constituted the central focus of both the Frankfurt as well as Marburg Schools, although their respective approaches to said critique took different paths. As far as their respective understandings of science were concerned, the Frankfurt School devoted itself primarily to the critical reflection of the manipulation of individual forms of desire and consciousness by late capitalism. For Marburg (and Abendroth in particular) on the other hand, the central question was to what extent the social sciences obstructed or facilitated working-class struggles and movements and in this way contributed to illuminating or obscuring the preconditions for a socialist transformation of society. With recourse to the memorable distinction established by the French theoreticians of capitalism Luc Boltanski and Ève Chiapello, Marburg tended to represent a type of 'social critique' whereas

---

133 On Hofmann's understanding of science see Boris 1999.
134 For one example see Hofmann 1961. See also several contributions on the critique of economics in Hofmann 1971f, as well as Hecker 1999.
135 Hofmann 1971f, p. 129.
136 Maus 1981a.
137 Maus co-edited a volume on the Emergency Acts with Werner Hofmann, Hofmann and Maus 1967.

Frankfurt gravitated more towards 'artistic critique', understood by the two authors as essentially emancipative endeavours oriented towards individual self-realisation, personal autonomy of action, creativity, and cultural freedom of options. Their conception of 'social critique' largely corresponds to the commonly accepted understanding of the term.[138]

The Frankfurt School's most important, lasting lesson is that an engagement with scientific modes of thought, theories, and methodologies devoted to legitimising the status quo is no intellectual luxury, but rather a constitutive element of social critique – precisely because the reality of domination does not exhaust itself in its economic and political relations, but rather manifests in the forms of thought and consciousness, scientific theories, and methodologies that symbolically reproduce, justify, and shield domination from critique. To have recognised and repeatedly emphasised this fact characterises the Frankfurt School's exceptional contribution.

From Marburg, on the other hand, we learn that one of scientific social critique's central tasks is not only to search for points of departure for practical social change but also to advocate politically for its realisation. This necessarily includes questions of who the collective actors of such change could be, what priorities political activity should set, and what forms of organisation and movement actors require in order to achieve their goals.

Both schools also shared certain deficits. Neither the Frankfurt nor Marburg Schools had anything substantial to say about gender relations as a central dimension of social domination. The relationship between humans and nature also remained underexplored by both schools. An ambivalent stance was reflected in the work of the Frankfurt School, oscillating between an Enlightenment-inspired rejection of nature and lamentations of its destruction. In Marburg, on the other hand, an optimism vis-à-vis the forces of production inspired by scientific-technical progress proved dominant, largely blind to the enormous risks and destructive consequences of modern energies, chemical materials, new technologies, and production methods. The processes of transnational and global socialisation as well as the accumulation of political power remained blind spots in the research and analyses of both schools' main representatives until at least around 1970, whose horizons of critique remained almost entirely limited to the relations, antagonisms, and discourses of the Western hemisphere. In Marburg, however, this would change drastically beginning in the 1970s.

---

138   Boltanski and Chiapello 2018.

Despite these deficits and blind spots, scientific social critique today could hardly manage without the insights and achievements of both schools. That said, a shift in the political balance of forces both in- and outside of the universities will be necessary if scientific social critique is to have any chance of remaining a factor in teaching, research, and public discourse in the future.

6   Dominance of the Marxist Paradigm

6.1   *Karl Hermann Tjaden*

Beyond the 'Triumvirate', a further representative of the Marburg School's second phase also worth noting is Karl Hermann (Kay) Tjaden. Born in 1935 and raised in Germany's northern coastal region, he first studied sociology under Adorno in Frankfurt before coming to Marburg in 1961 where he, as mentioned above, completed his dissertation under Abendroth's supervision. The borders between sociology and political science in Marburg at that time were fluid for both scientific as well as political reasons, where alternating between responsibilities at one of the two institutes – Abendroth's and the Sociological Seminar, respectively – was quite common.

Tjaden distinguished himself from the rest of the Marburg School protagonists through his specific intellectual approach to the demands of social-scientific analysis. This manifested itself primarily in his attempt to subject the foundations of Marx and Engels's theory, historical materialism, to a new systematic review and reflexive investigation in light of changed social conditions, demarcating himself from both idealistic and economistic interpretations on the one hand and ideological instrumentalisation on the other. Tjaden sought to grasp the inner structure and historical change of societies on the basis of historical materialist theory (his avoidance of the attribute 'Marxist' was no coincidence), and in doing so relate the concepts he developed to contemporary social and scientific problems without losing sight of fundamental social realities such as exploitation and domination. In this process of a historical materialist reformulation of social theory he worked his way up to the state of modern sociological theory, which he in turn made the object of critical analysis. No representative of German sociology – and certainly no one on the spectrum of left-wing social science – came even close to possessing such an expansive and profound knowledge of contemporary, primarily Anglo-American 'bourgeois' sociological theory as Tjaden.

The first major product of this endeavour emerged in his work on *Soziales System und sozialer Wandel* (Social System and Social Change), first published in 1969 in which he subjected practically the entire range of topically relevant literature to a systematic assessment in terms of their argumentative coherence, aporia, lacunae, and abstract constructs.[139] Historical materialist thought was not immediately manifest in this volume, but factually served as the theoretical subtext throughout. His historical materialist foundation was made explicit in an extensive introduction and lengthy afterword to the 1971 collected volume *Soziale Systeme*, as well as in the afterword to a new edition of *Soziales System und sozialer Wandel* published in 1972.[140] In doing so, Tjaden illuminated a fundamental weakness in all of the theories and attempts to explain the stability of social systems and social change he analysed, namely the abstractification of economically structured processes of socialisation of social systems rooted in nature into instances of interpersonal interactions, presuppositionless organisational activities, and system-generating constructs of social activity detached from all material points of reference.

Although Tjaden's work was quietly admired by insiders of mainstream sociology, it remained subjected to the discourse-specific effects of its time – despite its high reflexive level and methodological quality he failed to exert a decisive influence on the process of sociological research and discussion, but instead for the most part fell victim to the mechanisms of discursive selection and exclusion as subtly and powerfully described by Michel Foucault.

Following Hofmann's death, Tjaden served as professor of sociology in Marburg from 1970–4 before being appointed to the Gesamthochschule Kassel. Here, together with Margarete (Annegret) Tjaden-Steinhauer (born in 1936),[141] he would devote himself to the development and application of historical materialist theory as social and civilisational critique in which the necessity of preserving the biosphere[142] and sublating powers of social control determined by domination would constitute a central focus.[143] Characteristic for Tjaden and Tjaden-Steinhauer's efforts towards a further development of historical materialist social theory is a conscious and systematic updating of the material, energetic, and biotic preconditions for processes of socialisation, as well as the analysis of social and historical relations of violence while taking patriarchal domination into systematic account – aspects which were notoriously neglected in the tradition of Marxist thought *after* Marx and Engels and into the present.

---

139   Tjaden 1972 (slightly revised and expanded edition of the original 1969 edition).
140   Tjaden 1971a and 1971b.
141   Steinhauer 1966. Heinz Maus wrote a preface to this book (pp. V–IX).
142   Tjaden 1990.
143   Lambrecht, Tjaden, and Steinhauer 1998; Tjaden-Steinhauer and Tjaden 2001; Sperling and Tjaden-Steinhauer 2004; Mies and Tjaden 2009.

Tjaden's decision to leave Marburg in 1974 may have been related to dissonances in terms of his assessment of inter-departmental politics, and perhaps also due to concerns that the specific demands of scientific work could not be fulfilled when the borders between scholarship and politics began to blur – something which most certainly could not be ruled out in the politically-charged atmosphere of *Fachbereich* 03 at the time.

6.2 *Shifting Actor Constellations*

The number of left-socialist and Marxist-oriented staff and graduate students at both institutes began to increase considerably in the mid-1960s. As hinted at above, many of them came from SDS, such as Karl Hermann Tjaden, Margarete Tjaden-Steinhauer, Eberhard Dähne, Rüdiger Griepenburg,[144] Ursula Schmiederer,[145] Frank Deppe, Dieter Boris, Hans-Ulrich Deppe,[146] Georg Fülberth, Kurt Steinhaus, Gert Meyer, Jürgen Harrer, Herbert Claas,[147] Hellmuth Lange, and Lothar Peter. It was only at this point that something resembling an 'epistemic community' began to emerge based on the cultivation of socialist and Marxist theory as well as political activism going beyond the academic field. Some of the essentials of the group's self-understanding were the theory of

---

144 Born in 1937, Rüdiger Griepenburg was a member of SDS, Abendroth's assistant, and a major contributor to the drafting of *Einführung in die politische Wissenschaft* (Abendroth and Lenk 1968). He wrote his dissertation on the social-democratic resistance group Deutsche Volksfront and served as professor of social movement history at the University of Osnabrück from 1973–98. Griepenburg was widely respected in both the Marburg SDS chapter as well the national organisation for his wide-ranging knowledge spanning various disciplines. As Abendroth's assistant, he supported students and SDS members through diverse suggestions and discussions. That said, he failed to publish much of note after his time in Marburg.

145 Deputy SDS national chairwoman Ursula Schmiederer (1936–89) completed her dissertation under Abendroth on the Danish Socialist People's Party and was an adjunct researcher in Marburg from 1965–70. She completed her *Habilitation* in 1975 and was appointed to a professorship of international politics at the University of Osnabrück in the same year.

146 Born in 1939, Hans-Ulrich Deppe is the brother of Frank Deppe. He studied medicine, sociology, and political science and served as Werner Hofmann's assistant at the Sociological Seminar before receiving a professorship of medical sociology at the University of Frankfurt in 1972. Here, he would go on to direct the Institute for Medical Sociology until his retirement in 2004. He belonged to the group of those who continued to feel connected to the Marxist current of the Marburg School even after their time in the town.

147 Born in 1941, Herbert Claas was a member of SDS and initially served as Abendroth's research assistant, later as Werner Hofmann's. He completed his dissertation on Bertolt Brecht's aesthetics in 1975, joined the academic council at the sociology institute, and was elected vice-president of the Philipps University in 2002. In this position he was actively involved in implementing the Bologna Process and the new, six-semester Bachelor's degree system this entailed.

Marx and Engels as the foundation of their own academic work, intellectual loyalty to the workers' movement, theoretical and practical participation in trade union activity, solidarity with the anti-colonial liberation movements, and anti-capitalism.

After SDS reached its zenith with the 1968 student movement and rapidly collapsed before disbanding in 1970, countless members of the 'traditional-ist' Marburg SDS chapter joined the DKP's student organisation, MSB Spar-takus. Encouraged by Abendroth and Hofmann, some non-professional teach-ing staff from the two institutes also began to move towards political posi-tions facilitating cooperation with the DKP, implying a fundamentally posit-ive attitude towards the GDR as an alternative to capitalism[148] and arguing for a 'trade-union orientation' (*Gewerkschaftliche Orientierung*, nicknamed '*GO-Politik*') among the academic intelligentsia. Nevertheless, this development was by no means shared by all members of the left-wing staff milieu. Several Mar-burg protagonists, such as Rüdiger Griepenburg, Ursula Schmiederer (one of the few women in the male-dominated academic milieu which also encom-passed the Marburg School), Jörg Kammler, and Wolf Rosenbaum[149] cultivated a vehement demarcation vis-à-vis 'orthodox Marxism' whether real or alleged, rejection of the policies of the Soviet Union and the GDR, as well as an (albeit vague) conception of a non-bureaucratic, non-statist socialism, and kept their distance from the group of staff sympathising with the DKP and socialism in the GDR.[150] That this sometimes led to mutual personal animosities was of course

---

148   This was soon reflected, for example, in a collected volume comparing the social sys-tems of the Federal Republic and the GDR featuring, among others, Karl Hermann Tjaden, Frank Deppe, Georg Fülberth, Peter Römer, and Reinhard Kühnl that became the subject of intense, and in some points justified criticism (See Jung et al. 1971).

149   Born in 1941, Wolf-Sighard Rosenbaum came to Marburg with Werner Hofmann in 1966, taking on an assistant's position. Yet he completed his dissertation on 'natural and pos-itive law' in 1970 under Abendroth's supervision. He became a professor of sociology in Marburg as early as 1972 before being appointed to the University of Göttingen in 1973. Following Germany's so-called 'reunification', he served as one of the founding deans of sociology at the University of Jena. Rosenbaum had already begun to distance himself from the Marxist positions of the Marburg School's second generation – specifically from those of the author of this volume, see the unpublished interview conducted by Joachim Fischer and Stephan Moebius in the context of the project *Audio-visueller Quellenfundus zur deutschen Soziologie nach 1945* (Fischer and Moebius with Wolf Rosenbaum on 13 Feb-ruary 2013).

150   The group of scholars with a fundamentally positive attitude towards the GDR certainly acknowledged the enormous economic and political problems confronting East Germany both externally as well as domestically, but hoped for a possible remedying of these deficits to the extent this external pressure became weaker and international isolation receded. Ultimately, they underestimated both their extent and depth.

in the nature of things and, in light of similar positional disagreements and splits within other intellectual currents, by no means a unique negative characteristic of the Marburg School. On the other hand, figures such as Reinhard Kühnl began a more intensive engagement with Marxism relatively late despite working for Abendroth for quite some time, and quickly gravitated towards the positions of Frank Deppe and others.[151]

As was the case for practically the entire social-scientific field in West Germany at the time, the Marburg School remained dominated by male patterns of thought, action, and behavioural codes in many respects, making it exceedingly difficult for women to assert themselves intellectually and professionally under these conditions. Ursula Schmiederer was by and large the only woman who served at either the political science or sociological institutes, with the exceptions of staff researcher Heidi Rosenbaum,[152] Gisela Burbach's brief tenure as Werner Hofmann's assistant, and several of Abendroth's and Maus's graduate students. Although Abendroth treated men and women with the same degree of good will and any notion of male superiority was deeply alien to him,[153] the topics, political themes, and forms of social interaction among the Marburg School remained blatantly male-connoted despite its socialist normativity. In this respect political science and sociology in Marburg were largely the same.

Due to both the personal charisma, scholarly competence, and public political presence of its two decisive protagonists as well as the impressive achievements and practical political engagement of its students and staff, the Marburg School had a remarkable impact on both the academic sphere as well as other, non-academic fields. The 'Abendroth Institute' held something of a monopoly on the further education of hundreds of Hessian teachers in the subject of civics for many years,[154] and many Marburg graduates went on to work as school teachers. Contact and cooperation with trade-union organisations and functionaries, sometimes organised through the Arbeitsgemeinschaft für gewerkschaftliche Fragen (AgF), were warmly received and developed into a

---

151   In retrospect, Kühnl concluded that 'in terms of a theory of science, I understood myself as a Marxist as early as 1969–70, yet looking back I see that I was still quite far off from a deeper understanding of this theory of society. Frank Deppe and Georg Fülberth, coming from SDS, were much better acquainted with it' (Kühnl in Hecker et al. 2001, p. 218).

152   Heidi Rosenbaum composed, among other things, an important work on the sociology of the family, see Rosenbaum 1973.

153   His doctoral student at the time Vera Rüdiger, for example, a Social Democrat and later founding president of the Gesamthochschule Kassel, Hessian Minister of Culture and Senator for Health in Bremen, praised Abendroth's respectful, tolerant conduct towards her in the aforementioned 1987 WDR television documentary.

154   See Mück 2001.

praxis within the trade union movement that often cultivated a critical attitude towards social partnership and corporatist arrangements between trade
union leaderships, functionary groups, and corporate executives and their associations, seeking to develop a willingness to engage in conflict among the membership. Cooperation with the DKP and its think tank, the IMSF (Institut für
Marxistische Studien und Forschung), also resulted in the Marburg School's
research having an influence on the consciousness and actions of politicised
groups of blue- and white-collar workers particularly in larger workplaces.[155]
The trade unions themselves would become the occupational field of many of
Abendroth's students, while others became active in the left wing of the SPD.
Lastly, one ought not to forget in this 'second generation' context the former
students and graduate students of the Triumvirate or Tjaden who went onto
academic careers outside of Marburg, some of whom developed impressive
reputations in their field. This group included Hans Manfred Bock as a political scientist (and Romanicist) in Kassel, Erhard Lucas as a labour historian in
Oldenburg, Heiko Haumann as an historian of Eastern Europe in Frankfurt am
Main and Basel, or Alfred Oppolzer as a Marxist labour sociologist and labour
scholar in Kassel and Hamburg.

Following Abendroth's retirement in 1971 and Reinhard Kühnl's controversial appointment (opposed quite vehemently by the historian Ernst Nolte),
massive controversies accompanied by the student-led campaign 'Marx an
die Uni, Deppe auf H-4!' resulted in former sociology student Frank Deppe's
appointment to a professorship of political science, Peter Römer and Georg
Fülberth's full professorships, and temporary lecturer positions for the assistant
Gert Meyer, an expert on the history and structure of the socialist states, and
Jürgen Harrer, a knowledgeable labour historian. Herbert Claas, Hans-Ulrich
Deppe, and Dieter Boris became teaching staff or rather assistants at the Sociological Seminar, where Karl Hermann Tjaden had received the second pro-
fessorship alongside Heinz Maus as Werner Hofmann's successor in 1970.

Abendroth's retirement signalled the conclusion of the Marburg School's
second phase. By this point, the group of scholars devoted to Marx and Engels's
theory and the socialist project occupied relatively influential positions in the

---

155   See IMSF 1988. Formally an independent research institute, the IMSF was forced to dis-
band in 1990 as its funding from the DKP dried up. Several of the institute's publications
were acknowledged in the non-Marxist social sciences, such as the three-volume study
Klassen- und Sozialstruktur der BRD, 1950–1970, impressive in terms of both its wealth of
material as well as its systematic approach (IMSF 1973; IMSF 1974; IMSF 1975). Multiple
protagonists of the Marburg School contributed to the study including Karl Hermann
Tjaden, Margarete Tjaden-Steinhauer, Eberhard Dähne, and Christof Kievenheim.

new *Fachbereich* 03, which had been reorganised in 1971 and now encompassed pedagogy and philosophy alongside political science and sociology. This position would initially appear reinforced by the controversial appointment of Hans Heinz Holz (1927–2011), an early student of Ernst Bloch, outstanding Leibniz scholar, and expert in philosophical problems of dialectics. Yet Holz, who did not align with the profile of the Marburg School either in terms of his practical-political engagement nor his tendency towards scholarly abstraction, would leave the Philipps University after receiving a professorship of philosophy in 1978 to accept a professorship in Groningen, Netherlands, much to the disappointment of Abendroth's students. He would resign himself to a form of 'Leninist' ultra-dogmatism following the collapse of state socialism, seeking reassurance in his role as the 'chief theoretician' of the rump organisation that remained of the DKP.

CHAPTER 4

Third Phase: Continuity and New Challenges. Abendroth's Retirement to the Early 1980s

1   Social and Political Context

The long period of uninterrupted economic prosperity (beyond the brief lapse in 1966–7) and the 'Fordist regulation regime' based on a tripartite corporatism between capital, labour, and the state would reach its definitive end in the mid-1970s. Accumulation of West German capital began to stall, economic growth slowed, and unemployment soared to heights long considered unimaginable under the ideological spell of continuous prosperity. This development went hand-in-hand with a technological and organisational restructuring of the social labour process in West Germany, eroding the industrial working class and facilitating processes of objective and subjective individualisation across broad swathes of the population. The traditional social and cultural contours of capitalism in the country began to shift, albeit without altering its underlying economic logic. On the contrary, this logic would manifest in new, rigorous post-Taylorist strategies of exploitation resulting in ever-growing levels of mass unemployment, a sinking relation of distribution tipping the scales against wage labourers, along with deregulation and privatisation measures enacted by the liberal-conservative government under Chancellor Helmut Kohl elected in 1982. This dynamic placed increasing pressure on the associations and representative organisations of the wage-earning class. Although IG Metall and IG Druck und Papier mobilised a strike for the 35-hour week in 1984, the economic effects of crisis and social-structural ruptures also carried implications for the trade unions' base. The 'proletarian milieu' collapsed, as the hitherto collective identity of interests began to differentiate into heterogeneous group interests, and alienation – particularly on the part of the younger generation – vis-à-vis collective forms of trade union and political representation and organisation increased. As a result, resistance and protest against the destructive consequences of the capitalist economy began to migrate away from the core industrial sectors towards other fields of social contradiction and the emerging 'new social movements' such as the women's movement, the peace movement, and the environmental movement. The liberal-conservative government's agenda of budget consolidation, privatisation (of telecommunications and the postal service, for example), and cuts to the social safety net along with the consequences of unemployment made the broad outlines of a 'two-thirds society' clearer than before, even if the levels of social-political hardship and decline failed to reach those of Thatcherism in Great Britain or austerity policies in France. Nevertheless, unemployment in West Germany rose alarmingly quickly between 1980–3, from 3.8 to 9.1 percent.[1]

The political state of the already weak West German left grew increasingly precarious. The influence of the left wing remained limited within the SPD, while left-wing functionaries and members of the trade unions found themselves caught in a 'war on two fronts' against both their leaderships' willingness to adapt to capital's demands as well as the consolidation of the post-Fordist regime of boosting workplace productivity on a mass scale.[2] Although the DKP – an increasingly important point of reference in the thinking of the post-Abendroth protagonists of the Marburg School – managed to stabilise organisationally and recruit large numbers of workplace activists, it remained utterly irrelevant in parliamentary terms beyond several local council seats. The DKP's student wing, the MSB Spartakus, along with the left-socialist Sozialistischer Hochschulbund (SHB) successfully consolidated their position at a number of universities in cities like Marburg, Bremen, and Hamburg. Alongside Marburg, the newly-founded University of Bremen was most notable, where several professors including former students of Abendroth and Hofmann like Hellmuth Lange[3] and Lothar Peter[4] identified with the DKP's politics and joined the party.

---

1 See Görtemaker 1999, p. 608.
2 On the problems confronting the trade unions as a result of post-Fordism's consolidation see Deppe 2012a, esp. pp. 32–57.
3 Born in 1942, Hellmuth Lange studied sociology, political science, and German philology in Munich and Marburg. He completed his dissertation on the 'new working class' in France (Lange 1972) under Abendroth's supervision and temporarily worked as a researcher at the Institut für politische Wissenschaft. Lange was appointed to a professorship of industrial and scientific sociology at the University of Bremen in 1973. He was an active member of the DKP, participated in the BdWi, and belonged to the local party leadership in Bremen where the party was relatively strong. Following German reunification and the collapse of the DKP, Lange distanced himself from Marxist positions and moved towards the Greens, albeit without joining the party. Lange would later serve for years as the spokesperson for the environmental sociology section of the German Sociological Association.
4 Born in 1942 and a member of SDS from 1965–70, Lothar Peter studied sociology, political science, and German philology in Marburg and Geneva. He worked as Abendroth's student assistant from 1965–6 and was a student tutor under Werner Hofmann. After completing his dissertation in 1971 with a thesis on the relationship between authors and political activity supervised by Abendroth and Maus (Peter 1972), he worked as an *assistant associé* at the University of Paris III from 1971–2 and was a lecturer in Marburg for a time, before being appointed to a professorship of industrial and workplace sociology (later also general sociology) at the University of Bremen. He worked closely with the IMSF in Frankfurt beginning in 1970.

This remained an exception in the nationwide university landscape, however, other than the case of Munich DKP member Horst Holzer (1935–2000) who was dismissed from his position and even had his publications removed from the university library in accordance with the 1972 *Radikalenerlass*, or 'Anti-Radical Decree'.[5]

Following a brief uptick, overall political room to manoeuvre grew increasingly narrow for the DKP and other left-wing groups. On one side, neoliberal crisis management, fear of job losses and precarity, along with cutbacks to social-political standards dampened wage-earners' willingness to engage in actions, while on the other side serious political competition to the left emerged in the form of the 'new social movements', citizens' initiatives, and the Green Party – not least because these formations proved far more capable of articulating the observable shift in values towards 'post-materialism', individualisation, and pluralisation of lifestyles in which scepticism vis-à-vis collective organisation and action intermingled among the growing social groups and milieus in a way the Left, widely suspected of being 'traditionalist', could not.[6] Multiple tendencies began to emerge that made conditions for left-wing politics more difficult following Willy Brandt's resignation in 1974. Although Helmut Schmidt's subsequent government enacted some traditional Keynesian crisis management measures, supply-side economics became increasingly influential in policy-making. These policies strengthened businesses' capital profitability while pushing trade unions onto the defensive by forcing them to rely on adaptation rather than conflict-oriented resistance by their membership. The escalation of terrorist actions by groups like the Red Army Faction (RAF), which reached a bloody highpoint during the so-called 'German Autumn' in 1977, also helped to discredit left-wing thought and activity in the public eye. Following

---

Having joined the DKP in the meantime, he formed a group of professors that cooperated closely with the DKP and remained active in academia and university politics for many years until 1990. This group included figures like economist Jörg Huffschmid, sociologist Hellmuth Lange, the lawyer Gerhard Stuby who was influenced by Abendroth and served as a visiting professor at the Philipps University for a time, sociologist Susanne Schunter-Kleemann, philosopher Hans Jörg Sandkühler, literature scholar Thomas Metscher, and others. Some were DKP members while others were not. The author left the DKP in 1991 and has remained unaffiliated with any party ever since. In his academic work he now seeks to bring Marxist ideas and non-Marxist socially critical theories and discourses (particularly the sociology of Bourdieu, but also the 'left' communitarianism of Charles Taylor, aspects of feminism and other theoretical elements) into dialogue with one another.

5 The so-called *Radikalenerlass* was a 1972 federal law banning members of 'radical' organisations from the civil service, including teaching, officially in response to the threat posed by the Red Army Faction. Many German states have since repealed the law.

6 See Beck 1992.

Helmut Kohl's rise to power in the wake of a successful no confidence vote by the federal parliament in 1982, a neo-conservative shift and general transition towards market-liberal economic policies began to set in.

2   The Political Sociology of Worker Consciousness and the Trade Unions (Frank Deppe)

The actual, albeit informal successor to Abendroth's professorship (tellingly reserved for the non-Marxist Theo Schiller) was Frank Deppe, born in Frankfurt am Main in 1941. Following an intermediate diploma in sociology in Frankfurt, he went to Marburg to continue his sociology studies under Heinz Maus before soon encountering Abendroth in a political science course. Deppe completed his dissertation under Abendroth's supervision on the aforementioned topic of Blanqui before going on to work at the Sociological Seminar as a research fellow. He completed his *Habilitation* in 1971, again under Abendroth, prior to his appointment to a professorship of political science in Marburg in 1972 (succeeding Ernst-Otto Czempiel).

Deppe cultivated a close intellectual and political relationship with Abendroth and appears to be the student who most deeply internalised and practiced the latter's understanding of Marxist political science. Like Abendroth, Deppe understood himself as a political intellectual who refused to retreat into the academic ivory tower but rather actively intervened into social and political movements in various forms. Although this was also true of other Marburg School representatives, Abendroth and Deppe arguably exhibited the greatest degree of shared intellectual and political overlaps, as was also reflected in their overriding interest in the workers' movement extending beyond purely theoretical motivations.

Deppe's closeness to Abendroth began as early as his time in the leadership of SDS, and was reflected in his participation in the founding of the Sozialistisches Zentrum in 1967, an attempt to gather up the fragmented Left beyond the SPD including the still-banned Communists that largely failed.[7] Major focuses of Deppe's work since 1970 covered the problems of the trade unions, collaboration with the IMSF in Frankfurt (he later served on its academic advisory council), the social position and political orientation of the intelligentsia and intellectuals, as well as the field of higher education policy. Deppe, who was (and remains) extraordinarily productive, wrote about all of these and other

---

7   On this see Heigl 2008, p. 216 ff.

topics, delivered public addresses on them, and participated in related conferences, public debates, and political actions.

As was true of his contemporaries, Deppe's early work was inspired by other Marxist theoreticians beyond Abendroth such as Ernest Mandel, a prominent member of the Trotskyist Fourth International, as well as Western European socialist debates on 'anti-capitalist structural reforms' (André Gorz),[8] 'workers' control' (Tom Man, Ken Coates, Tony Topham, Serge Mallet),[9] and conceptions of socialism like those of the Italian Lelio Basso, many of which found a forum in publications like the *International Socialist Journal*.

Deppe's work attempted to relate to the developments of left-socialist and Marxist theory in Western Europe and make them useful for the situation in the Federal Republic. This initially led to a first group of publications centred around the themes of trade union co-determination, the role of the technical intelligentsia in 'organised capitalism', and the consciousness of the industrial working class.[10] In methodological terms, these publications can be credited for making consistent reference to sociological findings and even being formulated in a sociological format, thereby representing a form of political sociology in an even more explicit sense than was the case for Abendroth.

Driving Deppe's research was the question of how forces and movements capable of far-reaching social transformation with a socialist perspective could be initiated among a West German working class under conditions of a prosperous capitalism in which a majority either acquiesced to or even supported capitalism, and in which a Left of national significance failed to exist. Deppe published *Das Bewußtsein der Arbeiter* (The Consciousness of the Workers)[11] in 1971, a wide-ranging study based on empirical findings and the state of international scholarship seeking to extrapolate the collective forms of worker consciousness from its context of a contradictory process of capitalist socialisation, the shifting social composition of the working class, and trade union

---

8   Gorz 1967.
9   On the British debate around 'workers' control' see the countless citations from British authors collected in Kuda 1970. Renowned French sociologist and leading member of the left-socialist Unified Socialist Party (PSU) Serge Mallet published the internationally influential empirical study *La nouvelle classe ouvrière* in 1963, which appeared in German as *Die neue Arbeiterklasse* in 1972 and in English as *The New Working Class* in 1975. Hellmuth Lange's afterword to the German edition (pp. 353–83) evidently had to appear anonymously for reasons of political opportunity, and was not even noted by the publisher in the table of contents.
10   Deppe et al. 1969; Deppe, Lange, and Peter 1970. This volume contained texts by, among others, Serge Mallet, Ernst Mandel, and Alain Touraine.
11   Deppe 1971.

policies post-1945. He concluded that barring several exceptions the empirical studies taken into account confirmed the generalisable conclusion that workers' dichotomous situational awareness had not dissipated despite shifting working conditions and rising mass consumption; instead, the contradiction between subjectively latent social insecurity and a relatively high level of systemic stability was reflected in the ambivalence of working-class consciousness.[12] According to Deppe, empirically verifiable tendencies towards a 'privatisation' of worker behaviour and an 'instrumental', de-politicised attitude to work and wages did not disprove the notion that workers perceived capitalism's existence, but rather pointed to the experience of powerlessness vis-à-vis the capitalist regime over labour power.

Deppe complemented this finding with the hypothesis that worker consciousness derived not only from immediate working and living conditions but rather was also always constituted and reproduced as a moment of a comprehensive relation of socialisation. Immediate experience was insufficient to develop class consciousness in the sense of an awareness adequate to the objective situation capable of guiding subjective action – farther-reaching initiatives 'from without' would be necessary. Deppe cited relevant deliberations in the work of Lenin and Lukács to back up this argument – albeit not in a literal, dogmatic way as authoritative instructions to be followed blindly (as was quite common for the Left at the time), but rather ascribed to them a heuristic function appropriate to the contemporary moment. This became most evident when Deppe discussed the growing discrepancy between many workers' and low-level white-collar employees' spontaneous identification with socialist slogans post-1945 and the glaring absence of a socialist project transcending immediate interests.[13]

As would be confirmed in coming years, both his studies on worker consciousness as well as other, prior works indicated that Deppe's scholarly and political attention would be drawn primarily to the problems, challenges, and prospects of the trade unions. His study on *Autonomie und Integration* published in 1979 helped to cement his reputation in the Federal Republic as a Marxist trade union theorist.[14] The study was characterised by several major aspects, beginning with his development of the economic function of the trade unions from the Marxian analysis of the international contradictions of cap-

---

12   Deppe 1971, p. 112 f.
13   Deppe 1971, p. 189.
14   Deppe 1979. This book was published by the Marburg publishing house Verlag Arbeiterbewegung und Gesellschaftswissenschaft, founded by Frank Deppe, Georg Fülberth, and Karlheinz Flessenkemper.

ital movement, namely from the relation between surplus-value production and workers' wages. Here, he emphasised trade unions' indispensable role in securing the reproduction of labour power, although they remained subjugated to the respective conditions of the capitalist mode of production despite the opposition to capital this role entails.[15] Nevertheless, it remained both possible and necessary – particularly given capitalism's expanding socialisation, which increasingly extended beyond wage labour into ever more areas of life – that trade-union demands and struggles become part of a general and thus political movement challenging the capital relation, without suspending or replacing the specific function and competencies of the political organisations of the working class. Deppe thus understood trade union autonomy as an expansion and politicisation of the functions of economic protection and security within a general movement directed against the logic, structure, and consequences of capitalism. He contrasted this to 'integration', the process of the trade unions' material and cognitive incorporation into the capitalist system, as well as 'integrationism', the ideologies and strategies serving such an incorporation.

This touched on the study's second important aspect, namely the difference between a conservative hypothesis of integration and a specific left-wing interpretation that assumed an irreversible subjugation of the trade unions to the goals of the capitalist order. Exemplary concepts of the former included the notion of the 'fortified trade unions' (Goetz Briefs) and the 'institutionalisation of class struggle' (Theodor Geiger), of the latter the notion of the trade unions' 'loss of autonomy' (Joachim Bergmann, Otto Jakobi, and Walther Müller-Jentsch). However, the left-wing explanation in some ways amounted to the same as the first hypothesis: according to Deppe's interpretation of the loss of autonomy argument, the trade unions had made their peace with the capitalist system, meaning that even initial sparks of a 'conflict-oriented trade union policy' would be absorbed by the mechanisms of the system.[16] How the abruptly introduced term of the 'revolutionary trade union' could be justified under such conditions remained as unclear as the blatant assumption that this aforementioned 'loss' had emerged following a stage of 'autonomy' – an idealised assumption that contradicted the trade unions' actual historical emergence and development.[17]

Deppe laid out the contradictions and limits of a 'socialist' critique of the trade unions that postulated the trade unions' institutional pacification on one hand, while (paradoxically) believing to have discovered the potential for

---

15   Deppe 1979, p. 91.
16   Deppe 1979, p. 179 ff.
17   Deppe 1979, p. 184.

system-transcending actions in precisely the same unions on the other. Here, Deppe saw himself confronted with the problems of a neo-syndicalist discourse, a tendency represented in West Germany by authors like Rainer Zoll, Joachim Bergmann, and Walther Müller-Jentsch, and in France by André Gorz and Serge Mallet. Deppe's concept of autonomy could on the one hand refer to exponents of left-wing trade union policies like the prominent Italian union leader Bruno Trentin of the CGIL, who advocated overcoming the traditionally rigid division of labour between trade union and political organisations, without conflating this with a neo-syndicalist de-legitimation of the political parties of the working class.[18] In Deppe's view, the possibility of developing and fighting for trade union autonomy was rooted in the process of 'antagonistic socialisation', which could potentially lend the struggles of wage-earners an autonomous political quality in the present: 'The more trade union struggles move into the political space and the more immediately the political parties, the institutions of the system of political domination, are confronted with this autonomous, political quality of the trade union movement, the more the movement is capable of developing political initiatives which have effects on the political parties – and, above all, the activity of trade union members involved in party politics'.[19]

The study's third major aspect were the results of Deppe's theoretical analysis of both concrete historical developments in the trade union movement as well as the contemporary situation as it presented itself at the end of the 1970s. He rejected fatalistic interpretations of the trade union movement as a history of decline by incorporating empirical findings primarily from industrial sociology, while upholding the possibility of trade union autonomy despite evidence of the social fragmentation of the working class as well as the corporatist tendencies dominating trade union policy, which he never denied.[20] He regarded this autonomy as increasingly urgent the more wage-earning employees' reproductive interests expanded beyond the workplace. Whether or not the 'loss of utopia' he decried would have to be remedied in order to develop trade union autonomy, something he clearly believed in the rich study on *Ende oder Zukunft der Arbeiterbewegung?* (End or Future of the Workers' Movement?) published at the beginning of the Kohl era in 1984, would necessarily remain an open question, as Deppe never provided further clarification or concretisation of the term itself.[21]

---

18   Deppe 1979, p. 178.
19   Deppe 1979, p. 190.
20   Deppe 1979, p. 229, fn. 88.
21   Deppe 1984a.

3   The History of German Social Democracy (Georg Fülberth and
       Jürgen Harrer)

While Deppe concentrated primarily on the trade union movement during
the 1970s and 1980s, Georg Fülberth devoted himself to the history of Social
Democracy and the Communist parties in Germany. Born in 1939, Fülberth
first studied history and German philology in Frankfurt am Main where he
became a member of SDS. He had maintained an assistant's position under
Abendroth since 1967 and completed his dissertation under the latter's supervision in 1970. He was then segued into a professorship of political science at the
Philipps University in 1972 that he held until 2004.[22] In contrast to the other
key representatives of the Marburg School, Fülberth joined the DKP around
1974 after demonstratively resigning from the SPD in 1967, and represented the
Marburger Linke coalition as a city councillor for several years in Marburg's
municipal assembly, where he remained until 2011. A brilliant speaker, Fülberth
also made a name for himself as a sharp and humorous journalist alongside his
many political activities. He regularly composed columns for the *Frankfurter
Rundschau* and occasionally for *Die Zeit* until its publishers grew tired of his
political invective, and regularly appeared in various left-wing publications.[23]

   Like Deppe's work on the trade unions, *Die deutsche Sozialdemokratie, 1890–
1933* by Georg Fülberth and Jürgen Harrer (who also completed his dissertation
under Abendroth) reflected the typical focus of the Marburg School in its post-
Abendroth phase and the desire to contribute to a West German left independent of Social Democracy and incorporating the Communists.[24] The volume
built on Abendroth's 1964 *Aufstieg und Krise der deutschen Sozialdemokratie*
(Rise and Crisis of German Social Democracy), yet distinguished itself through,
among other things, an unevenly more intensive use of source materials. Fülberth and Harrer's decision to dedicate the book to four colleagues who had
fallen victim to the occupational ban, largely enforced by Social Democratic
Chancellor Brandt despite infringing on basic constitutional rights, speaks to
the intellectual climate of the Federal Republic in which it emerged.[25]

---

22   Fülberth provided several bits of biographical information in a round table discussion
      marking the 50th anniversary of the Marburg *Institut für wissenschaftliche Politik* (later
      the Institute for Political Science). On this, see Hecker et al. 2001, p. 173 f.
23   Fülberth 1997; Fülberth 1999b.
24   Fülberth and Harrer 1984 (the book appeared as the first volume in the series *Arbeiterbe-
      wegung und SPD* published by Luchterhand Verlag).
25   Born in 1942, Jürgen Harrer studied political science, sociology, and German philology. He
      completed his dissertation under Abendroth with a thesis on the primary driving forces
      of the Mexican Revolution in the early twentieth century. His dissertation was published

The volume's analysis rested on an assumed distinction between two fundamental political-ideological categories, namely 'reformism' and 'revisionism'. By reformism the authors understood a current in the Social Democratic workers' movement that pursued improvements for the working masses within the existing system, whereas revisionism denoted a distancing from or even rejection of Marxism as a theoretical point of reference as could be seen in the thought of Eduard Bernstein, who abandoned the Marxist notion of revolution, the idea of base and superstructure, and the labour theory of value.

Reformism in turn could be divided into two currents in Fülberth and Harrer's eyes: a 'social liberal-integrationist' current (taking the concept of 'social liberalism' from Reinhard Opitz),[26] which not only passively tolerated the maintenance of the existing capitalist order but actively pursued it, and a modification which restricted itself to parliamentary means but did not fundamentally exclude the possibility of a general transcending of capitalism.[27] At the time of the book's publication in 1974, the essentially unchanged 'dual structure' of these two currents reproduced itself within the organisational structures of Social Democracy, which had in turn been shaped by them since World War I.

The distinction between these two variants of reformism that rejected a schematic contrast between 'reformist' and 'revolutionary' served as a guiding conceptual difference for the critical reconstruction of the history of the spd up to the Nazi dictatorship. In the authors' eyes, the tension-fraught relationship between the two currents pervaded this history from World War I to 1933, while the system-stabilising function of the social liberal-integrationist current proved dominant (particularly among the leadership) especially in situations of heightened economic and political tension like 1923 or post-1929. Towards the end of the Weimar Republic, a deeply-rooted legalism already vir-

---

by the Pahl-Rugenstein Verlag in Cologne in 1973 as *Die mexikanische Revolution 1910–1917*. He worked as a lecturer at the Institute for Political Science from 1972–8. After being rejected as a professor in Bremen for political reasons despite having been offered a position and not kept on in Marburg, he became an editor at Pahl-Rugenstein Verlag. He founded the left-wing PapyRossa Verlag in Cologne in 1990 that he ran successfully until recently, and to which he continues to actively contribute. Harrer published multiple studies on the German workers' movement. His publishing house issued numerous titles by, among others, Frank Deppe and Georg Fülberth.

26   Born in 1934, Reinhard Opitz was an sds member and completed his dissertation in Marburg in 1973 on German social liberalism. He was an editor at Paul-Rugenstein Verlag in Cologne and co-editor of the *Blätter für deutsche und internationale Politik*. Intellectually cutting and rhetorically gifted, Opitz devoted extensive attention to research into the relationship between liberalism, fascism, and neo-fascism until his early death in 1986.

27   Fülberth and Harrer 1974, p. 14.

ulent during Bismarck's anti-socialist laws[28] combined with an authoritarian-
militaristic interventionism,[29] anti-revolutionary, primarily anti-Communist
attitudes, fear of action, and economic illusions[30] to constitute a style of politics that was ultimately forced to capitulate in the face of rising nationalist
and fascist forces. Yet the thoroughly majoritarian and only temporarily mod-
ified system-conforming tendency within Social Democracy could only fulfil
its integrative function as long as the capitalist economy and state institutions
were not yet fully destabilised. According to Fülberth and Harrer, the party was
doomed to fail as the logic of the 'lesser evil' with which the SPD hoped to tame
the crisis would not only fail to prevent the 'greater evil', but in fact facilitated
its advance. The result was not only the victory of fascism but the practically
total self-disempowerment of the workers' movement. The KPD's oscillation
between a 'united front from below' strategy, the 'social fascism' thesis, and
overtures to the SPD leadership to practice unity in action may have facilitated
Social Democracy's willingness to capitulate but did not cause it. This was an
essential distinction that could not be forgotten.

Looking back on Fülberth and Harrer's study in light of the current state
of research, one can conclude that the subjective dimension of the object of
investigation was illuminated poorly and in a peripheral fashion. Although the
authors worked through wide-ranging material including both economic and
social history, they failed to depict the forms of consciousness, value orientations, attitudes, and behavioural patterns – that is to say, the collective habitus
of the working class, its fractions, and the 'proletarian milieu' (Josef Mooser) –
without which one cannot satisfactorily explain why large parts of the German working class never broke with the SPD before the Nazi takeover despite
their increasingly difficult social situation.[31] Although not necessarily disprov-
ing the political substance of Fülberth and Harrer's line of argument, this deficit restricted their analytical and interpretive depth of perception and power
of explanation. That said, one should also keep in mind that methodological
innovations such as the heuristic principle of 'history from below', the history
of mentalities, and 'oral history' had not yet emerged or at least not established
themselves in West German scholarship at the time of the book's publication.

Fülberth and Harrer would subsequently continue their studies of SPD history. Together with other authors, some of whom belonged to the SPD's Marx-

28   Fülberth and Harrer 1974, p. 55.
29   Fülberth and Harrer 1974, p. 179.
30   Fülberth and Harrer 1974, p. 231.
31   Mooser 1984.

ist wing, they expanded the timescale of their investigation into both the party's origins as well as the post-1945 period into the mid-1970s.[32] Wolfgang Abendroth composed a preface to this collective publication in which he stressed that the SPD's Friedrich Ebert Foundation had thus far failed to achieve what the Marburg School's authors had, namely to provide an all-encompassing depiction of SPD history into the present day.

Following the book's second printing, an expanded third edition would appear a decade later including developments into the late 1980s, which – at least for the period after 1945 – integrated findings from recent research but remained methodologically largely the same. Neither the development of consciousness nor the shift in attitudes among the party base were subjected to deeper investigation, nor were relations between capitalist modernisation (such as the social process of labour) and Social Democracy's political self-understanding subjected to fundamental analysis.[33] Nevertheless, this third edition contained an impressive amount of information and clearly fulfilled the standards of social critique conducted in the context of the Marburg School.

4   Studying Fascism (Reinhard Kühnl)

Reinhard Kühnl would also choose a thematic focus first established by Abendroth as his primary if not exclusive area of research – namely the study of fascism, successfully evoking an enormous response and having a massive impact in the very literal sense, with over 200,000 copies of his publications in circulation and translated into numerous languages.[34] Born in 1936 in what was then Czechoslovakia, Kühnl completed his dissertation on the 'left wing of the NSDAP' under Abendroth's supervision, served as his assistant, and was appointed to a professorship of political science in 1971.[35] In 1973 he was awarded a one-year guest professorship at the University of Tel Aviv. He was a major participant in the 1972 reactivation of the BdWi, and served as a member of its executive board for over three decades. Kühnl died in February 2014.

---

32   Freyberg, Fülberth, Harrer, Hebel-Kunze, Hofschen, Ott, Stuby 1975.

33   Freyberg et al. 1989.

34   Kühnl cited this figure in his 'biographical supplement' found in Hecker et al. 2001, p. 217. This supplement also contains additional biographical information.

35   His dissertation appeared as the sixth volume of the series *Marburger Abhandlungen zur politischen Wissenschaft* under the title *Die nationalsozialistische Linke 1925–1930* (Kühnl 1966).

Kühnl's research on fascism attracted such a wide readership not least because of its contrarian position vis-à-vis the dominant teachings on the subject in West Germany at the time – particularly its intellectual historical, personalising, or historical variants such as Ernst Nolte's *Der Faschismus in seiner Epoche*, published in English as *The Three Faces of Fascism* (Nolte would later spark major controversy in the 1980s during the so-called *Historikerstreit* as a major proponent of totalitarianism theory, which sought to relativise the crimes of the Nazis). Kühnl countered these views with a diametrically opposed interpretation of fascism that articulated a critique of domination and rejected any whitewashing or justification thereof.

For Kühnl, the specificity of fascism – particularly in its German form, which self-identified as National Socialism – consisted not only of the fact that he neglected to regard it as the absolute Other of bourgeois society, but that it was a totalitarian system of domination emerging out of bourgeois society's internal historical contradictions and crises that, although not possessing a teleological inevitability, certainly was inscribed with catastrophic consequences in light of its social preconditions. In this sense, fascism constituted an (albeit exorbitant) element in the historical continuity of bourgeois capitalist society rather than its negation, even if it suspended the principles of parliamentary-democratic legitimation of the state order in a terroristic fashion.

As far as fascism was concerned, Kühnl demarcated himself from competing interpretations in a dual fashion. On the one hand, he categorically rejected all attempts to separate fascism from its capitalist relations of property and power, while also opposing the simplifying thesis of fascism as a political 'bailiff of capital' postulated by proponents of 'vulgar materialist theories'.[36] Instead, he insisted that fascism manifested as a 'spontaneously emerging mass movement' while also appearing as an 'independent factor of power' in relation to the 'ruling class'. Because the bourgeois parties had proven no longer capable of solving the economic and political crisis by themselves, 'substantial segments of the ruling class' – the big bourgeoisie, the military, the state bureaucracy, the nobility, and the churches – had entered into an 'alliance' with the fascist movement to secure the ruling system from left-wing attacks and revolutionary upheavals.[37] By defining fascism as an alliance between the fascist movement and fractions of the ruling class which for their part 'acknowledged the party's assertion of political leadership', Kühnl moved towards the sort of 'Bona-

---

36   Kühnl 1971, p. 104.
37   Kühnl 1971, p. 103.

partist' theory of fascism widely accepted on the Left.[38] However, his theory
also encountered an intense critic on the Left in the form of Reinhard Opitz,
a 'freelancer' from Cologne who cooperated with the Marburg scholar Rainer
Rilling.[39] Opitz raised the relationship between monopoly capitalism and fascism onto a qualitatively new level in light of the contemporary international
debate around fascism, and sought to demonstrate that fascism had indeed
been a function of monopoly capitalism to the extent that it always forced the
transition to a fascist dictatorship at the point 'when the monopoly capitalist
mechanisms of integration threatened to break down'.[40] Nevertheless, a direct
debate between Kühnl and Opitz concerning this disagreement never came to
pass.

That Kühnl's interest in studying the topic of fascism was not limited to
academic motivations but rather corresponded to the aim of contributing the
results of his historical investigation to a critical understanding of the present
can be seen in the wide-ranging study of the neo-fascist NPD conducted by
Kühnl, Rainer Rilling, and Christine Sager published by Suhrkamp in 1969.[41]
The study's concrete occasion was the alarmingly rapid rise of the NPD since
the mid-1960s, having surpassed seven percent in several regional elections,
reaching 8.8 percent in Bremen in 1967 and nearly ten percent in Baden-
Württemberg in 1968.[42]

The study's approach to the topic exhibited a differentiated methodological
awareness that avoided both a mono-causal, deterministic attempt to explain
the NPD phenomenon as well as reductive, alarmist interpretations of the
NPD's successes limited to a critique of its ideology. Kühnl, Rilling, and Sager
presented their methodological premises with a level of clarity that only few

---

38   Kühnl 1971, p. 145.

39   Born in 1945, Rainer Rilling completed his cumulative doctorate with a focus on economic
       sociology in 1974 under the author's supervision at the University of Bremen, completed
       his *Habilitation* in sociology in 1980 at the University of Marburg, and worked as a lec-
       turer in Marburg and Münster. He was the executive secretary of the BdWi from 1983–98
       and afterwards the leading researcher at the Rosa-Luxemburg-Stiftung in Berlin. The Uni-
       versity of Marburg appointed him to an extraordinary professorship in 2002. His book
       Theorie und Soziologie der Wissenschaft. Zur Entwicklung in der BRD und DDR (Rilling 1975)
       remains one of the best investigations of the subject to this day.

40   Opitz 1999, p. 187.

41   Kühnl, Rilling and Sager 1969. As the authors of this study demonstrate, one of the charac-
       teristic traits of the Marburg School was to integrate even very young authors into research
       and publishing. Rainer Rilling, for example, was only 24 years old and still a student at the
       time.

42   Kühnl, Rilling and Sager 1969, p. 71 (table).

later contributions from the Marburg School would be able to match. Invoking Habermas and Adorno, they felt obligated to a 'dialectical method' taking into account two constitutive aspects: *firstly*, the mediated nature of all concrete problems through structural relations of social 'totality', and *secondly* the historicity of totality and its individual moments.

Building on this foundation, the study first investigated the prehistory of the NPD before addressing the ideological continuity between Nazi and NPD ideology, the social and political backgrounds of functionaries, members, and voters, public responses to the party, and the connections between social structure and fascism or rather neo-fascism. Drawing on wide-ranging source materials and diverse methodological instruments (elements of empirical social research, sociological theories and political science, historical and ideology-critical studies, etc.), the authors characterised the NPD as a largely middle-class political organisation essentially dependent on fascist ideology but tactically conforming to the existing relations of parliamentary democracy that exploited the economic instability, social insecurity, and deficits of parliamentarism and offered solutions to its target audience which did not exclude transitioning into a new fascist dictatorship.

Kühnl, Rilling, and Sager inquired as to the 'possibilities of resistance' in the closing chapter, yet astonishingly limited themselves to legal and juridical aspects. They fully supported a legal ban on the NPD and criticised objections to such a move. Given the authors' unmistakable claim to hold a decisively left-wing standpoint, it is surprising that their line of argument adhered to the formal, institutionalised plane, mentioning possibilities and challenges of a collective social and political movement against German neo-fascism in passing at best, but never exploring them in any depth.

5   The Political Sociology of Latin America (Dieter Boris)

Dieter Boris occupied a new field of research for the Marburg School that only began to emerge through the work of several graduate students during the Triumvirate's era. Born in 1943 in what was then the Upper Silesian town of Bielitz (Bielsko-Biała, Poland today), he studied sociology and political science in Marburg where he was an active member of SDS and contributed to its education programme. He became Werner Hofmann's assistant after completing his studies and was considered an expert in economic, social, and political problems of the 'Third World' and national and anti-colonial liberation movements quite early in his career. His dissertation completed under Heinz Maus's supervision, however, focused on the political sociology of Karl Mannheim.[43] He was particularly interested in Mannheim's notion of social planning – notoriously underestimated in receptions of Mannheim's work and dismissed by Karl Raimund Popper as 'utopian' – which in turn was linked to discussions within the Marburg School around possibilities of planning within and the transformation of 'organised capitalism' (Abendroth had spoken of 'transitional planning'). Boris was transferred to a professorship of sociology at the Philipps University in 1972 and officially appointed in 1973, making him the fourth such professor alongside Maus, Tjaden, and Rosenbaum.

Alongside his 1971 book on Chile,[44] typical studies in terms of Boris's methodological construction and line of argument as he began to specialise in the field of political sociology of Latin America included a study on Argentina's political history and present co-authored with his student Peter Hiedl in 1978.[45] The immediate occasion for the volume was certainly not least the fact that the 'second phase' of Peronism (1973–6) had ended with its total collapse and a bloody military putsch, claiming tens of thousands of victims and etching itself into the 'collective memory' of the Argentinian population to this day.

The authors identified the country's relatively early modernisation through capitalisation and monopolisation in the agricultural sector, the development of industries, and urbanisation as the essential characteristic distinguishing Argentina from other Latin American states. This explained the swift rise of an industrial working class playing a central role in the country's history, irrespective of shifting and contradictory conditions. The book's noteworthy insights included the conclusion that Peronism, a specific phenomenon possessing decisive influence on the country's fate for 40 years, could not be explained without the existence of this working class and, correspondingly, the relatively strong influence of the workers' movement and trade unions in particular. This topic attracted the authors' closer attention, emphasising the contradictory nature of 'classical Peronism' (1946–55). On the one hand, Peronism facilitated the independent national development of Argentinian capitalism while basing itself primarily on the working class as the social bearer of this development (and ally of the industrial bourgeoisie). On the other hand, however, Peronist policies were directed against the accumulation regimes of the agricultural

---

43   Boris 1971.
44   Boris, Abendroth and Ehrhardt 1971.
45   Boris and Hiedl 1978. The book was dedicated to 'our academic and political teachers Wolfgang Abendroth and Werner Hofmann'.

monopolists while nevertheless remaining dependent on them. Moreover, Peronism had limited the influence of foreign capital while reaching concession agreements with major US corporations at the same time.[46]

Boris and Hiedl identified the limits of classical Peronism in its inability to continue living up to its claim to represent the national 'public interest' as economic and political conditions began to undergo dramatic shifts. This occurred over the course of the 1950s, a period that initially brought noteworthy improvements in the conditions of material reproduction for wage-earners and industrial workers in particular, but then transitioned into a phase of stagnation and weakening state control.[47]

In the chapter on the post-Perón 'Argentinian cycle' from 1955–73 during which one government followed the next, Boris and Hiedl focused primarily on the development of the Peronist workers' movement, which remained significant and powerful but was divided between right- and left-wing currents, and in (or alongside) which non-Peronist socialist actors proved unable to develop meaningful influence. The authors put forward a detailed elaboration of Peronism's major hegemonic impact as a socially integrative ideology even after Perón himself was overthrown by demonstrating that subsequent governments were consistently forced to enact corrections in economic and social policy and at least partially take the interests of the working class into account despite occasional neoliberal advances. The Frondizi government that followed the radically anti-Peronist *Revolucion Libertadora* in 1958, for example, initially accepted wage increases and abolished legal restrictions on the trade unions before enacting a neoliberal agenda in line with the demands of the International Monetary Fund.[48]

Boris and Hiedl explained the fact that all short-lived governments between 1955–73 were forced to deal with Peronism through the 'specificity of economic cycles and class alliances emerging from them' as an 'important source of the conservation and support of the Peronist ideology'.[49] Its persistence could only be truly broken when Peronist policies were transformed into an instrument of capitalist denationalisation, yet utterly failed under the pressures of neoliberally dominated global economic conditions during the 'second phase'. This established the preconditions for the military coup and the dictatorship of General Videla and his successors (1976–83).

---

46   Boris and Hiedl 1978, pp. 76–88.
47   Boris and Hiedl 1978, p. 98.
48   Boris and Hiedl 1978, p. 131 f.
49   Boris and Hiedl 1978, p. 144.

Boris and Hiedl's study not only went beyond the Marburg School's typical scholarly focus in thematic terms, but also broke new methodological ground by attempting to systematically investigate the relationships between certain types of capitalist accumulation and political and social developments. A more profound politico-economic line of argument was apparent than in other Marburg contributions from this period. Nevertheless, the book on Argentina shared several weaknesses with the work of other Marburg Marxists. The entire dimension of actors' activity – their subjective experiences, forms of habitus, cultural and gender-oriented value orientations – was absent between the analysis of politico-economic developments and the political-ideological tendencies of organisations and institutions. The latter would have been particularly worthy of analytical interpretation given Peronism's stylisation of Perón's first wife, Evita, into a mass political icon. A deeper discussion of the intellectual architecture and functional mode of Peronist discourse was also missing. Although Boris and Hiedl by no means adopted a simple base/superstructure schematic and expressly acknowledged misalignments between economic processes and political balances of forces, their study remained within the methodological limits typical of the Marburg School in the 1970s.

6 External Pressure, Administrative Interference, Difficult Encounters

Alongside the professors of the Marburg School appointed in the early 1980s – Deppe, Kühnl, Fülberth, and Boris – additional professorships in the disciplines of political science and sociology were occupied over the course of the decade by individuals who were neither intellectually socialised in the Marburg School nor shared its intellectual premises. Relations between the two groups varied depending on individual dispositions and circumstances. Some protagonists of different scholarly and political orientations worked together quietly as was necessary for the sake of tests and doctoral examinations, but sometimes voted for different or alternative proposals and measures at the university and departmental levels and organised themselves in competing faculty factions. Their cooperation was thus anything but trusting.[50] Although conflicts generally remained latent, occupational interaction was empirically speaking more or less palpably structured by a tension-fraught relationship, the causes of which went far beyond the university itself. This tension resulted from the

---

50   On this see the round table discussion in Hecker et al. 2001, pp. 171–212.

fact that pressure on the Marxist faculty members at *Fachbereich* 03 grew to the same extent that the short-lived dynamic of social-political reform died down and initial reforms to higher education – irrespective of how their individual intentions are to be retrospectively evaluated – began to be rolled back.[51] Although internal departmental procedures would not be conducted in perfect harmony, they generally remained fairly bearable for the parties involved. After all, the new group of professors were neither left-wing socialists nor Marxists, but at least representatives of their discipline who largely tended towards social-liberal positions, meaning that antagonisms in the department rarely clashed directly as was the case at other institutional levels of the Philipps University.[52] Outside of the department, however, the non-Marxists participated in alliances and ostracisation against their Marxist colleagues. The situation in the political science and sociology departments thus remained more or less bearable for both sides despite the occasional irritation, with the exception of a later spectacular attack by the sociologist and political scientist Michael Th. Greven, who went to the press with the (utterly unproven) allegation that one of his Marxist colleagues was perhaps working for the East German state security, the Stasi.[53]

Despite the increasingly raw climate both in- and outside of the university, the representatives of the Marburg School – which alongside the aforementioned professors also included lecturers such as Jürgen Harrer, Gert Meyer, and Rainer Rilling along with researchers at the Institute for Scientific Politics like Wolfgang 'Harry' Hecker – continued their project of 'operative' social critique and remained politically active in various activities (outside of university politics) such as the BdWi, in collaborations with the trade unions, with the IMSF in Frankfurt am Main, the DKP, and left-wing student groups.

Christof Kievenheim stands out among Marburg's left-wing students, acknowledged as an authority within MSB Spartakus and admired for his obsession with his work by classmates who themselves often appeared less so with their own.[54] Although still quite young, Kievenheim made a significant contribution to the ISMF's major study on the 'class and social structure of West

51 For an example of the demonisation of Marburg School representatives see an article by professor Wilhelm Nikolai Luther, responsible for teacher examinations in the State of Hessia at the time (Luther 1976).
52 This was true of, for example, Theo Schiller and Hans Karl Rupp, who initially considered himself a Marxist before later cultivating a distance to the Marxists of the Marburg School.
53 See Hecker et al. 2001, p. 196, fn. 258.
54 Born in 1946, Christof Kievenheim studied political science and sociology in Marburg and Berlin. He belonged to the executive committee of the DKP's student league, MSB Spartakus, and was a fellow at the IMSF in Frankfurt. He sympathised with the Eurocom-

Germany', where his profound studies on the social status and function of the academic-technical intelligentsia stood out.

Although the 'epistemic community' of Marburg's Marxist intellectuals remained small, those who felt a sense of attachment to it continued to work together quite closely. After publishing a collected volume comparing the social systems of West and East Germany in 1971 (widely derided by critics as little more than apologia for the GDR) they continued to publish studies together, speak together at conferences, and engage in shared activity in university politics such as in the Sozialistische Hochschullehrer faction.[55] The degree of their cohesion in this situation was essentially in reverse proportion to their minority position within the Philipps University as a whole, and soon within *Fachbereich* 03 as well.

Given the degree of external political pressure they faced, the fact that Marburg's intellectual milieu sympathising with the DKP exhibited symptoms of an ideological 'circling of the wagons' was practically sociologically inevitable. But why did the Marburg Marxists feel politically attracted to the DKP, a party widely labelled as 'Stalinist' in the bourgeois camp, criticised as ossified by left-wing social-democratic groups like the Sozialistisches Büro, and derided as 'revisionist' by ultra-leftists? In order to avoid useless stereotypes and sweeping ideological generalisations, a series of moments must be taken into account.

Unlike the other left-wing (and particularly ultra-left) groups which threw around terms like 'proletariat' and 'revolution' almost like a kind of socialist monstrance while in reality recruiting almost entirely students and intellectuals, the DKP based itself in the industrial workplaces and the tertiary sector with a respectable number of members who enjoyed the respect of their work colleagues as representatives of their interests. In this sense, although never counting more than 40,000 members the DKP was by all means 'rooted' in layers of wage-earning workers, namely the industrial working class. While ultra-left organisations issued blanket denunciations of the trade union leaderships as 'traitors', the DKP sought – invoking the principle of the *Einheitsgewerkschaft* (One Big Union) – to mobilise the 'base' within the trade unions for resistance against the power of capital owners and management as well as question system-conforming 'integrationist' trade union strategies (such as those of IG Chemie). The DKP rejected a schematic polarisation between membership base and trade union leadership along with a blanket labelling of Social Democracy as political 'bailiffs' of monopoly capital as delusional. Rather, the party

---

munist current and founded the Arbeitskreis Westeuropäische Arbeiterbewegung in the mid-1970s. Tragically, Kievenheim took his own life in 1978.

55   Jung, Deppe, Tjaden and Fülberth et al. 1971.

sought (albeit often unsuccessfully) to expand the degree of shared interests and goals between Social Democrats and Communists. In doing so, it simultaneously took into account the historical experience of the fateful split in the pre-1933 workers' movement and adhered to a political line that corresponded to Abendroth's thought and his advocacy for united action within the workers' movement.

The DKP's programme and its project of an 'anti-monopolist democracy',[56] which exhibited parallels to the French Communist Party's (PCF) advocacy for an 'advanced democracy' (*démocratie avancée*),[57] was aligned in its ambitions in a dialectic of 'reform' and 'revolution' reflective of the conditions of modern capitalism – although the DKP understood 'revolution' not as violent overthrow but rather as the political transformation of capitalist relations of production. As in other Western European Communist parties, this corresponded to an explicit renunciation of the 'dictatorship of the proletariat'.

Further motivating factors can be identified along with these reasons to explain the sympathies for the DKP within the Marburg School. These included the principled affirmation of the GDR as an alternative system to the capitalist Federal Republic, support for international disarmament as called for by the state-socialist bloc, and not least solidarity with anti-colonial and national liberation movements. The Marburg Marxists shared the DKP's outlook on all of these questions. Although they were aware of the party's problematic ties to the SED, they regarded this fact as secondary in relation to the party's concrete activities and political goals, not to mention they remained unaware of the party's financial dependence on East German funding.

The political and ideological pressure exerted on the protagonists of the Marburg School and the *Fachbereich Gesellschaftswissenschaft* must be viewed as a symptom of anti-Communist hysteria typical of the situation in the Federal Republic in the 1970s yet practically unthinkable in other Western European parliamentary democracies, particularly in countries with strong Communist parties.

Both the CDU and to some extent the SPD, government ministries, the education bureaucracy, the media, along with various individuals and intellectual circles such as the Bund Freiheit der Wissenschaft did everything in their power to remove the shameful stain of the insubordinate *Fachbereich* at the Philipps

---

56   On questions of an 'anti-monopolist democracy' as a transitional stage towards socialism and the conditions of the 'anti-monopolist struggle' in the Federal Republic, see Gerns and Steigerwald 1973.

57   Comité Central du Parti Communiste Français 1970.

University from the otherwise flawless landscape of academic conformism, and to protect other institutions and organisations like schools and trade unions from Marburg's Marxist virus.[58]

To the Hessian CDU, the most efficient method of dealing with the issue appeared to be shutting it down entirely as if it were a clinic infected with a dangerous plague. CDU state parliamentarian Bernhard Sälzer justified this martial intent to the lively applause of his parliamentary group with the argument that 'such a Soviet-Marxist party college could not be permitted' to exist, and the state must prevent 'the training of professional revolutionaries for Communism in our country with our citizens' tax revenues' at all costs.[59] Yet because another advocate of closing down the department, CDU parliamentarian Friedrich Bohl, was forced to admit that the 'orthodox Communists' failed to command a majority in their own department let alone at the University of Marburg as a whole, he resorted to the claim that this majority would be established through the aid of a 'popular front' of fellow-travellers. Although by no means suspected of sympathising with the thought of the Marburg Marxists, the SPD-FDP government refused to submit to the CDU's adventurous demands and rejected the party's proposal at the state parliament's committee level.

The members of the *Fachbereich Gesellschaftswissenschaften*, including a group of non-Marxist professors, defended themselves against the accusations of one-sidedness and indoctrination levelled by the CDU and other opponents by providing concrete evidence of instructional content's thematic diversity, course assessments, and examinations.[60] The attacks on the department and the Marburg School in particular emerged not only from the conservative end of the political spectrum, however, but were also supported by prominent political scientists like Iring Fetscher from Frankfurt am Main. He had already been alarmed by the ominous influence of a 'militant, tightly organised and dogmatic Party Marxism of Soviet orientation' on the hiring policies of Marburg's *Fachbereich Gesellschaftswissenschaften* after Hans Heinz Holz was appointed to a professorship of philosophy over a candidate from the ranks of the Frankfurt School, Alfred Schmidt, in 1971.[61] Regardless of whether or not

---

58   On the following see Vorstand der Sektion Marburg des Bundes demokratischer Wissenschaftler (BdWi) 1977.

59   See Bernhard Sälzer's speech in the Hessian state parliament, in Vorstand der Sektion Marburg des Bundes demokratischer Wissenschaftler (BdWi) 1977, p. 53.

60   Letter from professors Wilfried Freiherr von Bredow, Ingrid Langer-El Sayed, Peter Römer, Hans-Karl Rupp, and Theo Schiller to the *Oberhessische Presse* on 20 September 1976, see Vorstand der Sektion Marburg des Bundes demokratischer Wissenschaftler (BdWi) 1977, pp. 75–7.

61   Iring Fetscher, 'Koexistenz oder Kaderschule? Marxismus an den deutschen Universit-

Holz was really the better choice, there was nothing faulty or suspicious about the hiring process itself, which not even Fetscher himself dared claim.

Another protagonist from the academic field, Fritz Vilmar, professor of political science at the Free University of Berlin since 1975, would launch a truly ideological crusade against the Marburg Marxists. Often writing in the *Frankfurter Rundschau*, he derided the 'DKP groups' skilful infiltration' of the 'social-scientific section of the Marburg university' along with 'a totalitarian Communist demagogy especially at several colleges', above all the University of Marburg, and called for resistance to the perceived threat.[62] In doing so he invoked the principle of 'academic pluralism', which in his thinking had undergone a mutation characteristic of the situation in the Federal Republic as a whole at the time. In Vilmar's and others' reinterpretation, the principle restricted itself to the legally guaranteed freedom of research and teaching less and less, and was instead subtly transformed into an ideological battle cry and a tool with which to marginalise unpopular scientific theories by administrative means, which in this case meant Marxism and any approach suspected of being influenced by it. Initiated by a Social Democratic minister, interventions into the hiring process at Marburg's *Fachbereich* 03 by the Hessian education bureaucracy represented a grave attack on academic pluralism, of which Jürgen Harrer's case, a lecturer hired as a temporary lecturer at the Institute for Scientific Politics, serves as a particularly stark example. His university-approved transfer to a tenured position was sabotaged by the Ministry of Education arguing, among other things, that one of Harrer's essays on the development of economic policy in the GDR had 'utterly no epistemological value ... viewed from the economic-theoretical[63] standpoint of critical rationalism'.[64] In doing so, a ministry – that is to say, a state institution – presumed the right to pervert a certain epistemological worldview into a criterion of exclusion for applicants to an academic position who favoured epistemological conceptions diverging from said criterion. This was further compounded by the fact that the ministry cited expert assessments in its letter of rejection to Harrer, yet refused to make them public.[65] In doing so, the Hessian Ministry of Education behaved in a man-

äten', *Süddeutsche Zeitung*, 20–1 February 1971, cited in Vorstand der Sektion Marburg des Bundes demokratischer Wissenschaftler (BdWi) 1977, p. 114.

62   See Vilmar 1977.

63   Author's note: they actually meant 'epistemological' (!).

64   Statement by the Fachbereich Gesellschaftswissenschaften on the notification of Jürgen Harrer's rejection by the Hessian Ministry of Education, from which the quoted passage is taken. See Vorstand der Sektion Marburg des Bundes demokratischer Wissenschaftler (BdWi) 1977, p. 185.

65   Vorstand der Sektion Marburg des Bundes demokratischer Wissenschaftler (BdWi) 1977,

ner otherwise used to characterise the academic policies of the GDR, namely restricting scholars to a certain theoretical and methodological paradigm.

This does not deny the thematic and methodological selectivity implied in the individual views of Marburg School protagonists, the cultivation of a degree of isolation from 'bourgeois science', and a questionable one-sidedness in their assessment of certain social and political realities. If these existed – and, in the author's opinion, they most certainly did – then they should have been made the object of scholarly critique. Instead, attempts were made to administratively discipline and ideologically stigmatise the Marburg Marxists.

7   A Controversial History of the Trade Unions

The escalating conflict both in- and outside of *Fachbereich* 03 around the positions of the Marburg School, discredited as in thrall to the DKP, would reach a new highpoint in the disputes triggered by Deppe, Fülberth, Harrer and others' 1977 *Geschichte der deutschen Gewerkschaftsbewegung* (History of the German Trade-Union Movement),[66] emphatically praised by Abendroth as a 'major social-scientific and pedagogical achievement'.[67] On the one hand, the book was received with interest by many members and functionaries in trade unions like IG Metall, HBV (representing commerce, banking and insurance employees), and the printers' union IG Druck und Papier. On the other, however, it provoked a storm of public controversy characterised by an intermingling of prejudiced, denunciatory polemics, and elements of scholarly critique. The backdrop for this event was the political atmosphere typical of the Federal Republic at the time, which – influenced by the Anti-Radical Decrees, hysteria around terrorism, and a virulent anti-Communism extending deep into the trade unions themselves – began to take the shape of a West German McCarthyism. Both opponents as well as defenders of Deppe, Fülberth, Harrer, and the rest articulated their views in countless articles both within and beyond the pages of trade-union publications.[68]

---

p. 183. The Ministry of Education would only publish its decision later, after Harrer initiated legal proceedings with the help of the teachers' union, GEW, making the matter public.

66   Deppe, Fülberth and Harrer 1978. The editors took various disagreements and criticisms they considered valid into account in a fourth, updated and revised edition published in 1989.

67   Abendroth 1979.

68   Ernst Günter Vetter, responsible for trade union coverage at the *Frankfurter Allgemeine Zeitung* at the time, felt compelled to warn readers of looming Communist infiltration

The authors sought to refrain from presenting a 'celebratory history', instead taking up the 'failures and maldevelopments' of the trade unions, particularly as these 'unfortunately were overlooked far too often'.[69] If, like the authors, one sought to hold true to the goal of trade union 'autonomy' then an analysis taking contradictions and defeats into account was indispensable. The comprehensive volume covered the development of the German trade unions from their beginnings in the nineteenth century into the 1970s. It also contained a brief chapter on the development of the FDGB in the Soviet zone and the GDR that tended to paper over rather than analyse real problems, and concluded with critical reflections on the contradiction between the 'comfortable path into integration' in the capitalist system and the 'difficult path of organising autonomous resistance'.[70] Drawing on extensive sources as well as economic and social historical data, the authors sought to live up to their stated goal of producing a comprehensive account with an adequate discussion of organisational history.

The authors themselves were perhaps surprised by the massive reactions their book provoked after being published by the DKP-friendly Pahl-Rugenstein Verlag in Cologne. The *Frankfurter Rundschau*, the leading daily newspaper among the entire West German left at the time, extensively documented the controversy it first unleashed by publishing a full-page polemical denunciation by an ultra-left author.[71] Putting aside the crude anti-Communist rhetoric of conspiracy and infiltration characterising most of the book's reviews, several lines of argument and points of controversy can be distilled from the polem-

---

of the trade unions in the alarmist rhetoric of the Cold War: 'The fifth column of Communism is on the march. True to Lenin's instructions, they have only one goal in their sights: to transform the society of the Federal Republic in the image of the GDR and the Soviet Union, with revolutionary means if necessary' (Vetter 1979). In light of the facts that the DKP always remained below one percent in federal elections and there were hardly any Marxist professors outside of Marburg and Bremen, let alone active professors who were members of the DKP, the anti-Communist tirades of the time appear rather absurd. On the other hand, however, they most certainly fulfilled a political-ideological function, branding any fundamental political opposition with the curse of Communism's hostility to democracy.

69   Deppe, Fülberth and Harrer 1978, p. 12.
70   Deppe, Fülberth and Harrer 1978, p. 467.
71   The author in question was Manfred Scharrer, a founding member of the Maoist KPD/AO in 1969–70 and an assistant in the sociology institute at the Free University of Berlin from the mid-1970s onward. The *Frankfurter Rundschau* documented the controversy extensively on 2, 3, 4 and 5 January 1979, publishing numerous letters to the editor on the topic. That said, it was clear that the newspaper stood behind the critics.

ical but substantial critique by renowned social-democratic historian Helga Grebing, and the response by *Gewerkschaftsgeschichte* editors Deppe, Fülberth and Harrer.[72]

Grebing's comprehensive review focused one of its major criticisms on the book's alleged rigid opposition between a 'reformist' (or rather 'revisionist') current in the workers' movement on one hand, and a 'revolutionary' current on the other. This opposition pervaded the entire book, brazenly overlooking the actual, multi-faceted differentiations and crossovers existing within the workers' movement. Such an approach corresponded to a theoretical orthodoxy that claimed the mantle of Marx and Engels yet neglected empirical research and replaced real historical analysis with ideological projections.[73] Furthermore, Grebing added, the book whitewashed and trivialised the Communists' problematic relationship to the trade unions. Ultimately, the authors distorted the real nature of the contemporary trade union programme in order to endow their own political orientation with the desired level of distinction.

As the editors of *Gewerkschaftsgeschichte*, Deppe, Fülberth, and Harrer answered with an equally comprehensive response. They rejected the accusation of construing a rigid opposition between a 'revisionist' (or 'reformist') and 'revolutionary' current by arguing that rather than the opposition of which they were accused, the central focus of their research was in fact the tense relationship between 'social partnership' and 'autonomous interest representation' which was substantially different from what Grebing had in mind.[74] As far as the question of theoretical orthodoxy was concerned (what Grebing called their 'system of ideological premises'), they not only enthusiastically reaffirmed the theory of Marx and Engels as the foundation of their understanding of history and society, but also retorted by deriding the grave absence of a concept of society as such in Grebing's own work.[75] However, the authors failed to respond to Grebing's assertion that they neglected to take the current state of research adequately into account and in turn took recourse to wooden, simplifying interpretations of the complex social composition of the working class and the workers' movement.

Unlike Grebing, they refused to interpret the relationship between Communists and the trade unions as a 'quasi-ontological antagonism', arguing that

---

72 Grebing 1979; Deppe, Fülberth and Harrer 1980. The *Gewerkschaftliche Monatshefte* was unwilling to print their response. Generally speaking, it proved difficult to find outlets willing to allow them to present counter-arguments.

73 Grebing 1979, p. 206.

74 Deppe, Fülberth and Harrer 1980, p. 85.

75 Grebing 1979, p. 206.

historical reality spoke against such a view and citing examples like the practical unity between both currents in other European countries post-1934 or the attempts at German trade union unity in British exile and after 1945.[76] Nevertheless, Deppe, Fülberth, and Harrer admitted that the theory of 'social fascism' and the policy of 'revolutionary trade union opposition' (*Revolutionäre Gewerkschaftsopposition*, or 'RGO') towards the end of the Weimar Republic had weakened the unity of the workers' movement and its ability to resist fascism, facilitating the unions' inaction in the face of the looming Nazi takeover.[77] They rejected Grebing's accusation of dismissing both the progressive demands of the German Trade Union Confederation (DGB)'s 1949 Munich basic programme as well as trade union efforts towards a 'humanisation of labour' in the 1970s as empty, symbolic policies by explaining that although they failed to see the Munich programme as a 'foundation for a socialist order' as some Social Democrats had at the time, they described the programme's character as a 'reform programme with anti-capitalist elements'.[78] Their book contained several pages on the 'humanisation of labour' evaluating the project in emphatically positive terms.[79] In conclusion, Deppe, Fülberth, and Harrer defended themselves against the accusation of preaching a 'thesis of betrayal' based on a schematic dichotomy between trade union base and leadership, and the alleged passivity and defeatism of a trade union leadership that failed to exercise its potential power. They were not interested in an abstract polarisation between union 'base' and 'leadership' so much as the problem of how trade unions' 'fitness for struggle' and 'solidary counter-power' could be developed out of the antagonistic conditions of capitalism and its crises.[80]

Peter van Oertzen also participated in the controversy around the book, initially sparked by a sharply negative review by historian Manfred Scharrer. Von Oertzen was a political scientist from Hanover, a member of the SPD party leadership, the Minister of Education for Lower Saxony from 1970–4, and a fervent supporter of banning radicals from the civil service at the time – a fact he evidently came to regret later in life.[81] How deeply the anti-Communist virus had crept into the circles of self-identified socialist intellectuals could be

---

76   Deppe, Fülberth and Harrer 1980, p. 92.

77   On the circumstances and contradictions of the KPD's 'RGO' policy in the late Weimar Republic see Peter 1980, pp. 40–55.

78   Deppe, Fülberth and Harrer 1980, p. 98.

79   Deppe, Fülberth and Harrer 1978, pp. 432–8.

80   Deppe, Fülberth and Harrer 1980, p. 101.

81   See the obituary published by the board of trustees of the Rosa-Luxemburg-Stiftung in 2008, of which he was a member after leaving the SPD in 2005 (Kuratorium der Rosa-Luxemburg-Stiftung 2008).

seen not only in the tone in which von Oertzen addressed the volume's editors, but also in the fact that his response to the book functioned as a call to
arms against Communist influence in the trade unions attracting the attention of the national union leadership.[82] Von Oertzen's choice of words for
the Marburg trade union history was characterised by a curious antinomy: on
the one hand, the author of a classic study on workers' councils in the German Revolution presented plausible criticisms of a series of points which the
Marburg authors had, in his view, either incorrectly, contradictorily, or insuf-
ficiently taken into account.[83] On the other hand, however, he privileged an
anti-Communist witch-hunt over scholarly debate, beginning his written comments not with substantial or methodological disagreements but a litany of
accusations describing the book as primarily an instrument of Communist
Party strategy. Von Oertzen described the book's weaknesses as inevitable consequences of the 'guiding interests' of the DKP. In other words: because the
DKP saw itself as the 'sole inheritor' of the 'democratic, peace-loving, anti-
imperialist, socialist and Marxist traditions of the German workers' movement',
the Marburg authors associated with this party had delivered a corresponding
version of trade union history, branding revisionism and reformism as failures
of the workers' movement while greatly inflating the KPD's importance to the
trade-union struggle during the interwar period at the same time.[84]

This airing of political prejudices was followed by a number of accusations,
allusions, and problematisations which would have deserved serious discussion in their own right, yet were devalued through their association with an a
priori blanket political judgement. This was true, for example, of the role of
revisionist Social Democratic politicians in the pre-1914 'mass strike debate',
the weakness and isolation of the Spartacus League in the great strikes of 1917
and 1918, and the problem of the West German trade unions' anti-Communist
Revers policy in the 1950s.[85] By denying the scholarly integrity of the Marburg
authors from the outset, however von Oertzen robbed even those arguments
which could have provoked an interesting academic debate of their credibility.

---

82   See the documentation in the *Frankfurter Rundschau*, 'Wie lässt sich Geschichtsschrei-
     bung im DKP-Stil messen?', 11 April 1979, p. 10f. The author possesses a copy of von
     Oertzen's letter to the DGB executive in the form of an undated typewritten letter (prob-
     ably from March or April 1979).
83   von Oertzen 1963.
84   Peter van Oertzen in the *Frankfurter Rundschau* documentation, 11 April 1979, p. 10.
85   In the early 1950s DGB functionaries attempted to force KPD members to sign a declara-
     tion (*Revers*) distancing themselves from a KPD resolution. Those who refused would lose
     their trade union positions, while those who agreed to sign were expelled from the KPD.

That he was less interested in such a debate than in politically comprom-
ising and isolating the Marburg authors could be seen in the fact that alongside
his critique of the book, his letter to the trade union leadership also included
observations on an article Wolfgang Abendroth had published concerning the
dissident trials against figures like Rudolf Bahro in the state-socialist countries.[86] In the article, Abendroth called for limiting politically motivated trials
under socialism to extreme cases that endangered the socialist order, while noting that disproportionate criminal prosecution made it difficult for left-wing
forces in the West to expand the socialist movement's ability to build coali-
tions. Von Oertzen found exceedingly harsh words for Abendroth, whom he
knew quite well, accusing him of supporting the suppression of the opposition in socialist states and only demanding unrestricted exercise of the right to
free speech from 'bourgeois democracy'. Abendroth only accepted a critique of
'actually existing socialism' that stood in solidarity with it, while suspecting any
principled critique of complicity with the class enemy. Von Oertzen concluded
his notes on the article with a damning evaluation of Abendroth: 'Abendroth's
outlook is at any rate irreconcilable with the fundamental tenets of democracy, the goals of socialism and the traditions of the freedom-loving workers'
movement'.[87] This in turn provoked a resolution from the department advisory council of the *Fachbereich Gesellschaftswissenschaften* 03 at the Philipps
University signed by dean Dieter Boris, stating that von Oertzen's statement
had been 'acknowledged with extreme disconcertment and outrage', pointing
to Abendroth's 'invaluable merits' as a scholar and contributor to 'the development of democracy in the Federal Republic', and promising Abendroth the
council's 'unqualified solidarity'.[88]

Theo Pirker, professor of sociology at the Free University of Berlin, continued the themes raised by von Oertzen in a letter published in the *Frankfurter
Rundschau*.[89] In contrast to von Oertzen, however, Pirker made no effort whatsoever to accuse the volume's authors of concrete failures, mistakes, or untenable assertions, instead preferring to question the scholarly integrity of the
Marburg School as a whole, giving the impression that the authors behaved
like 'candidates for an Academy of Social Sciences and History of the Workers'
Movement in Actually Existing Socialism'.[90]

---

86   Abendroth 1978.
87   Von Oertzen's letter to the DGB.
88   Fachbeirat des Fachbereichs Gesellschaftswissenschaften 1979.
89   See 'Solange es noch keine Akademie nach Moskauer Vorbild gibt ...', *Frankfurter Rund-
     schau*, 4 January 1979, p. 14.
90   Ibid.

Deppe's letter of reply was also published in the *Frankfurter Rundschau*.[91] Because Pirker's article had expressed only a general sense of disgust at the authors' scholarly position, Deppe countered Pirker's assault on the level of theoretical and methodological problems by laying out the book's conception once again and making several comments on accusations that they rejected academic pluralism. The trade union volume neither denied the legitimacy of other scholarly approaches nor the right to be critical of the volume itself. When Pirker drew connections between him and the other authors and Stalinism and conditions in 'actually existing socialism', however, he merely adhered to the 'classical pattern of denunciation'.[92]

In retrospect, the controversy – continued in countless further statements, newspaper and magazine articles, interviews, and letters to the editor – reveals the disconcerting instrumentalisation of the principle of 'academic pluralism', a phrase that was readily invoked when certain worldviews refused the mainstream consensus and, like the Marburg School, sought to justify their refusal to accept capitalism and bourgeois democracy as history's ideal state. The hypertrophic reactions to the book (which certainly was not above critiques of methodology and substance) showed that in this case academic pluralism was deployed as a welcome means with which to prevent the feared growing influence of the book that was obviously greeted by quite a few, particularly younger, trade union members.

The debates around *Gewerkschaftsgeschichte* attracted so much attention that the DGB saw itself compelled (although not admitting the true reason) to organise an academic conference in October 1979 under the theme 'Learning from History', at which Frank Deppe spoke. Yet even this failed to defuse the conflict. A televised debate was broadcast on Norddeutscher Rundfunk as late as 1981 between Fritz Vilmar and Wolfgang Rudzio, both professors of political science and co-authors of a book with the compelling title *Der Marsch der DKP durch die Institutionen* (The DKP's March Through the Institutions),[93] and professor Josef Schleifstein, director of the IMSF in Frankfurt, former Gestapo inmate and Communist, along with Frank Deppe to discuss the role of West German Communists in the trade unions. During the debate, the two latter figures were met with invectives accusing them of 'whitewashing', 'propaganda', and 'well-poisoning' in the interests of a totalitarian Communist ideology.[94]

---

91 See 'Ich habe nicht die Absicht, diesen Notenwechsel fortzusetzen', *Frankfurter Rundschau*, 5 January 1979, p. 16.
92 Ibid.
93 Flechtheim, Rudzio, Vilmar and Wike 1980.
94 Vilmar 1981.

As little as the controversy around *Gewerkschaftsgeschichte* met the standards of rational, scholarly discussion – an exception being the contribution by Jörg Kammler, Hartfried Krause, Dietfried Krause-Vilmar and Paul Oehlke[95] – it nevertheless demonstrates in its own way that the Marburg School's activities after Abendroth, Hofmann, and Maus continued to meet with lively public interest and that its representatives sought to live up to the goal of academic and political intervention into social processes inherited from their forbearers. The controversy also evidenced the absurdity of the infiltration accusations, precisely because the Marburg scholars did exactly that which was normally expected of political institutions and their representatives as ideally democratic: they presented their views for public discussion while neither concealing their party standpoint nor violating the rules of academic discourse.

Looking back, there seem to be two primary reasons behind the massive and even irrational, aggressive reactions to the Marburg trade union volume. Firstly, as mentioned above, the book received a warm reception among a significant number of union members and functionaries disappointed with the social partnership policies of the DGB and large individual unions, and in search of alternatives. Secondly, several critics sought to exploit the opportunity to finally rid the academic field of Marburg's *Fachbereich Gesellschaftswissenschaften* as a threat to the dominant academic 'doxa' (Pierre Bourdieu). This is evidenced not only by the tight relationship between literary critique and sharp polemic against the department itself, but also by immediate political steps such as the CDU's attempt in the Hessian state parliament to abolish the 'red cadre factory' at the Philipps University.

8   Theoretical Conflict: The Identity of Marxism

The controversy around the trade union volume took place primarily in the political-ideological arena, as their opponents were mostly concerned with publicly vilifying and isolating its authors and with them the entire Marburg School. Scholarly arguments were of secondary importance.

---

95   A nuanced, critical discussion of *Geschichte der deutschen Gewerkschaften* can be found in Kammler, Krause, Krause-Vilmar and Oehlke 1979. The authors criticise, for example, that Deppe and his co-authors failed to adequately explain why 'unity and autonomy of the trade unions broke down at key junctures' (p. 688), but also reject the methods of their critics (marginalisation of the Left in the workers' movement, selective perception of problems and 'historical untruths', p. 693 ff.).

Yet the Marburg Marxists were also caught up in debates which bore political implications despite playing out on theoretical terrain. One example of such a theoretical controversy was the discussion flaring up in the early 1980s between the journal *Das Argument* and its spiritus rector, editor, and primary author Berlin philosopher Wolfgang Fritz Haug, and a group of authors that included leading representatives of the Marburg School like Hans Heinz Holz, Frank Deppe, and Georg Fülberth. This conflict damaged the hitherto friendly relations between the journal and the Marburg intellectuals. Although Karl Hermann Tjaden, Kurt Steinhaus, Frank Deppe, Jürgen Harrer, and Dieter Boris had written for *Argument* in the past, the disagreement soon boiled over into a sharp antagonism between opposing perspectives, made all the more regrettable by the fact that *Das Argument* had played an influential role in the West German intellectual left for years and both Haug and his group of colleagues as well as the Marburg School claimed to work on the basis of Marx and Engels's theory. This began to change as the Marburg Marxists cooperated more closely with the Frankfurt-based IMSF and the DKP, and *Das Argument* distanced itself from the Communist current in the Left following an initial period of relative openness. The understanding of Marxism emerging in the journal would soon appear increasingly incompatible with that of the Marburg School.

The immediate occasion for the controversy was provided by several essays in *Argument* largely authored by Haug, postulating the necessity of a 'plural Marxism'. Although not explicit, it clearly constituted a critique of Marxism's looming ossification and sanctification at the hands of the DKP and its intellectual cadre. In a programmatic article on the 'Crisis or Dialectic of Marxism', Haug argued that the existence of a 'polycentrism' in 'world Marxism' could no longer be denied without suggesting that this state of affairs corresponded to a unity of Marxist discourse worthy of the name.[96] These reflections were accompanied by recognition of the emergence of 'authoritarian state socialism' and incidences of open hostilities between socialist states (the war between China and Vietnam) or between populations and apparatuses of state rule (military rule in Poland), which brutally held back a plurality of Marxisms.

Haug's sharply reasoned thoughts largely related to three problems: firstly, the question of the 'identity of Marxism'; secondly, the 'articulation of Marxism as science'; and thirdly the outlines of a 'pluri-centrist Marxism'.

Haug saw the 'identity of Marxism' threatened primarily by the prospect of the 'nagging unfinishedness and radicalism of the project associated with Marx's name' being obscured and repressed by canonisation into a rigid ideo-

---

96   Haug 1983, p. 9.

logical system.[97] He opposed this move with two main arguments: Marxist theory's connection to a political apparatus, the party, restricted the necessary space for developing and exploring critical Marxist thought. Moreover, the party – by which he implicitly meant the CPSU, SED, DKP, and other 'orthodox' Communist parties – sought to assert an ideological monopoly that dissident Robert Havemann once ironically described as the 'central administration of eternal truths'.[98]

In contrast to many other left-wing critics, Haug did not regard the expression 'scientific socialism' as undiscussable as such, but instead was far more concerned with its perversion into an empty ideological formula. What really mattered was respecting the scientificness of socialism, and with it the willingness to not extinguish its inner plurality but rather apply it as the method to decode and understand change (within the sciences as well). In Haug's view, the repeated danger to 'scientific socialism's project character' of 'regressing into religious and other forms of the ideological' was caused by a self-reproducing tendency towards historical-philosophical determinism.[99] In doing so, he identified 'two opposing interpretations' of Marxism. While a historical and philosophically determinist interpretation drew on the topoi of natural historical necessity and abstract universalism, the second interpretation (favoured by Haug) sharpened an analysis corresponding to the concrete situative forms of actions, experiences, and struggles along with 'regional specifics'.[100]

The central category a 'scientific socialism' worthy of the name must address was that of the socialisation of science and labour: 'the formula "scientific socialism" is essential, but its content must be energetically developed, and must keep pace with the sciences and concrete problems of socialisation'.[101] Marxism would only be capable of productively adopting the 'irreversible reality' of 'polycentrism' by breaking with its obligation to extol eternal truths and instead understand itself as an internally differentiated theory and method of mediating contradiction and unity.

Haug's considerations contained a number of aspects pointing to the weaknesses and dogmatisations of the Marxism dominant in the state-socialist countries and some Communist parties in the West. These arguments deserved thorough-going discussion, but were met with little enthusiasm by the intellec-

---

97   Haug 1983, p. 12.
98   Haug 1983, p. 14.
99   Haug 1983, p. 20.
100   Haug 1983, p. 23.
101   Haug 1983, p. 29.

tuals around the DKP, IMSF, and the Marburg School due to their overall tone of missionary self-righteousness. They certainly felt attacked by Haug's formulation of 'the party's claim to monopoly', thereby ensuring a discussion burdened with mutual accusations of guilt.

Be that as it may, a group of authors – several of whom occupied leading positions in the DKP or represented the Frankfurt IMSF and the Marburg School – responded to Haug's critique with a massive reaction in the form of a collected volume which appeared in the DKP's publishing house, Verlag Marxistische Blätter.[102] Although their preface acknowledged that *Das Argument* had made an important contribution to the development and dissemination of critical thought in the Federal Republic in prior years, they criticised its turn away from the journal's former path and turned the accusation of a 'claim to sole representation' in the field of Marxism back on Haug himself. Depending on personal disposition, horizon of biographical experience, political function, and academic habitus, the individual articles spanned a spectrum ranging from polemical-dismissive to categorical intellectual flights and sober-rational lines of argument structured around certain problems.

More than anyone else, philosopher Hans Heinz Holz (who no longer taught at Marburg) contributed an abstract, moralising declaration on what Marxism was, was not, and was to be, which ended up confirming several of Haug's suspicions of an ossification and dogmatisation of Marxist theory.[103] Holz had nothing more to offer Haug than pithy ideological rhetoric, which sounded as follows:

> From dialectical and historical materialism follows the struggle for a socialist society, that is to say partisanship in the class struggle; Marxism is the reflected form of a political praxis which does not occur independently of this theoretical determination of itself. As a concept of social praxis – whether in the struggle of the oppressed and exploited working class for its liberation, or in the building of socialism – Marxist theory is oriented not towards the probation in the particular of the cognitive individual, but in the generality of the social process: for this reason, in Marxism and for Marxists the question of truth is always simultaneously a question of organisation. For it is not a matter of the pluralism of possible models of thought, but rather of theory as an historical agent.[104]

---

102   Holz, Metscher, Schleifstein and Steigerwald 1984.
103   Holz 1984.
104   Holz 1984, p. 37.

Holz repeatedly brought up the so-called 'fundamental question of philosophy' (by which he obviously meant the relation between material and ideal, or rather material being and consciousness), in which he opposed to Haug and his scepticism the 'ontological status of the dialectic' as the 'key to the further development of theory', yet without demonstrating how this key was to be concretely applied in analyses of the oft-invoked praxis. When Holz deployed terms like theory, praxis, or class interest – of which his article largely consisted – he moved in the thin air of an equally abstract and voluntarist normativity climaxing in, among other things, the notion that the 'ideal construction' of philosophy 'which asserts its claim to historical truth' stands 'in a specific relationship to party discipline as an indispensable moment of revolutionary class struggle'.[105]

Georg Fülberth, by contrast, responded to Haug's critique in a sober and relaxed fashion.[106] Looking back on labour history articles in the pages of *Argument*, he charted an erratic development beginning in the early 1970s with the publication of Marxist essays on the topic before increasingly favouring non-Marxist authors and ultimately pursuing a pluralist line which, although opening itself up to newer approaches (everyday history, regional history, oral history, lifeworld-orientation), in doing so abandoned the elaboration of a Marxist research perspective.[107] Marxist historical studies from the GDR in which everyday history and regional social structural differentiation of the proletariat posed a central dimension of research (such as in the work of Jürgen Kuczysnki and Hartmut Zwahr) were ignored. Ultimately, Fülberth sought to identify in *Argument*'s approach to problems of the workers' movement less an intrinsic, specific line so much as a 'symptom' of a general intellectual tendency towards subjectiveness, resignation, and abandonment of the political struggle.

Frank Deppe, who recalls participating only hesitantly as an author in the volume against Haug and *Das Argument* and considered the opening of a new 'front' of conflict on the Left to be counterproductive, situated his reflections in the context of a changed relationship between the intellectual, the working class, and the workers' movement.[108] Beginning with the decoupling of the development of socio-economic crises and a theoretically acquired 'working-class standpoint' whose expectations of a mass mobilisation had not been fulfilled, Deppe pointed to the following weaknesses in Haug's ambitious attempt

---

105   Holz 1984, p. 50.
106   Fülberth 1984.
107   Fülberth 1984, p. 123.
108   Deppe 1984b.

to articulate the 'standpoint of the intellectual' anew: Haug reified intellectuals' critical stance to forms of 'autonomy' and 'resistance', rather than placing the processes of intellectual reflection and critique in relation to the concrete conditions and movements of the class struggle. His sharp and polemical formulation that socialist and Communist parties would 'throw wayward intellectuals to the dogs like populist scraps' (Haug's actual words) simplified the complicated tensions and animosities between intellectuals and the political organisations of the Left, which were by no means the fault of the parties alone.[109] Although the latter's approach to intellectuals was by no means deserving of constant applause neither were intellectuals free of all suspicion, having often distinguished themselves through an 'opportunism' and 'individualism' running counter to the needs of political praxis.[110]

Deppe identified Haug's concept of 'structural hegemony' as a further weakness, that is to say a 'hegemony without a hegemon' that constituted itself as a 'pluri-centric activation structure' and forbid a reduction to the standpoint of the working class. Deppe illustrated his criticisms with several examples: Haug's oft-invoked Antonio Gramsci had left no doubt that the revolutionary party and not a plural discourse was obliged to exercise hegemony in social and political struggles. Haug's reference to Lenin was similarly misleading, in the sense that the 'democratic movement' of which Lenin spoke was no mere end in itself, but rather located in the 'focal point' of politics of the revolutionary party. Lastly, contrary to Haug's assumption a synthesis of 'class constitution and hegemonic capacity' could not be derived from British historian E.P. Thompson's study of the historical emergence of the English working class. In fact, the exact opposite was the case: it posed the question the other way around, namely why the English working class had *not* become hegemonic.[111] Deppe's arguments converged in the thesis that the standpoint of the intellectual could not limit itself to theoretical reflection and scholarly work, but rather must be repeatedly redefined and evaluated in its relation to the real processes of class contestation. Should this fail to be the case, intellectuals risked stylising themselves as judges of a tribunal over the workers' movement, mechanically conflating theoretical reflection and political praxis and consolidating themselves as 'free-floating intellectuals'.[112]

The Marburgers' contributions to the volume on *Das Argument* also included the author of this book, who came from the Marburg School and re-

---

109   Haug 1983, p. 32, fn. 1.
110   Deppe 1984b, p. 106.
111   Deppe 1984b, p. 109.
112   Deppe 1984b, p. 116.

tained his connection to its protagonists after leaving for Bremen, often mediated through projects, events, and publications for the IMSF. The author's article oscillated between similarly abstract statements and postulates and an attempt to illustrate the deficits of Haug's line of argument on the basis of specific points.[113] Although a contemporary reading of the contribution reveals a partially unconvincing critique of Haug, it also raised several points evidencing Haug's argumentative weaknesses and untenable claims. This was true for his hypostatisation of 'the party' and 'the apparatus' and their isolation from all concrete pressures of their social and political environments.[114] This was also true of Haug's assessment of Friedrich Engels as an alleged propagator of blind technological euphoria. The author pointed out that Engels had warned against the catastrophic consequences of unrestrained scientific-technical domination over nature with almost prophetic clarity, calling for a sublation of this domination through a non-capitalist mode of production. In light of these facts, Engels could not be accused of an uncritical *Produktivkraftoptimismus*.[115]

Looking back on the debate between *Das Argument* and the intellectuals in and around the DKP of whom Marburg Marxists comprised a significant portion, we can conclude that both sides were deeply involved in the argumentative forms, categories, and patterns that dominated the struggle for hegemony in the Marxist intellectual sphere at the time. Both sides found it difficult to leave the plane of ideological confrontation behind in order to break new ground in socially critical analysis without being coloured by political-ideological competition from the outset. This did not mean, however, that the controversy failed to raise important questions for left-wing intellectual discourse as a whole.

---

113   Peter 1984.
114   Peter 1984, p. 60f.
115   Peter 1984, p. 65f. Here, Peter referred to Engels's *Dialectics of Nature* (Engels 1987), esp. pp. 461–4.

CHAPTER 5

The Marburg School since the 1980s

1   A Premature Farewell

The conflict around the Marburg *Gewerkschaftsbuch*, the unsavoury conflict with Wolfgang Fritz Haug and *Das Argument*, as well as other conflicts either forced onto the representatives of the Marburg School or which they allowed themselves to be drawn into did not, however, lead to the retreat their political opponents and some of their intellectual critics may have hoped for. On the contrary: the Marxist Marburg School's scholarly productivity continued without interruption. In many ways, one could even say it reached a higher level of academic quality than in the preceding period.

This contradicts the hypothesis put forward by historians Christoph Hüttig and Lutz Raphael that its 'fixation on an orthodox Marxism and a DKP intellectually emaciated by "Eurocommunist" heresies'[1] definitively sealed the fate of Marburg's 'Red Bastion' by the late 1980s. Noteworthy about Hüttig and Raphael's depiction of the Marburg School as a 'scientific thought collective' is that while it describes internal institutional developments, constellations of actors, and the factionalisation of discourse in astonishing detail, the substance of the Marburg School's scholarly work is itself categorically ignored. Had they refrained from this, they would have been able to conclude that the actors of the Marburg School continued to produce academically respected work well into the 1980s and beyond, continuing in their own work the relationship between theory and praxis the school's founders established.

One example that demonstrates how Marburg's left-wing social scientists remained remarkably active during the years on which Hüttig and Raphael's necrology of the School is particularly focused is Frank Deppe's major study of Machiavelli (1987),[2] a truly impressive work in terms of both its substantive complexity as well as analytical stringency. Its publication proved that he was not only an expert in trade union research or EU policy, but also a competent scholar of classical political theory who had no reason to shy the academic competition, such as Herfried Münkler's book on the same topic.[3] That said, with few exceptions Deppe's volume was largely greeted by academic silence.

---

1   Hüttig and Raphael 1992, p. 24 f.
2   Deppe 1987. Published in a new edition in 2014.
3   Münkler 1982. According to a letter sent to the author by Frank Deppe, a debate was held in

Deppe was moved to study Machiavelli by the question as to how the indi-
viduation of the state out of the development of bourgeois society could be
explained, and what operative status the political dimension takes in this process. This line of inquiry forced itself onto Deppe insofar as the Marxist state
debate dominant at the time, with its abstract derivation procedures and ritualised economistic explanations, had reached its limits. At the same time,
he was confronted by the irritating fact that Machiavelli's theories of power
and the state were not only adopted as a classic work on the philosophy of
the state by representatives of a conservative and even fascist-inclined Neo-
Machiavellianism (Georges Sorel, Gaetano Mosca, Vilfredo Pareto and others)
for their own worldview, but were also positively reviewed by a pioneer of Western Marxism, Antonio Gramsci, in his depiction of the relationship between
the state, politics, and society. In his thematically diverse study incorporating
the historical development of the Northern Italian city states as well as the
role of Renaissance intellectuals, Deppe focused on Machiavelli's political theory as an action-oriented political solution to the early bourgeois economic,
social, and moral crisis rocking Florence and other cities. He worked out that
Machiavelli was above all interested in controlling and integrating the destabil-
ising centrifugal forces of competition, egoistic desires, and sectional interests
with the aid of what he saw as a morally indifferent, ruthlessly forceful state.[4]

According to Deppe's reading, Gramsci invoked Machiavelli because he
understood his activist political philosophy as a comprehensive attempt to
interpret the crisis of ruling-class hegemony,[5] which could only be solved
'organically' if a new hegemonic formation replaced the old, exhausted one.
The recourse to a 'new leader', in Machiavelli's words the 'new prince', was in
Deppe's view merely proof that such a hegemonic force did not yet exist. In light
of 1920s and 1930s Italian society at the time, this could only develop as a collective movement – and only under the leadership of a revolutionary Marxist
party. Here, Deppe pointed out the limits of Gramsci's reading of Machiavelli,
tracing his mistaken perception of Machiavelli as a revolutionary and an early
Jacobin back to a false identification of Northern Italian Renaissance society
with the alleged existence of developed bourgeois class and production relations.[6]

Marburg between him, Herfried Münkler, and the Romance studies scholar August Buck in
1988.
4   Deppe 1987, p. 289.
5   Deppe 1987, 422.
6   Deppe 1987, p. 427.

2   A Contribution to Constitutional Law (Peter Römer)

Just how threadbare Hüttig and Raphael's claim of a 'dreary end' to the Marburg School after the departure of Abendroth, to which both authors (utterly disregarding Marburg sociology) ascribe a style-forming function for West German political science in order to more effectively discredit the subsequent generation of Marburg social scientists, can be proven with the work of Peter Römer. Römer chose one of Abendroth's scholarly priorities as a central focus of his work: the function of the legal system, the constitution, fundamental rights, and democracy caught in the tension between antagonistic social interests.

Born in 1936, Peter Römer studied law and political science in Berlin, Göttingen, and Marburg. He completed his dissertation in 1964 at the Philipps University Department of Law on 'the criminal problem of bribing parliamentary deputies'. He then went on to work as an assistant to Abendroth from 1966–70, before being appointed to a H-2 level professorship of political science at the Philipps University in 1972. He was involved in the founding of both the journal *Kritische Justiz* in 1968 as well as the editorship of *Demokratie und Recht*, which began publication by Pahl-Rugenstein Verlag in 1973.

Römer's substantive identification with Abendroth was reflected in among other things a text that already referred to Abendroth by name in its title and took up his conception of law and democracy.[7] By way of introduction, however, Römer transforms Abendroth's quote that 'good praxis without theory can exist as little as no theory beyond this relation to praxis is truly theory worth taking seriously' into the apodictic conclusion that the 'rightness or wrongness of a theory' is proven 'out of the connection of theory with praxis'.[8] This somewhat coarse rhetoric proclaiming Marxism's allegedly unquestionable epistemological superiority – quite common across the left spectrum at the time – did not prevent Römer from taking up an informative and differentiated exploration of Abendroth's views on law, the state, and democracy in the context of contemporary discourses on constitutional law. It is surprising to note that Römer sought to cast Abendroth as a proponent of 'legal positivism' (*Rechtspositivismus*), albeit to make the specific character of this legal positivism as an expression of Marxist social critique plausible over the course of his line of argument. Like other representatives of (legal) positivism, Römer's Abendroth also viewed law as something humans 'established' and created, whereas explanations of law based on concepts of natural law were derived from a religious, Enlightenment, or anthropological human nature as

---

7   Römer 1986.
8   Römer 1986, p. 7.

such: 'In this sense, then, in which he acknowledges and takes seriously as such the valid and effective, that is to say positive law, Abendroth is a positivist'.[9]

Whereas in bourgeois legal positivism the law made and established by humans takes on a life of its own as a 'neutral' object to be viewed as 'impartial' independently of its historical and social conditions of emergence and intentions, Abendroth inquired in direct opposition to this notion as to precisely these conditions and conflicts of interest from which legal and constitutional norms emerged. This allowed him, for example (and as Römer repeatedly reminds us), to understand the Basic Law of the Federal Republic as a product of certain balances of social forces and a legal product of the 'class compromise'. In doing so, Abendroth not only differentiated himself from traditional legal positivism but also from approaches within Marxist legal theory that identified constitutions as ideological systems of the ruling classes with corresponding balances of social power. Overlooking the repeated, analytically irrelevant declarations that only 'scientific socialism' is capable of understanding reality,[10] Römer managed to lay out the multi-faceted legal, constitutional, and political implications of Abendroth's thought, providing clear contours to the latter's opposition to the dominant teachings of West German state and constitutional theory.

Similar to the example of legal positivism, with view to the problem of an 'identarian democracy' Römer critically depicted that Abendroth as well as Carl Schmitt on one hand and the legal positivism of Hans Kelsen or Rudolf Smend's theory of integration on the other advocated the principle of an 'identitarian democracy'.[11] The concrete substance thereof, however, constituted something qualitatively different than the *Identitätslehre* propagated by Schmitt, Kelsen, and Smend. While Schmitt called for a totalitarian conflation of *Volk*, state, and law, Hans Kelsen defined democracy as an 'identity of leaders and led' under the 'rule of the people over the people', and Smend hoped for social integration through the constitution and state, Abendroth – as Römer demonstrated – understood democracy as a process of approximation between the interests of the dependent social classes and a government accountable to them, pointing beyond the class division of society.[12]

Reading and interpreting Abendroth's constitutional theory comprised the foundation for countless numbers of Römer's works. This was the case in *Im*

---

9   Römer 1986, p. 8 f.
10   See Römer 1986, such as p. 7, p. 15, p. 39.
11   Römer 2001.
12   Römer 2001, p. 27.

Namen des Grundgesetzes (In the Name of the Basic Law),[13] in which he returns to the problem of an 'identitarian democracy' in Abendroth's sense. By defending the necessity thereof against the status quo-affirming stance of prominent contemporary constitutional experts like Ernst-Wolfgang Böckenförde, who rejected the notion of a deficient, not-yet-realised democracy in need of permanent improvement as risky, he emphasised the processual nature of 'identitarian democracy' which could first be unfolded through political praxis.

Römer's attempts can be summarised to the effect that oriented towards Abendroth he counterposed to the methodological dualism of legal system and society (such as in Ernst Forsthoff's work) the notion of its nevertheless contradictory, conflict-prone relation in order to derive from this the need for an approximation between social reality and the constitution realised through the will and activity of the people. Such a conception of constitution and democracy prevented one from legitimising and orienting oneself towards constitutional norms through the dominant social relations – such as the capitalist 'market economy'.[14]

3   Marburg in the *Historikerstreit* (Reinhard Kühnl)

The mid-1980s witnessed the emergence of a major public debate in the Federal Republic focused on the country's Nazi past. Known as the *Historikerstreit* or 'historians' dispute', it occupied the academic and political spheres intensively and placed the questionable approach to dealing with German history (particularly between 1933 and 1945) back onto the public agenda. Participating in the debate on the conservative historians' side were above all Ernst Nolte, Andreas Hillgruber, Michael Stürmer, and Klaus Hildebrand; from the social-democratic and liberally oriented side were Jürgen Habermas, Hans Mommsen, Kurt Sontheimer, and Heinrich August Winkler (among others). At its core, the debate revolved around Ernst Nolte's relativisation of fascist terror as an historically understandable reaction to the Bolshevist 'Gulag archipelago'. Auschwitz and the fascist system of rule which allowed it to occur thereby lost their historical unprecedentedness as a machinery for the destruction of millions of human beings in order to accommodate an implicit downplaying and justification of the past. Nolte revised the theory of totalitarianism already common at the time into a specific, more apologetic and extreme version in

13   Römer 1989.
14   Römer 1989, p. 124.

which Bolshevism and fascism were not equated (as was usually the case), but rather the former was declared to have caused the latter. In doing so he ascribed a certain historical consistency to Hitler's invasion of the Soviet Union and the Holocaust that, although not endorsing it, sought to 'normalise' it to some degree.

It was no surprise that the Marxist scholar of fascism Reinhard Kühnl would take sides against the conservative historians, yet what stands out about his contribution is the fact that he also examined the consistency of the arguments put forward by Nolte's critics.[15] Although he acknowledged the liberal participants' political and moral stance and corroborated many of their arguments, Kühnl also identified several weaknesses. He concurred with their estimation of the uniqueness of the system of fascist terror that the conservative historians sought to relativise and exculpate, but insisted on the need for an analysis of the socio-economic and political conditions that made this system possible in the first place. He could find no such analysis among the liberal critics, nor a nuanced discussion of their proclaimed commitment to the values of Western culture. If Habermas invoked the spirit of an 'Occidental understanding of freedom, responsibility and self-determination'[16] and Sontheimer accused his conservative opponents of abandoning the post-1945 democratic consensus, then one could not forget, Kühnl demanded, that the 'opening to the West' had also meant 'restauration of capitalism', West German rearmament, and NATO membership. In their inclination to idealise the 'Western bond' and West Germany's post-1945 democratic consensus, Habermas and other liberal intellectuals risked overlooking the fact that the West's actual historical development was insolubly tied not only to the values of the Enlightenment but also to imperialist policies, colonialism, Hiroshima, Vietnam, and the overthrow of Chile's Salvador Allende in 1973. This side of the West was no contingent phenomenon, no 'coincidental lapse', but rather the result of its capitalist 'social and property order', as Kühnl expounded with idiosyncratic linearity.

Kühnl also problematised the liberal critics' certain proximity to the hypothesis of German 'collective guilt'. He argued that although the position that 'we Germans' were responsible for the Nazis' crimes was morally honourable, it simultaneously impeded a nuanced inspection of the proportion of different population groups involved in these crimes. Even if a majority of the German people carried a degree of shared responsibility for the fascist crimes through their 'actions or tolerance', it was necessary to distinguish between the elite

15   Habermas 1991, p. 240.
16   Kühnl 1987.

groups who actively organised the fascist system on the one hand, 'followers', and in particular the 'hundreds of thousands' who rejected the Nazi regime or even risked their lives to resist it. A historiography adhering to a sweeping hypothesis of 'collective guilt' renounced the opportunity to raise awareness of this 'other Germany'. In this sense, Habermas's talk of 'constitutional patriotism' also fell short, for although it identified a substantial foundation for democratic identification it excluded identification with the 'needs, feelings, and goals' of 'the European peoples' anti-fascist liberation struggles or the liberation movements in the Third World'.[17]

Kühnl interpreted the *Historikerstreit*, as did the conservative historians, as an eminently political 'battle for the understanding of history' relevant to the contemporary moment,[18] yet drew diametrically opposed conclusions from it. While Nolte, Stürmer, Fest, and others used the 'normalisation' of fascism to provide legitimatory meaning to a neo-conservative style of politics emerging under the banner of a 'spiritual-moral turn', Kühnl for his part saw his task as summoning the potential of historical analysis for the struggle against newly emerging tendencies towards a politically ominous supremacy of the Federal Republic in Europe.

4 Activities and Interactions in the Academic Sphere

The protagonists of the Marburg School thus did not reduce the intensity of their activity in the 1980s, in fact their rhythm of production continued to move on quite a high level. This was true not only for research and publishing but also, for example, for the supervision of graduate students, the number of which was comparable to those of their colleagues. The dissertations they supervised were often published by the Marburg publishing house Verlag Arbeiterbewegung und Gesellschaftswissenschaft, founded by Frank Deppe, Georg Fülberth and Karlheinz Flessenkemper in 1977 to take the place of the *Marburger Abhandlungen zur Politischen Wissenschaft*. The titles published here certainly converged with the Marxist views of the dissertation supervisors to a higher degree than had been the case among the more pluralistic spectrum of the *Marburger Abhandlungen*. Beyond the publications of the new publishing house, also contributing to the profile of the Marburg School was the Marxistische Arbeitskreis (MAK), a working group initiated by Deppe in the mid-1980s which, as

---

17   Kühnl 1987, p. 281.
18   Kühnl 1987, p. 282.

Deppe wrote in retrospect,[19] offered an alternative to the increasingly obvious 'theoretical flattening and stultification of a growing part of MSB members and DKP people'[20] and sought to link up with the state of international Marxist discourse through, for example, Gramsci or the French regulation school (Alain Lipietz, Michel Aglietta, Robert Boyer, and others). Several professors (like Klaus Dörre[21] and Hans-Jürgen Bieling)[22] as well as a range of trade unionists would emerge from this group, including Hans-Jürgen Urban, a member of the IG Metall executive board, Witich Roßmann, a representative of IG Metall in Cologne, and Thorsten Schulte, a staff member at the Economic and Social Scientific Institute of the trade union-aligned Hans-Böckler-Stiftung.

The declining significance of MSB Spartakus and the rise of the Greens (particularly its 'Realo' wing) at the Phipps University since the early 1980s ate away at the influence of left-wing student GO-Politik. This reduced the Marburg School's scopes of action among the student body, but did not lead to it reducing its efforts towards a development and application of Marxist theory commensurate with changing conditions. Frank Deppe in particular cultivated contacts to internationally renowned social scientists of 'Western Marxism' such as Perry Anderson, Göran Therborn, Bob Jessop, Leo Panitch, and Eric Hobsbawm, but also to Peter Heß, a scholar of capitalism living in East Berlin whom he invited to Marburg for lectures and workshops. He actively participated in the strike movement for the 35-hour work week in 1984, partly in an informal capacity as an expert policy advisor, and also published on the movement.

---

19   Frank Deppe made this retrospective comment in an unpublished letter dated 6 October 2001 to Hans-Jürgen Bieling, Klaus Dörre, Jochen Steinhilber, Hans-Jürgen Urban, and Klaus Pieter Weiner, the editors of a collected volume to commemorate Frank Deppe's 60th birthday (Bieling, Dörre and Steinhilber 2001).
20   Ibid.
21   Born in 1957, Klaus Dörre studied political science and sociology in Marburg and wrote his dissertation under Frank Deppe's supervision. He then worked as a research fellow at the SOFI Göttingen, before becoming the managing director of the Forschungsinstitut Arbeit, Bildung, Partizipation at the Ruhr University in Bochum. He completed his *Habilitation* in 2002 in Göttingen and has been a professor of sociology at the University of Jena since 2005. Here he has succeeded in developing a distinctive, socially critical brand of 'Jena sociology' together with Stephan Lessenich and Hartmut Rosa. Dörre was also a founding member of the Institut Solidarische Moderne, a left-wing think tank.
22   Born in 1967, Hans-Jürgen Bieling studied economics and sociology in Marburg, where he completed his dissertation and *Habilitation* under Frank Deppe's supervision. He initially worked as a junior professor in Marburg and was appointed to a professorship at the University of Bremen in 2010, before receiving a position as a professor of political economy at the University of Tübingen in 2011.

Deppe had turned to the European dimension of social and political struggles fairly early on, an aspect which took on new and specific contours with the Europe research initiated by him beginning in the mid-1970s.[23] Deppe successfully called into being a research group that analysed the problems and contradictions of European integration in the form of diverse projects and publications for years. The theoretical approach of this capitalism-critical Europe research was comprised of the mediation of a 'regulation-theoretically expanded Neo-Gramscianism'[24] with the concept of 'international political economy', seeking to overcome the conventional division between politics and economy. Hans-Jürgen Bieling and Frank Deppe characterised this approach as follows:

> At its core, the Neo-Gramscianism of international political economy seeks – similarly, by the way, to the other, primarily neo-realist inspired conceptions of hegemony – to figure out the causes and fundamental structures of transnational relations of cooperation, power, and violence. However, in contrast to these, hegemony is understood not as the domination of an economically and militarily powerful nation-state, but rather as a consensually supported mode of transnational socialisation, including the relations of class, ideological relations, and structures of domination and consensus underlying it.[25]

It would appear that the atmosphere inside *Fachbereich* 03, or at least in the disciplines of political science and sociology, began to relax after the 1970s when 'liberality was not popular' – something one participant perceived not as an 'identity crisis' of political science but certainly an 'uncomfortable time'.[26] The causes of this lack of liberality and 'uncomfortableness', however, were interpreted in highly contradictory ways depending on one's scholarly and political point of view. Here, it is worth noting that the personal statements and recollections of non-Marxists in the department exhibit a certain inclination towards retrospective lachrymosity, although they – unlike their increasingly institutionally marginalised opponents – did not have to fear massive political pressure. Dirk Berg-Schlosser, a political scientist appointed to a position in Marburg in 1985, noticed 'certain frontlines' but simultaneously detected a 'climate of "peaceful coexistence"'.[27]

---

23   See on this the unpublished report Bonfert and Ehling 2015.
24   Ibid.
25   Bieling and Deppe 1999.
26   See Hecker et al. 2001, p. 212.
27   Ibid.

That said, a productive exchange between the representatives of different academic approaches would never materialise. Instead, the 'normalisation' of scientific and higher education policy after the brief post-1968 reform period (with its structural defects, some of which certainly were in need of correction) facilitated the recovery of a mainstream social science that rejected fundamental social critique, also expressed in quantitative shifts of the balance of power within departments and academic bodies. The group around the Marburg School lost three qualified and dedicated colleagues when Jürgen Harrer, Gert Meyer,[28] and Rainer Rilling were not appointed to teaching positions for political reasons.

The antagonisms were less prominent in Marburg sociology than they were in political science, although Dieter Boris adhered to the principles of the Marburg School in both his research and teaching. But because he remained in the minority in his department after Tjaden went to Kassel and thus had less influence over internal institutional affairs, his cooperation with non-Marxist colleagues such as the sociologist Renate Rausch[29] proved less conflict-prone. Friendly relations would later even develop between Dieter Boris and Dirk Kaesler, a well-known Max Weber scholar and editor of respected edited volumes on both the classics of sociology as well as internationally renowned contemporary theoreticians, who was appointed to a position in Marburg in 1995.

---

28   Born in 1943, Gert Meyer is a political scientist and historian. He completed his doctorate in 1971 under Abendroth with a dissertation on relations between town and countryside in Soviet Russia at the beginning of the New Economic Policy. He was then, as already mentioned, a lecturer at the Institute for Political Science in Marburg. He later took on teaching assignments at the Gesamthochschule Kassel and the University of Marburg, yet despite his impressive academic talents never managed to succeed in an academic career – not least for political reasons. Today he lives in Marburg.

29   Renate Rausch (1930–2007) was a professor of empirical social research in the sociology department at the Philipps University beginning in 1975, was active among other things in feminist scholarship, and shared with Dieter Boris (with whom she also published) a research interest in Latin America where she previously lived.

CHAPTER 6

Fourth Phase: From the 'Epochal Rupture' of 1989–90 to the Early 2000s

1 Social and Political Context

The collapse of state socialism not only altered the global balance of forces between systems, but also for Germany in particular brought forth a fundamentally new social situation when a new state emerged from the two previously existing German states – albeit one which retained the title 'Federal Republic'. The GDR's incorporation into the West German Federal Republic extended the country's influence as a 'centre of accumulation' (Georg Fülberth) of European capitalism to the east. This development was expedited by the neoliberal restructuring of the welfare state that already began, albeit haltingly, in the 1980s. Under the banner of strengthening Germany as a site of economic production against global competition, Helmut Kohl's government attacked significant welfare-state standards by sinking the level of statutory sick pay, weakening dismissal protection laws, and cutting unemployment benefits in order to simultaneously drive forward the privatisation and commodification of public services. The Deutsche Bahn became a kind of joint-stock company, the Federal Post Office was dismembered, and the once publicly-owned Deutsche Telekom entered the stock market as a privately owned major corporation. Cuts to the 'social net', market liberalisation, and the deregulation of labour relations led to deepening social division (the 'two-thirds-society'), impacting the territory of the former GDR particularly hard. The economic upswing following 'reunification' proved to be hollow and short-lived, and Germany tumbled into a deep recession by 1993 expressed in shrinking GDP as unemployment climbed to nearly ten percent. However, it was not until the Red-Green coalition under Social Democratic Chancellor Gerhard Schröder that government policies would cause the previously existing welfare state system's 'dam to break' (Georg Fülberth), and allow a 'financial market-driven' capitalism to become dominant over the productive real economy.

That said, the forces and actors standing in opposition to the ideology and reality of unfettered neoliberalism had little to offer in its place. While the 'new social movements' lost their dynamic and the Green Party majority began to favour neoliberal policies, the trade unions participated in fortifying the 'competitive state' through 'alliances for work' and 'co-management' in the workplace, while tolerating the 'Hartz IV' laws that paved the way for the creation of a 'new industrial reserve army'. An important exception to this process of neoliberal *Landnahme* (Klaus Dörre)[1] and the marginalisation of an effective opposition were the mass protests against the Federal Republic's involvement in the 2003 Iraq War. Only then did parliamentary and extra-parliamentary resistance gradually begin to grow, leading to among other things a strengthening of the Party of Democratic Socialism (PDS) and later Die Linke, which understood itself as the tribune of the socially excluded. Its pro-peace orientation also lent the party a degree of support among the population.

2 Confronting the 'Epochal Rupture' (Georg Fülberth)

One could have expected that the 'epochal rupture' unleashed in the West in the late 1980s by the collapse of state socialism, the shift in the global economic and political balance of forces, as well as the political and intellectual crisis of the workers' movement and Marxism as a whole would have driven the protagonists of the Marburg School to conduct a critical evaluation of their theoretical self-understanding and their own role as militant left-wing intellectuals. Yet for the most part the Marburg Marxists neglected to engage with questions such as the extent to which the Marxist theory they represented was capable of adequately analysing these fundamental ruptures and breaks, whether Marxism's conceptual methodological arsenal was in need of thorough re-evaluation, and why the working class in both Eastern as well as Western Europe no longer chose to occupy the leading role Marxist theory so decidedly ascribed to it – or if they did, only hesitantly. One important exception to this trend, however, ought to be noted: Georg Fülberth, who undertook an attempt to analyse the failure of state socialism and the Communist movement and work out its implications for his own thinking across a range of publications.[2]

Searching for causes of this failure that had done away with all previous historical certainties and left only the distant hope for an end to capitalism, Fülberth's 1991 *Sieben Anstrengungen, den vorläufigen Endsieg des Kapitalismus zu*

---

1 Coined by Klaus Dörre, the German term *Landnahme* is often translated as 'land-grabbing'. Dörre retains the German in order to capture the full range of activities implied by the broader term which go beyond the appropriation of physical land, see Dörre, Lessenich and Rosa 2015.
2 Such as in Fülberth 1994 and Fülberth 2010.

begreifen (Seven Attempts to Understand the Tentative Final Victory of Capital-ism)[3] was devoted to, among other things, the following four topics: firstly, the period of capitalism's development; secondly, variants and projects of 'counter-societies' to capitalism; thirdly, organisations and movements opposed to cap-italism; and fourthly, several post-1990 intellectual self-assurances.

Because Fülberth proceeded from the assumption that due to its intrinsic irresolvable antagonisms capitalism could not offer humanity an acceptable prospect for the future but rather threatened it with its own demise, its triumph after 1990 could logically not appear to him as a definitive, stable condition. In order to better understand the 'tentative final victory', he felt moved to inquire as to why all hitherto attempted counter-projects – first and foremost actu-ally existing socialism – were unable to triumph historically. Disposing of solid understandings of both the writings of Marx and Engels, Marxist economic the-ory building on them, and actual historical events, Fülberth believed to have discovered the 'tentative defeat' in the following reasons.

According to Fülberth, the absence of a proletarian revolution in the West after 1917 and the restriction of the USSR's sphere of influence after 1945 brought forth a situation in which the existing form of socialism was unable to solve its apparent problems despite catch-up modernisation.[4] Under conditions of systems rivalry and military build-up, the lack of industrial productive forces in comparison to the capitalist West inevitably exceeded the economic and technological possibilities of the USSR and the other socialist states. Despite this fact, the socialist bloc underestimated not only the material but also the social sources and integration potentials of capitalism and dedicated itself to the competition for technological superiority. Internally, this had the con-sequence that actually existing socialism applied models of economic manage-ment which with respect to the actually available resources took on a veritably utopian life of their own. The real *clou* lay in Fülberth's argument that endo-genous factors had not primarily or even solely led to socialism's collapse, but rather its failure was to be situated as a historically nevertheless meaningful episode within the total context of capitalism's development.

In the last section of *Anstrengungen*, Fülberth reviewed several attempts at (self-)critical surveys by left-wing social-scientific intellectuals. Discussing Uwe Wesel's 1990 essay 'Innerlich erröten',[5] for example, he observed that although it ascribed to Marx concepts which now required a critical reformulation,[6] on

---

3   Fülberth 1991.
4   Fülberth 1991, p. 107 ff.
5   Wesel 1990.
6   Fülberth 1991, p. 169.

the other hand it left the question as to whether certain 'humanisation achieve-ments' under capitalism had not at the same been paid for by the 'Third World' through exploitation and 'plundering of natural resources' unanswered.[7] Wesel also neglected to discuss to what extent future humanisation and gentle use of natural resources would be possible through modifications within capitalism or rather required a systemic rupture. When Habermas spoke of 'the need for new thinking on the Left',[8] he was obviously referring to the non-Communist left that allegedly had no cause for political depression. Fülberth viewed the welfare-state regulation and control of unfettered markets by the public envi-sioned by Habermas to be inadequate, both because they limited themselves to the internal dimension of capitalism and because they ignored the relation between humans and nature. Bischoff and Menard attempted to make 'market economy and socialism' compatible, yet ignored whether forms of non-state public property could be developed under existing conditions of casino capit-alism and unemployment in the first place. Fülberth appeared most impressed by Karl Hermann Tjaden's reflections on deepening the scientific understand-ing of the human-nature relation. In particular, he was interested in Tjaden's argument that although socialist societies offered more favourable precondi-tions for independent catch-up development, their factual failure raised the question of what alternative political options could potentially exist within capitalism. Although Tjaden's call to counter capitalism's destructive dynam-ics with a 'total economic direction of total social labour'[9] resembled left-wing 'programmatic Keynesian approaches' in some aspects, it went qualitatively beyond this approach. By taking up Abendroth's concept of 'transitional plan-ning' (*Überleitungsplanung*), Tjaden proposed a perspective of social plan-ning and at the same time raised the question of whether coordinating total labour could even be possible within the limits imposed by the capitalist sys-tem.

     In conclusion, Fülberth sketched out the situation of the Left in a global capitalist environment as the project of a current better described as a 'proto-left' distinguishing itself from reformist elements in that it opposed the causes and not the symptoms of capitalist devastation and was oriented towards a 'type of society interested in use values and reproduction'.[10] Yet Fülberth did not explain what concretely distinguished reformist economic and ecological politics within capitalism, and his claim that the downfall of 'actually existing

7   Fülberth 1991, p. 170.
8   Ibid; Habermas 1990.
9   Fülberth 1991, p. 183.
10   Fülberth 1991, p. 190.

socialism' must be ascribed to substantial deficits in Marxist political and economic theory itself appears rather questionable.

3   Reacting to a Changed Situation

The collapse of actually existing socialism – which in the Federal Republic led to a dramatic decline in DKP membership, the disappearance of the MSB from the universities, and the dissolution of the IMSF – affected several important markers in the Marburg School's political system of coordinates but failed to destabilise it. After all, the thinking of the Marburg protagonists had always been oriented towards actually existing socialism in a secondary manner, as the group was primarily interested in its own society and capitalism in its national and international forms and functions. This prioritisation was disturbingly confirmed by neoliberalism's triumphal march and the processes of social polarisation, segmentation, and precarisation it brought forth as well as the emergence of a new 'industrial reserve army' (Marx) in the metropolises on the one hand, and processes of post-colonial exploitation, immiseration, and devastation in the 'Third World' on the other. How did the Marxist Marburg School respond to this fundamentally changed situation?

Fülberth's growing interest in politico-economic and economic-historical themes had already become evident in works such as *Sieben Anstrengungen*. This corresponded to the informal Forschungsgruppe Politische Ökonomie he initiated at the Institute for Political Science in 1997,[11] and also served as a pendant to Deppe's MAK. Composed largely of students and emerging researchers in economics and political science, the research group's central focus lay in studying the 'mutual interactions between economic and political systems' in capitalist society.[12] The group conducted a number of activities addressing both classical theoretical approaches as well as problems of methodology and historiographical dogma. The group held a meeting in 1999 to commemorate Georg Fülberth's 6oth birthday resulting in an edited volume that was practically a festschrift,[13] although Fülberth sought to avoid this honorific title.[14]

Frank Deppe continued his work in and with the MAK, began to develop an interest in the Party of Democratic Socialism (PDS) – he would later join Die

11   Compare to this group Wolf, Reiner and Wolf-Eicker et al. 2001, pp. 285–90.
12   Wolf, Reiner and Wolf-Eicker et al. 2001, p. 288.
13   Wolf, Reiner and Eicker-Wolf 1999.
14   Wolf, Reiner and Wolf-Eicker et al. 2001, p. 287.

Linke – and often published articles in the pages of *Sozialismus* and *Z. Zeits-chrift Marxistische Erneuerung*, founded in 1990 by Heinz Jung, the last director of the IMSF who died in 1996, and continued today by former IMSF staff such as André Leisewitz in Frankfurt am Main. Deppe took on responsibilities in *Sozialismus* as well as *Z.*, serving as a member of the 'Forum Gewerkschaften' in *Sozialismus* and in the editorial advisory board for *Z.* A central focus of his activity to this day remains the trade-union left, for which he regularly appears as a lecturer, discussant, and public advocate.

4   Excursus: A Conversation between Ulrich Beck and Frank Deppe on the State of Political Opposition in Germany

Several exceptions aside, the Marburg Marxists did not seek out scholarly exchange with their colleagues from other paradigms in order to critically compare each other's research findings or cooperate with them. One of these few exceptions was an extensive conversation between Frank Deppe and Ulrich Beck, the renowned author of *Risk Society*, which appeared in the *Blätter für deutsche und internationale Politik* in 1991.[15]

Frank Deppe's student at the time, Klaus Dörre, put forward a profound critique of Beck's book (which became the most widely-read social science publication since the 1980s) only shortly after its appearance.[16] Where Beck was only able to perceive a diffuse power structure of risk production on the path towards 'reflexive modernity', Dörre pointed to the 'specific mode of socialisation of highly-developed capitalist societies' as the decisive structural cause,[17] without which the 'hazardous global situation' could not be adequately explained. Where Beck saw individualisation and with it the dissolution of the class structure typical of traditional industrial capitalism, Dörre sought to prove that the empirically undeniable individualisation processes Beck described remained consistently integrated into the reproduction of capitalism. Although Dörre praised Beck's unconventional approach and awareness of concrete threats, he argued that his 'catastrophic scenarios and theories of collapse' were an unsuitable 'foundation for a socially transformative praxis'.[18]

---

15   Beck and Deppe 1991.
16   Dörre 1987.
17   Dörre 1987, p. 22.
18   Dörre 1987, p. 89.

Building to some extent on themes developed in *Risk Society*, Beck and Deppe's conversation focused on the question as to the political opposition's ability to act in Germany. Beck opened with the hypothesis that no political opposition existed in reunified Germany. His focus, however, was primarily on the Green Party, whose core issues had in the meantime become generalised within society but which had lost its unique oppositional characteristics. Previously, the Federal Republic and the GDR had in some ways functioned as '*counter-state opposition for one another*' within Germany,[19] to which, however, the 'old left-wing opposition' had responded not with a fundamental reappraisal of Stalinism and totalitarian socialism but rather with an unrealistic 'ideal abstraction' taken from academic theory.

Deppe rejected this assertion by on the one hand assigning responsibility to objective reasons – specifically, the conditions of Fordism and that the Left was unable to surpass a certain level of political development – while on the other hand reminding Beck that a by all means critical discussion of 'actually existing socialism' had been taking place in the Federal Republic since the 1960s, pointing to the West German debate on Eurocommunism and the reception of Antonio Gramsci's thought as examples. Beck's thinking drew on these debates, initially developing them before altering or correcting them. He adopted the topos of the 'end of history' and deduced from this a 'loss of opposition',[20] only to develop the diametrically opposed notion that the '*society of individuals*' stood in opposition to the '*society of institutions*'[21] while at the same time 'subterraneously' transforming it several sentences later. Deppe refused to accept a monocausal explanation for the 'crisis of the Left' reduced to the failure of 'actually existing socialism', and emphasised the objective socialisation tendencies and general political developments which had also put oppositional politics on the defensive in other Western countries: the modernisation of capitalism, ruptures in the social structure, declining significance of the workers' parties, and more.[22]

Beck found this diagnosis to be too shallow, as it overlooked the qualitatively novel character of the 'reflexive modernity' now emerging. This was true of both left-wing theory as well as 'functionalism' and 'modernisation theories' in the social sciences. In both cases it was a matter of theoretical patterns of meaning from a 'halved modernity',[23] blind to new tendencies of indi-

---

19   Beck and Deppe 1991, p. 404.
20   Beck and Deppe 1991, p. 406.
21   Ibid.
22   Ibid.
23   Beck and Deppe 1991, p. 408.

vidualisation and subjectification. Deppe counterposed this with the unchanged structural dependency of processes of social individualisation and
differentiation on capitalist relations of production and property which could
not be understood without referring to Marxist theory, as proven by things
such as the divide between modernisation's 'winners' and 'losers'.[24] However,
the problem posed by this divide was not limited to Germany alone but rather
continued on in processes of the transnationalisation of capital. Beck's approach, by contrast, was far too focused on Western capitalism's 'internal structures'.

Further along in the conversation, Beck laid out the conditions of the 'risk
society' under which individuals' possibilities to act were enormously changed.
By this he primarily meant 'insecurity', changes to the 'networks of the institutions of power', and the emergence of 'new political arenas'.[25] Society's 'old
structure of opposition' characterised by the dominance of the social question was being replaced by the 'conflict of two modernities', namely of *self-
insecurity vs. perfecting*.[26] Deppe opposed to this another contradiction scen-
ario, comprised of four prognosed 'fields': firstly, processes of social division;
secondly, the critique of the dominant capitalist 'model of growth and civilisa-
tion'; thirdly, a politics of both internal and external violence; and fourthly, the
role of 'great power Germany' in the context of transnational relations. If the
question of social justice had been dominant in the 1970s and that of 'flexibil-
isation and individualisation' in the 1980s, then primary attention in the 1990s
would shift to problems of 'transnationalisation'.[27]

Towards the end of the conversation Beck attempted to develop a perspective of 'intermediate politics', building on the assessment he shared with Deppe
that the 'new social movements' had lost their momentum.[28] He conceived
this politics as a process initiated and guided by 'new norms' in which institutions would be prompted to develop a capacity to learn. This must primarily
be achieved through 'establishing *accountability*' across different institutional
levels.[29] In this 'intermediate politics' unfolding beneath 'big politics' the path
must lead to an 'ecological democratisation', as ecology and democracy were
linked by an 'elective affinity'.[30] Beck's concept of 'intermediate politics' had

---

24   Beck and Deppe 1991, p. 410.
25   Beck and Deppe 1991, p. 411 ff.
26   Beck and Deppe 1991, p. 415 f.
27   Beck and Deppe 1991, p. 418.
28   Beck and Deppe 1991, p. 420 ff.
29   Beck and Deppe 1991, p. 421.
30   Beck and Deppe 1991, p. 424.

no place for problems of economic interests, extreme inequality in access to resources, and the growing power of production and markets with its inevitable consequences for working and living conditions of large groups of people, as Deppe repeatedly emphasised.

The conversation between Beck and Deppe was not only a confrontation between two different political approaches but also between two different ways of thinking about social science: although both exhibited a tendency towards 'grand theories', they backed them up with opposing arguments. While Beck sought to explain social conflict and rupture through a specific problem of condition, namely that of risk and insecurity, Deppe continued to adhere to the foundations of a classical Marxist socialisation paradigm. Following one of the moderator's formulations, one could say that Beck represented a concept of a 'grand theory' with micro-political consequences ('subpolitics', 'intermediate politics'), while Deppe also built upon a 'grand theory' – Marxism – but developed his political arguments on a macro-level. Although Beck's deliberations sometimes lacked internal stringency or got lost in stimulating phenomenological insinuations, he not only managed to identify new problems which had been largely overlooked but also grasped them empirically and provided vivid descriptions. That said, a certain distance to the concrete-empirical that one could almost describe as a general characteristic of the Marburg School's epistemological orientation was reflected in Deppe's arguments, who nevertheless appeared better than his conversation partner when it came to an analytically consistent explanation of socio-economic processes and political balances of power.

Both agreed that ecology had become a field of social contradiction and politics of the first order with global implications. That this agreement was backed up with different arguments lay in the nature of their opposing social-scientific axioms. The conversation took place in an atmosphere of collegial respect and a complete abstention from the ideological clichés and accusations that dominated the Left's discursive rituals in the 1960s and 1970s. Moreover, Frank Deppe's contribution disproved the common accusation that the protagonists of the Marburg School were in principle neither willing nor capable of engaging in a scholarly conflict of opinion or face their critics.

Nevertheless, it certainly would have contributed to the academic and political influence of the Marburg Marxists had they done more to seek out and more intensively pursue cooperation, exchange, and controversial debate with their academic competitors – although their opponents did little to facilitate such an exchange either. Hans Jürgen Krysmanski, an early student of Schelsky, and the social scientists around him at the University of Münster are exemplary of other Marxist social scientists in the Federal Republic who pursued a different path, insulating themselves less from 'bourgeois' discourse than Marburg and putting forward their views within the scientific community, including the German Sociological Association.[31]

---

31   See, for example, H.J. Krysmanski and Peter Marwedel's edited volume *Die Krise in der Soziologie* (Krysmanski and Marwedel 1975), a critical appraisal of the 17th congress of the German Sociological Association held in Kassel in 1974. Alongside other Münster scholars, the volume featured contributions from Karl Hermann Tjaden, Urs Jaeggi, Sebastian Herkommer, and Hanns Wienold. The Marburg School's Rainer Rilling participated in the activities of Krysmanski's Münster circle within the German Sociological Association several times.

CHAPTER 7

Scholarly Focuses since the 1990s

1 Research Activity and a New Conflict

Reinhard Kühnl continued his research on fascism and neo-fascism[1] and spent many years as an editor of the *Blätter für deutsche und internationale Politik*. In academic politics he participated in the Bund demokratischer Wissenschaftler-innen und Wissenschaftler, making a significant contribution to its profile and serving on its executive board until his retirement in 2001. Frank Deppe, Georg Fülberth, and the sociologist Rainer Rilling published an edited volume in 1996 titled *Antifaschismus* commemorating Kühnl's 60th birthday, featuring contributions from numerous well-known left-wing academics including Georg Bollenbeck, Christoph Butterwege, Wolfgang Fritz Haug, Jutta Held, Kurt Goss-weiler, Karl Heinz Roth, Gerhard Schäfer, Gerhard Stuby, and Johannes Weyer.[2]

Dieter Boris concentrated on Latin America research, where he had organised several working groups around certain topics since the 1970s. The Arbeitskreis Zentralamerika that existed in the 1980s produced the highly successful edited volume *Zentralamerika*.[3] Boris led an examinations colloquium for over fifteen years and participated in a nationwide working group on 'development theory', in which Kay Tjaden, Margarete Tjaden Steinhauer, Peter Imbusch, and others also worked. One high point of his academic career was the Alexander and Wilhelm Humboldt guest professorship at the Universidad Nacional Autónoma de México and the Colegio de Mexico, an elite academic institution in Mexico City.

He often gave lectures at academic conferences such as the annual meeting of the Arbeitsgemeinschaft deutsche Lateinamerikaforschung. His work was reviewed and respected in the scientific community despite its decidedly Marxist orientation, as evidenced by an edited volume representing the 'state of the art' in research on social movements and political protest in Latin American history published in 2009.[4] His article 'Aktuelle Theorien der Soziologie' in Dirk Kaesler's edited volumes on sociological classics represented an instructive

---

1 See, for example, Kühnl 1988 and Kühnl 1990.
2 Deppe, Fülberth and Rilling 1996.
3 Boris and Rausch 1984. The book was ultimately printed three times.
4 See Mittag and Ismar 2009. This volume also contains a general overview by Dieter Boris, see Boris 2009.

contribution on Immanuel Wallerstein's sometimes difficult theory and 'world-systems analysis'.[5] As a long-serving academic trustee of the Rosa-Luxemburg-Stiftung, Boris also sat on the foundation's central selection committee and, along with Frank Deppe, the academic advisory board of the social movement organisation Attac and the editorial advisory board of the journal Z. Although he was not as politically active outside of the university as other Marburg School protagonists, he worked tenaciously in the spirit of this school until his retirement (and well after).

Controversy would again attract attention beyond the confines of Marburg in 2006 when the *Fachbereich* 03, which had long ceased to be dominated by leftists and was now led by the philosophy professor Peter Janich, had the idea quite against the Marburg School tradition to confer an honorary doctorate to former Chancellor Helmut Schmidt, the political embodiment of much of what Abendroth, Hofmann, Maus and their students had opposed.

On 14 April 2006, only several weeks before what would have been Abendroth's 100th birthday, Deppe addressed a lengthy letter to the doctoral board and the faculty council of *Fachbereich* 03 calling on these bodies to vote against Janich's proposal.[6] Deppe noted several weighty reasons to call for a 'no' vote. Firstly, the former chancellor's contributions to philosophy were practically undetectable. Jürgen Habermas's letter of evaluation, which said of Schmidt that 'something of a philosopher ... can be seen in the pragmatist',[7] failed to provide any evidence of the kinds of extraordinary philosophical contributions demanded by doctorate regulations. Schmidt's role in the so-called NATO Double-Track Decision in 1979 could not be reconciled with Schmidt's unity of 'ethics and politics' attested in the evaluation submitted by former State Minister of Culture Julian Nida-Rümelin. Secondly, the former chancellor's reputation as a 'major economist' was by no means uncontentious. Thirdly, Schmidt never seriously studied the 'critical rationalism' he occasionally invoked but merely deployed it as a polemical weapon against left-wing positions.

That Schmidt nevertheless received an honorary doctorate in Marburg despite student protests and opposing votes from the faculty vividly illustrated that this symbolic political act was intended to raze the last positions of the Red Bastion and definitively conclude the department's ideological cleansing, allowing it to present itself in academic competition as an attractive 'location' now freed of the stain of Marxism.

---

5   Boris 2005.
6   See the complete transcript of Deppe's letter in Freier Zusammenschluss von StudentInnen-schaften 2006.
7   Quoted from Deppe's letter in ibid.

2   Social Movements in Latin America (Dieter Boris)

A number of publications from the Marburg School's wide-ranging scholarly production in the 1990s demonstrate in exemplary fashion the direction in which its protagonists' thinking developed, where lines of continuity to previous phases became apparent, and where new aspects emerged.

Proceeding from the Western fixation on folkloric or catastrophic scenarios when it comes to Latin America, Dieter Boris's 1998 *Soziale Bewegungen in Lateinamerika*[8] took a bottom-up approach by focusing on the structures, action forms, symbolic self-interpretations, and social aims of social forces and political actors that cannot be seen or heard on the surface of social events as imagined by the media, but rather where they live, work, suffer, and seek to take their destiny into their own 'subaltern' hands. Boris's objects of study are thus the movements, initiatives, and associations which emerge outside of state institutions and do not delegate their concerns to representative organisations or authorities.

As Boris demonstrates, the specific situation of social movements in Latin America can be explained by among other things the fact that the continent continues to be ruled by still-existing traditionalist, semi-feudal, sharply hierarchised, authoritarian state structures to a large degree. According to Boris, coming to analytical grips with them and the movements opposing them requires a methodological approach that cannot be grounded in approaches inspired by rational choice theories, Jürgen Habermas, or Alain Touraine, for whom heteronomy caused by modernisation is central. Boris argues that the category of social classes and antagonistic class interests cannot be abandoned, even if – in superficial terms – concrete movements and struggles appear detached from class-structural determinants: 'In other words: not being reduceable to a "pure" class phenomenon by no means precludes being situated in class society and only being adequately determinable in its spaces to act and direction of development from there'.[9] That said, here it would have been useful to illuminate the *differentia specifica* in relation to social classes and the social movements which are no longer identical to them more closely, but he neglects to do so.

Dieter Boris not only critically addresses problems of methodological bias caused by theory imported from Europe or the US in this context, but also concepts of 'civil society' which although they may refer to Antonio Gramsci

8   Boris 1998.
9   Boris 1998, p. 18.

reduce his thinking to a class-neutral integration ideology. Instead, it is crucial to understand the chances and opportunities of social movements as 'elements of a "counter-hegemonic bloc" '[10] pursuing fundamental changes to the dominant social and political power relations.

One major insight of his study is that, on the one hand, the conception of social movements is kept quite broad, while on the other the individual analyses are consistently undertaken from the perspective of total social transformation. In doing so Boris avoids the one-sided preference for or absolutisation of certain movements, instead depicting a mosaic of social actors, cultural constructs, and forms of struggle and politics that, from different perspectives and in multiple ways, clearly elucidates the contours of social alternatives as well as the limits of micro-political self-sufficiency, ethnic-religious identities, and social inequalities.

Taking the example of 'indigenism', Boris shows how demands oriented towards cultural identity, ecological protection, recognition of autochtonous medical practices, etc. can be connected to demands for economic reforms (land redistribution) and political representation and participation. The transcending of local and regional limitations and isolation from the outside acquires a dynamising function in the political generalisation of new indigenous movements, as could be seen in the rapprochement between the traditionally hostile low- and highland Indians in Ecuador and Bolivia. A 'we feeling' emerging from this corresponded to 'new leadership personnel' no longer recruited from the group of 'traditional authority figures of the village community',[11] but increasingly from young educated urban Indians from outside who more or less articulated and politically represented the interests of the indigenous community as 'organic intellectuals' in the Gramscian sense. Boris explained why the Ecuadorian indigenous movement in particular developed such impressive strength while other actors like leftist parties and trade unions lost ground with causes that cast the nature of this movement in a new light: neither could the indigenous movements in Ecuador and other Latin American countries be conflated with an 'uprising of tradition' against modernisation, nor were their impacts restricted to the demands of their own ethnicity, for in the meantime 'parts of the non-indigenous, urban middle classes' had come to see the indigenous activities as a specific expression of a 'future Ecuadorian civil society'.[12] Boris dedicated two chapters of his book to the women's movement. One case concerns the connection between human rights and women's movements

10   Boris 1998, p. 37.
11   Boris 1998, p. 69.
12   Boris 1998, p. 80.

exemplified by the Argentinian Mothers of the Plaza de Mayo,[13] while the other discusses the Chilean women's movement, which did not experience growth during the formal 'democratic institutionalisation' after General Pinochet's dictatorship but was in fact even depoliticised to some degree.[14] That said, the analysis omits the aspect of *machismo*, which is not limited to private life but rather takes on structural significance in the cementation of male dominance across Latin American society.

Along with the indigenous and women's movements, Boris also studied movements such as those of the farmers and landless peasants, workers' trade unions, human rights groups, religious and social initiatives, and environmentalist groups. Unlike in his Argentina book and *Arbeiterbewegung in Lateinamerika* (Workers' Movement in Latin America),[15] the working class and the workers' movement no longer function as the central point of reference but rather are depicted as an equal collective actor among many, albeit one with unchanged significance.

By neither omitting nor reifying heterogenous aspects, Boris manages to deliver an overview of his object of study as concrete as it is differentiated, avoiding idealisations and mystifications. This constitutes a significant challenge for the kind of Marxist scholarly approach he stands for, insofar as one intends to avoid seeking refuge in either abstract political-economic categories or class reductionism. For this reason, the study's value lies not least in the insight – which can also be applied to Europe – that social critique can only be conducted if one approaches the resistances, disparities, and apparent paradoxes of the concrete with a spirit of intellectual openness.

3   Capitalism and *Kapitalistik* (Georg Fülberth)

Georg Fülberth undertook an original attempt to leave behind the entrenched habits of the Marxist analysis of capitalism in 2005 with his book *G Strich – Kleine Geschichte des Kapitalismus*.[16] The author begins his study by proposing the development of a new field of research and the introduction of a new discipline devoted primarily to studying capitalism but not identical with polit-

---

13   Boris 1998, pp. 103–21.
14   Boris 1998, p. 184.
15   Boris 1990.
16   Fülberth 2005. The expression *G Strich* refers to the symbol M' in the first volume of Marx's *Capital*. Here, M' signifies the expansion of invested money capital following the purchase of a commodity. The book appeared in a fifth, revised edition in 2014.

ical economy, instead fulfilling a kind of cross-section function with regard to other individual disciplines. He calls this new field 'Kapitalistik'. It relates to other disciplines such as mathematics and the natural sciences in line with the scholarly approach hitherto employed by philosophy. The central object of inquiry in *Kapitalistik* is 'the capitalist preconditions and consequences of human activity and thinking in the modern era' and the present.[17] *Kapitalistik* is tasked with studying the significance of capitalism's structural conditions for both the various spheres of society as well as its reflection in the various academic disciplines. As far as the latter is concerned, *Kapitalistik* could on the one hand contribute productively to a differentiation of social-scientific knowledge, while on the other also work against the loss of society as a unified social structure and the discipline's collapse into countless 'hyphenated' sociologies often derided by the field.

Proceeding from a definition of capitalism and the understanding thereof in the classics of social-scientific thought, Fülberth first approaches the problem of economic profit in capitalism. In doing so he claims to discover mistakes in Marx's own work concerning the transformation of values into prices. He also comes to the conclusion that profit cannot be deduced exclusively from surplus value generated in production, but possibly can appear in mixed forms and encompass sources such as profits from trade, entrepreneurial profits derived from productivity rises and innovation (Joseph Schumpeter), or monopoly profits.[18] For an author like Georg Fülberth who is sometimes accused of being dogmatic and far-left, these constitute remarkably unorthodox reflections and conclusions which question the authority of even Marx himself.

In order to sketch out the history of capitalism in its main outlines, he refers to the following criteria which any historical study of capitalism and societies permeated by it must take into account: the material and technical conditions of material reproduction, property and social structures, gender and generational relations, and ultimately the spatial, political-institutionally mediated organisation of society and its counter-movements.[19] Pointing towards the execution of a possible research programme for *Kapitalistik*, Fülberth's historical overview emphasises the differentiations and 'long waves' of capitalist development, the origins and initial elements of which he dates back to the pre-1200 period. He is unbiased enough to also incorporate ideas and findings of non-Marxist scholars when he considers them plausible.

---

17   Fülberth 2005, p. 7.
18   Fülberth 2005, p. 78 ff.
19   Fülberth 2005, p. 82 f.

Unconcerned that objective differentiations and the incorporation of non-Marxist authors could disturb notions of a closed system of Marxist categories, he repeatedly delves into processes and events that contradict a schematic depiction of capitalism's history and the model of a deterministic sequence of social formations. He refers to contributions by Max Weber, Norbert Elias, and Michel Foucault in order to more precisely grasp aspects of the transition from feudalism to capitalism, for which Marxism alone does not provide sufficient means to comprehend.[20]

In the concluding chapter on the 'end of capitalism?',[21] Fülberth himself neglects to give a concrete answer. Instead he chooses to situate this question in light of previous Marxist prognoses. Distinguishing between two conceptions of the end of capitalism, namely perspectives of transformation and collapse, he classifies the theories of Karl Marx, Rudolf Hilfderding, and Vladimir Lenin in the former and Rosa Luxemburg, Nikolai Bukharin, and Henryk Grossmann in the latter. Neither of them, however, have been proven correct by history. Newer scenarios such as that of Robert Kurz[22] were for their part not sufficiently grounded, and could only describe the preconditions for an end to capitalism but not reliably prognosticate which type of society would come after it. When Fülberth laconically states that 'we do not know how long capitalism will still exist',[23] this should by no means be understood as a recommendation for scholarly and political passivity. Rather, the already existing means of society's destruction must, according to Fülberth, be restricted as much as possible while existing alternative possibilities must be utilised as much as possible in the present. We will then see how long such a politics can be conducted before, as Fülberth says in the words of Marx, the material conditions for a society with 'new, higher relations of production' come to maturity 'in the womb of the old society'.[24]

4 Political Thought from the Late Nineteenth to the Early Twenty-First Century (Frank Deppe)

Frank Deppe undertook one last major individual project in the last decade of his academic career: a comprehensive study of the political thought of the

---

20   Fülberth 2005, p. 119 f.
21   Fülberth 2005, p. 293 f.
22   See Kurz 1999.
23   Fülberth 2005, p. 300.
24   Ibid.

twentieth and early twenty-first century. He published the first book of this four-volume, nearly 2,000-page work in 1999.[25] The series is devoted to critically reconstructing and developing an understanding of the political thought that intervenes in the real movements, conflicts, and struggles through all contradictions, ruptures, and historical catastrophes. The inspiration for this massive, imposing project arose out of initial reflections on the problems raised by the end of the global systems rivalry and capitalism's nearly total, worldwide triumph since the 1990s.

In one of the introductory chapters to the first volume, Deppe defines political thought as thought which is 'normative, value-oriented and in this sense related to political praxis',[26] ranging from classical political notions of the conception of 'civil society' all the way to theories of direction through the 'political system'. The first volume depicts a combination of specific intellectual currents (largely from the late nineteenth century to the end of World War I) and extensive individual studies of significant figures and their contributions to their respective political-social development and situation. The personalities chosen for this task are Max Weber, Vilfredo Pareto, Vladimir Lenin, and Sun Yat-sen although other philosophers, scientists, and writers are also included. This is preceded by an overview of transformations from traditional, pre-capitalist society to a 'mass society' characterised by the opposition between bourgeoisie and proletariat. Oriented towards the interconnections between socio-economic, political, cultural, and ideological processes and structures as developed in Marxist theory, Deppe engages with the thinking of the aforementioned figures by consistently asking whether and to what extent they pushed forward, blocked, or legitimised the suppression and deformation of tendencies of civilisational historical progress. One of the strengths of all four volumes of *Politisches Denken* is its refusal to employ schematic, black-and-white depictions, instead remaining sensitive to contradictions and ambivalences. The first volume concludes with the summation that the crisis of liberalism resulting from the convulsions brought forth by imperialism and World War I simultaneously led to a reframing of the concept of the political, which split off primarily into an authoritarian, dictatorial variant of elite rule on the one hand, and a socialist and revolutionary variant on the other. By its very nature, such an immensely complex object of investigation will not be without a degree of imprecision. Problems of selection with view to the figures discussed and the absence of others are also practically inevitable.

25   Deppe 1999.
26   Deppe 1999, p. 12.

The second volume published in 2003 addresses the period between the two World Wars.[27] It is similarly constructed to the first volume and foregrounds the following representatives of political thought: Carl Schmitt, Antonio Gramsci, Rudolf Hilferding, the representatives of the early Frankfurt School, John Maynard Keynes, Walter Lippmann, Mahatma Gandhi, and Mao Zedong. The volume includes several brilliant chapters such as the one on Gramsci, which takes into account all important aspects of this Marxist theoretician and political leader and mediates them coherently. Yet as with the first volume, disagreements can be raised concerning the author's selection of thinkers. One could question, for example, whether Horkheimer and Adorno were really as relevant prior to World War II as Deppe seems to think. This also touches on a further methodological problem that the author of this volume once described as follows:

> A systematic justification for the selection of representatives of political thought Frank Deppe deals with is lacking, along with a depiction of the relationships *between* the highly heterogenous discourses, historical-political positions, and contributions of the figures chosen by him. The first part of the studies containing an overview of the political, intellectual, and economic development of the (pre- and) inter-war period does not compensate for the methodological deficit I named; for it does not replace the systematic depiction of coordinates and criteria of the overall context in which the individual chapters stand.[28]

The third and most comprehensive volume on 'Political Thought in the Cold War' consists of two parts (2006, 2008) and follows a different methodological structure, at least in the first book.[29] It is primarily concerned with the depiction of real world-political processes of rupture and erosion, in which the functions and effects of political thought (such as of left-Keynesianism during capitalism's 'golden age' and simultaneous 'warfare capitalism')[30] are embedded, as it were. The structure of part two relates back to the first two volumes with its focus on 'system confrontation, Golden Age, and anti-imperialist liberation movements', that is to say the thinking of outstanding figures is contex-

---

27   Deppe 2003b.
28   See the review by Lothar Peter, Peter 2003, p. 31. Werner Goldschmidt expressed somewhat similar criticisms of Deppe's choice of political intellectuals (see Deppe and Goldschmidt 2011).
29   Deppe 2006b; Deppe 2008.
30   See Deppe 2006b, pp. 114–46.

tualised by an introductory chapter laying out the tension-fraught relations in which political thought has evolved since the 1950s, characterised by systems rivalry, Fordism, and modern liberalism and socialism. Deppe's attention is devoted primarily to Hannah Arendt, Wolfgang Abendroth, John Kenneth Galbraith, Jean-Paul Sartre, and Simone de Beauvoir. This time he attempts to explain why he chose these specific figures in the beginning of the second book, but this explanation is so brief that one cannot help but get the impression of a degree of arbitrariness. Nevertheless, the book's nearly 100-page chapter on Sartre and de Beauvoir constitutes a well-grounded analysis of these two 'engaged intellectuals' *par excellence*, both of whom greatly influenced the intellectual and political life of their era in terms of both the range as well as diversity of their thinking.[31] The chapter is a methodologically 'thick' intellectual-sociological 'description' that weaves biographical aspects, personal relationships, political constellations, literary production, theoretical-philosophical reflections, intellectual battles, and effective history (*Wirkungsgeschichte*) into an excellent study. Perhaps the only point that goes underemphasised is the fact that Simone de Beauvoir's impact on the women's movement went well beyond Sartre's ultimately very temporary contributions and continues to play a role in feminist discourses even today.[32]

The fourth and last volume published in 2010 poses the question of whether the world will collapse into barbarism or a new world order moving towards socialism can emerge right in its subtitle.[33] As in part one of the third volume, the contribution of political thought and its protagonists is integrated into an analysis of social and political tendencies, balances of forces, and contradictions, albeit without explaining the reasoning behind this methodological shift. In substantive terms, the connections between the emergence of a new global constellation (as a result of the 'erosion of Pax Americana', the rise of new state and economic actors like China and India, etc.), the crisis of modernity, and new approaches to emancipatory or socialist ideas, theories, and models (such as those of Immanuel Wallerstein, Heinz Dieterich, Michael Hardt and Antonio Negri, Alain Badiou, and Slavoj Žižek) are placed at the centre of the investigation. Deppe writes that opportunities for new movements also emerge along the 'new axes of contradiction', but they usually no longer emerge from the experience of wage-labour and capital antagonism but rather from experiences of the crisis in the human-nature relation, the effects of financial market

---

31   See Deppe 2008, pp. 196–284.
32   On this see the conference volume published by the Rosa-Luxemburg-Stiftung marking Simone de Beauvoir's 100th birthday (Böhlke 2009).
33   Deppe 2010.

capitalism, social precarity, and impoverishment. Nevertheless, the contradiction between wage-labour and capital remains the structural cause of all social crises and catastrophes. The book by no means ends on an optimistic note. Deppe does not discount the possibility that should conflicts, struggles, and the influence of socialist alternatives grow, the dominant regime of the capitalist system would have no qualms resorting to authoritarian and repressive solutions.[34]

Politisches Denken is an interdisciplinary work remarkable for its comprehensive thematic horizon, the complexity of the economic, historical, political, social, and intellectual aspects and levels studied, as well as its Marxist analyses and interpretations applied through all differentiations. It thereby distinguishes itself fundamentally and refreshingly from the countless self-referential and semantically pretentious social-scientific contributions of today, which eschew clear critique and preserve the status quo.

---

34   Deppe 2010, p. 410 f.

CHAPTER 8

Conclusion

Although the retirement of its last representatives brought the Marburg School to an institutional end in the early 2000s, its activity by no means ceased. Many of the students who studied, wrote their dissertations under, and worked with its representatives went on to positions at other universities, took on trade-union functions, worked in the media, the education system, or in political organisations where they continued to convey the thinking of the Marburg School and, in the case of figures like Klaus Dörre, further develop it on their own. Moreover, Frank Deppe, Georg Fülberth, and Dieter Boris themselves remained intellectually and politically active in various spheres. They continue to represent a current of critical social thought in today's Federal Republic seeking to establish a continuity between the history of the revolutionary socialist workers' movement and the problems of modern capitalism.

As this volume sought to demonstrate, the still pernicious myth that the Marburg School disqualified itself academically through intellectual orthodoxy and ideological instrumentalism is disproven by its actual contributions. In qualitative terms, its later work is by all means comparable to that of previous periods. That Abendroth and Hofmann could develop such exceptional influence can also be explained by the particular circumstances defining their lives, intellectual engagement, and scholarly activity. The years 1965–72 doubtlessly constituted a highpoint in which the social-political protest and reform movements, the 'renaissance' of Marxism in academic discourse, and the synergetic effects of the Marburg School's productivity facilitated by an 'epistemic community' cumulated. The social and intellectual conditions for the public acceptance of Marxist theory changed in the period after Abendroth, Hofmann, and Maus, in which its meaning was at times even fundamentally questioned. The protagonists of the Marburg School were partially pushed onto the defensive when confronted with the emerging hegemony of neoliberal thought, its homologous individualist economic and social science paradigms, and post-modern 'deconstructions' – not to mention the economistic standards of academic production and its symbolic rituals of evaluation. That they remained unfazed and continued to pursue their line of fundamental critique of capitalism and society can be interpreted as a kind of left 'conservatism', if you will, but also in quite opposite fashion as a form of single-mindedness incorruptible by the zeitgeist and fleeting intellectual trends. It meant defending that which one had understood to be true even when it meant swimming against the current and receiving neither material nor symbolic gratification.[1] In light of the massive institutional and intellectual pressure to conform exercised in the academic field today, this alone constitutes an attitude and contribution of the Marburg School deserving recognition and respect.

Social developments in the meantime have confirmed many of the Marburg School's political and intellectual positions, particularly since the 2008 financial crisis. The critique of capitalism is 'back' in German social science,[2] but reconciliation between various reformist and anti-capitalist movements and actors – one of the Marburg School's traditional goals – and with it a step towards the formation of a 'mosaic left'[3] (to use the metaphor of one of Deppe's well-known former students) remains difficult. That the Marburg intellectuals successfully diagnosed the last, most intense capitalist crisis for some time which is yet to be solved does not mean, however, that their scholarly work was shorn of deficits and blind spots.

The protagonists of the Marburg School have produced no fundamental theoretical or methodological innovations in the social sciences since the 1980s, and aside from isolated interventions (such as Georg Fülberth's) exhibited remarkable indifference to an epistemological or methodological reflection of their own activity. They only sporadically addressed gender relations as a social-structural category and neglected to engage in original empirical social research entirely, at least in the case of those who stayed in Marburg. Their research is of an exclusively theoretical and empirically secondary-analytical nature. At the very least, they engaged in no empirical social research of their own.

While the original Triumvirate attempted to stake out a position within the 'bourgeois' scientific community as much as they could despite their minority status, their successors adopted a more reserved and even intransigent stance. This occurred both because they obviously considered presence in this sphere to be irrelevant and because they were kept at a distance by the 'guild' itself, as a personal note from Dieter Boris suggests.[4] To what extent this had

---

1   It is thus all the more remarkable that Deppe, Fülberth, and Boris have evidently engaged in no concrete collaborations since the 1990s.
2   See on this, for example, the widely reviewed and discussed Dörre, Lessenich and Rosa 2015. The author of this volume also took part in the ensuing debate (see Peter 2011).
3   Urban 2009.
4   Note from Dieter Boris to the author, 2 March 2013. Although Frank Deppe was a member of the Deutsche Vereinigung für Politische Wissenschaft (DVPW) and was brought into the German Research Foundation's research group on European integration by the chairperson of the DVPW, he was otherwise not actively involved in the organisation (personal note from Frank Deppe to the author, 6 March 2013).

a negative impact on their own scholarly ambition and creativity is difficult to say in retrospect. On the other hand, they consistently strove to implement Abendroth, Hofmann, and Maus's postulate of connecting scientific analysis and political praxis with unflagging dedication. This distinguishes the Marburg School, its later phase included, from other social-scientific schools in Germany. Alongside the school's noteworthy scholarly contributions, it also constitutes its discourse-historical and political uniqueness and significance.[5]

In closing, it is worth mentioning the Marburg School's position in the field of international socialist movements and the discourses directly and indirectly reflecting them. Multiple overlaps and concrete contacts between the Marburg School and socialist debates, analyses, and positions in the neighbouring countries of Italy and Great Britain can be identified. Like other Western European left-socialist currents, political organisations, intellectual groups, and publications, the 'Marburgers' saw themselves as protagonists of an alliance between intellectuals and the workers' movement. They were primarily interested in connecting system-immanent and system-transcending 'anti-capitalist structural reforms', a confluence of extra-parliamentary and parliamentary activity, and an expansion of democratic control 'from below' in both the workplace as well as local, regional, and national levels. Similar demands can be found in the concepts of French 'workers' control', Italian factory councils, British 'industrial democracy', or the West German slogan of 'co-determination as marching orders'.

The Marburg School's situation diverged from that of other left-socialist forces due to the existence of two German states, pushing it to adopt a unique, conditional stance towards the state-socialist system. On the one hand the Marburgers defended the essential achievements in East Germany such as the abolition of the commodity character of labour power and social planning of the economy, while on the other hand believed the grave problems and contradictions emerging there would be solvable within the framework of the

---

5   Agreement with the Marburg School on many points can still be found in the University of Marburg's *Fachbereich* 03 today in the views of Ingrid Kurz-Scherf, born in 1949 and professor of political science in Marburg with a concentration in 'politics and gender' from 2001–15; Johannes M. Becker, born 1952, private lecturer in political science and managing director of the Zentrum für Konfliktforschung at the University of Marburg until 2017; as well as John Kannankulam, born in 1972 and a junior professor of political science (political economy and European integration) at the University of Marburg's Institute for Political Science from 2009–15, and professor of European integration and political economy since 2015. Kannankulam, whose scholarly thinking shares several commonalities with the Marburg School, came to Marburg from the milieu of the later Frankfurt School around Joachim Hirsch.

existing socialist order at least over the long term. This led to a phalanx of slander, ostracisation, and capriciousness towards the Marburg School and its supporters in a West German public sphere rattled by anti-Communist manipulation. This 'front line' naturally fell away with the annexation of the GDR into the capitalist West German Federal Republic, an event that would have ambivalent consequences for the Marburg Marxists. Tendencies towards their public marginalisation initially grew stronger, but soon points of commonality and connection with European and non-European representatives of Marxist and socialist thought began to expand and continue to this day. Frank Deppe regularly conducts exchanges with Marxist theorists like Bob Jessop and Leo Panitch who work with state-theoretical points of reference similar to his own (such as Gramsci's theory of state and hegemony, regulation theory). For Dieter Boris, the international dimension of his work is a product of the nature of his primary research interest, Latin America, and includes collaborations with colleagues and students in Argentina and Mexico. Georg Fülberth also maintains comparable international working relationships.

Students of the generation following the Abendroth, Hofmann, Maus Triumvirate stand out with their own transnational collaborations. This is most true of Klaus Dörre, who addressed questions of a contemporary class analysis informed by precarity and exclusion at conferences and in publications with Robert Castel, author of the internationally renowned *Les metamorphoses de la question sociale*, and is also the main reason why Michael Buroway's concept of 'public sociology' has been introduced to the broader academic public in Germany. In this sense ideas emanating from the Marburg School continue to interact with research and discussions in international left discourse even today.

What remains of the Marburg School for left discourse in the twenty-first century? What of that which characterises it will remain valid in the future? Many left-wing authors' contributions whether in Germany or internationally suffer from the deficit of subjecting capitalism to a fundamental critique, but having no answer to the question of how capitalism could concretely be changed and what forces and actors could be practically entrusted to enact such a change. Perhaps the most important aspect of the Marburg School is that it understood intervening into the seemingly uninfluenceable course of history as the central task of its unity of the concrete analysis of capitalism, analysis of the given balance of social forces and the search for collective subjects. The Marburg School protagonists' self-understanding of practically engaging their scholarly knowledge and political experiences in the struggles and movements of their time remains irrevocably tied to this reflexive and operative unity of Marxist analysis.

In that sense, the fundamental characteristics of the Marburg School will retain their actuality wherever in the world socialist discourses seek to engage capitalism in struggle and ultimately overcome it.

Bibliography

Abendroth, Wolfgang 1964, *Aufstieg und Krise der deutschen Sozialdemokratie*, Frankfurt am Main: Stimme-Verlag.

Abendroth, Wolfgang 1968a [1965], *Sozialgeschichte der europäischen Arbeiterbewegung*, 4th edition, Frankfurt am Main: Suhrkamp.

Abendroth, Wolfgang 1968b, 'Demokratisch-liberale oder revolutionär-sozialistische Kritik?', *Die Linke antwortet Habermas*, edited by Wolfgang Abendroth et al., pp. 131–42.

Abendroth, Wolfgang 1972a [1968], *Antagonistische Gesellschaft und politische Demokratie. Aufsätze zur politischen Soziologie*, Neuwied and Berlin: Luchterhand.

Abendroth, Wolfgang 1972b, 'Bilanz der sozialistischen Idee in der Bundesrepublik Deutschland', *Antagonistische Gesellschaft und politische Demokratie*, pp. 429–62.

Abendroth, Wolfgang 1972c, 'Die Alternativen der Planung: Planung zur Erhaltung des Spätkapitalismus oder in Richtung auf eine klassenlose Gesellschaft? Einige marxistische Bemerkungen zum Problem der Planung', *Antagonistische Gesellschaft und politische Demokratie*, pp. 463–93.

Abendroth, Wolfgang 1972d, 'Die soziale Struktur der Bundesrepublik und ihre politischen Entwicklungstendenzen', *Antagonistische Gesellschaft und politische Demokratie*, pp. 17–47.

Abendroth, Wolfgang 1972e, 'Ist der Marxismus "überholt"?', *Antagonistische Gesellschaft und politische Demokratie*, pp. 347–63.

Abendroth, Wolfgang 1972f, 'Zum Begriff des demokratischen und sozialen Rechtsstaates im Grundgesetz der Bundesrepublik Deutschland', *Antagonistische Gesellschaft und politische Demokratie*, pp. 109–38.

Abendroth, Wolfgang 1972g, 'Zur Einführung: Politische Wissenschaft als politische Soziologie', *Antagonistische Gesellschaft und politische Demokratie*, pp. 9–13.

Abendroth, Wolfgang 1976, *Ein Leben in der Arbeiterbewegung*, edited by Barbara Dietrich and Joachim Perels, Frankfurt am Main: Suhrkamp.

Abendroth, Wolfgang 1977 [1958], *Arbeiterklasse, Staat, und Verfassung: Materialien zur Verfassungsgeschichte und Verfassungstheorie der Bundesrepublik*, Frankfurt am Main: EVA.

Abendroth, Wolfgang 1978, 'Dissidentenprozesse in den sozialistischen Staaten, Propaganda der "westlichen" Staaten und westdeutsche Linke', *Das Argument. Zeitschrift für Philosophie und Sozialwissenschaften* 20 (111), pp. 716–18.

Abendroth, Wolfgang 1979, statement printed in the *Frankfurter Rundschau*, 3 January, p. 14.

Abendroth, Wolfgang 1985, 'Thesen zum Problem des marxistischen Menschenbildes im wissenschaftlichen Zeitalter', *Die Aktualität der Arbeiterbewegung. Beiträge zu ihrer Theorie und Geschichte*, edited by Wolfgang Abendroth and Joachim Perels, Frankfurt am Main: Suhrkamp, pp. 201–24.

Abendroth, Wolfgang 2019 [1965], *A Short History of the European Working Class*, translated by Nicholas Jacobs and Brian Trench, London: Verso Books.

Abendroth, Wolfgang and Kurt Lenk (eds.) 1968, *Einführung in die politische Wissenschaft*, Bern: Francke.

Abendroth, Wolfgang and Oskar Negt (eds.) 1968, *Die Linke antwortet Habermas*, Frankfurt am Main: Europäische Verlagsanstalt.

Abendroth-Gruppe 2006, 'Gibt es eine Abendroth-Schule? Frank Deppe zur Emeritierung', *Das Argument. Zeitschrift für Philosophie und Sozialwissenschaften* 48 (266), pp. 355–63.

Adorno, Theodor W. 2000 [1984], 'Sociology and Empirical Research', *The Adorno Reader*, edited by Brian O'Connor, Oxford: Blackwell, pp. 174–92.

Adorno, Theodor W. 2003 [1968], 'Late Capitalism or Industrial Society? The Fundamental Question of the Present Structure of Society', *Can One Live After Auschwitz? A Philosophical Reader*, edited by Rolf Tiedemann, translated by Rodney Livingstone et al., pp. 111–25.

Adorno, Theodor W. 2004 [1966], *Negative Dialectics*, translated by E.B. Ashton, London: Routledge.

Albers, Detlev, Werner Goldschmidt and Paul Oehlke 1971, *Klassenkämpfe in Westeuropa. Frankreich, Italien, Großbritannien*, Reinbek bei Hamburg: Rowohlt.

Anderson, Perry 1989 [1976], *Considerations on Western Marxism*, London: Verso.

Balzer, Friedrich-Martin, Hans Manfred Bock and Uli Schöler (eds.) 2001, *Wolfgang Abendroth. Wissenschaftlicher Politiker. Bio-bibliographische Beiträge*, Opladen: Leske + Budrich.

Barrow, Clyde 1993, *Critical Theories of the State: Marxist, Neo-Marxist, Post-Marxist*, Madison, WI: University of Wisconsin Press.

Bauer, Otto, Herbert Marcuse, and Arthur Rosenberg et al. 1967, *Faschismus und Antikapitalismus. Theorien über die sozialen Ursprünge und die Funktion des Faschismus*, edited by Wolfgang Abendroth, introduction by Kurt Kliem, Jörg Kammler and Rüdiger Griepenburg, Frankfurt am Main: EVA.

Bebnowski, David 2018, 'Grundlagen der Neuen Linken: Franz L. Neumann und amerikanisch-deutsche Netzwerke in West-Berlin', *Arbeit – Bewegung – Geschichte: Zeitschrift für historische Studien* 2, pp. 23–38.

Beck, Ulrich and Frank Deppe 1991, 'Chancen einer Zwischenpolitik. Betrachtungen zum Strukturwandel der Opposition. Ein Gespräch zwischen Ulrich Beck und Frank Deppe', *Blätter für deutsche und internationale Politik* 36 (4), pp. 402–24.

Beck, Ulrich 1992 [1986], *Risk Society*, translated by Mark Ritter, London: Sage.

Bergmann, Joachim et al. (eds.) 1966, *Politik und Kritik. Arbeiten zur Sozialwissenschaft. Wolfgang Abendroth zum 60. Geburtstag*, Marburg (hectographed manuscript).

Bieling, Hans-Jürgen and Frank Deppe 1999, 'Neo-Gramscianismus in der Internationalen Politischen Ökonomie', *trend, online zeitung* 06, www.trend.infopartisan .net/trd0699/t020699.html

Bieling, Hans-Jürgen, Klaus Dörre and Jochen Steinhilber (eds.) 2001, *Flexibler Kapitalismus. Analyse, Kritik und politische Praxis*, Hamburg: VSA.

Boccara, Paul et al. 1971, *Le Capitalisme monopoliste d'État*, Vol. 1 & 2, Paris: Éditions Sociales.

Bock, Hans Manfred 1969, *Syndikalismus und Linkskommunismus 1918–1923. Zur Geschichte der Freien Arbeiter-Union Deutschlands (Syndikalisten), der Allgemeinen Arbeiter-Union Deutschlands und der Kommunistischen Arbeiter-Partei Deutschlands*, Meisenheim am Glan: Hain.

Bock, Hans Manfred 2001a, 'Akademische Innovation in der Ordinarien-Universität. Elemente einer Gruppenbiographie der Abendroth-Doktoranden', *Wolfgang Abendroth. Wissenschaftlicher Politiker. Bio-bibliographische Beiträge*, edited by Friedrich-Martin Balzer, Hans Manfred Bock and Uli Schöler, Opaden: Leske + Budrich, pp. 271–88.

Bock, Hans Manfred 2001b, 'Ein unangepaßter Marxist im Kalten Krieg. Zur Stellung Wolfgang Abendroths in der Intellektuellengeschichte der Bundesrepublik', ibid., pp. 216–67.

Bock, Hans Manfred 2007, '"Frankfurter Schule" und "Marburger Schule". Intellektuellengeschichtliche Anmerkungen zum Verhältnis von zwei epistemic communities', *Das Feld der Frankfurter Kultur- und Sozialwissenschaften*, edited by Richard Faber and Eva Maria Ziege, Würzburg: Königshausen & Neumann, pp. 211–49.

Böhlke, Effi (ed.) 2009, *Freiheit, Gleichheit, Geschwisterlichkeit. Beauvoir und die Befreiung der Frauen von männlicher Herrschaft*, Berlin: Dietz.

Bonfert, Bernd and Janis Ehling 2015, *Die Marburger Schule der kritischen Europaforschung*, Marburg: Fachbereich 03 der Philipps-Universität Marburg.

Boltanski, Luc and Ève Chiapello 2018 [1999], *The New Spirit of Capitalism*, translated by Gregory Elliott, London: Verso.

Boris, Dieter 1971, *Krise und Planung. Die politische Soziologie im Spätwerk Karl Mannheims*, Stuttgart: Metzler.

Boris, Dieter 1990, *Arbeiterbewegung in Lateinamerika*, Marburg: Verlag Arbeiterbewegung und Gesellschaftswissenschaft.

Boris, Dieter 1998, *Soziale Bewegungen in Lateinamerika*, Hamburg: VSA.

Boris, Dieter 1999, 'Zu Werner Hofmanns Verständnis von Wissenschaft (Thesen)', *Werner Hofmann. Gesellschaftslehre in praktischer Absicht*, edited by Herbert Claas et al., Marburg: BdWi-Verlag, pp. 51–7.

Boris, Dieter 2005, 'Immanuel Wallerstein', *Aktuelle Theorien der Soziologie. Von Shmuel N. Eisenstadt bis zur Postmoderne*, edited by Dirk Kaesler, Munich: C.H. Beck, pp. 168–95.

Boris, Dieter 2009, 'Soziale Bewegungen in Lateinamerika: Bilanz und Perspektiven', *¿'El pueblo unido'? Soziale Bewegungen und politischer Protest in der Geschichte Lateinamerikas*, edited by Jürgen Mittag and Georg Ismar, Münster: Westfälisches Dampfboot.

Boris, Dieter, Elisabeth Abendroth and Wolfgang Ehrhardt 1971, *Chile auf dem Weg zum Sozialismus*, Cologne: Pahl-Rugenstein.

Boris, Dieter and Peter Hiedl 1978, *Argentinien. Geschichte und politische Gegenwart*, Cologne: Pahl-Rugenstein.

Boris, Dieter and Renate Rausch (eds.) 1984, *Zentralamerika – Guatemala, Nicaragua, Honduras, Costa Rica, El Salvador*, Cologne: Pahl-Rugenstein.

Bourdieu, Pierre 2000 [1997], *Pascalian Meditations*, translated by Richard Nice, Stanford, CA: Stanford University Press.

Buckmiller, Michael (ed.) 2006–, *Wolfgang Abendroth, Gesammelte Schriften*, Vol. 1 (2006), Vol. 2 (2008), Vol. 3 (2014), Vol. 4 (2015), Hanover: Offizin.

Canfora, Luciano 2006, *Democracy in Europe. A History*, translated by Simon Jones, Oxford: Blackwell.

Casanova, Antoine, Claude Prévost and Joe Metzger (eds.) 1970, *Les intellectuels et les luttes de classes*, Paris: Éditions Sociales.

Claas, Herbert, Joachim Hofmann-Göttig, Ralf Käpernick and Jan Limbers (eds.) 1999, *Werner Hofmann. Gesellschaftslehre in praktischer Absicht*, Marburg: BdWi-Verlag.

Claas, Herbert 1999, 'Praktische Politik im Reich der Vorstellung. Werner Hofmanns Eingriffe in das politische Geschehen', *Werner Hofmann. Gesellschaftslehre in praktischer Absicht*, pp. 221–9.

Claessens, Dieter, Arno Klönne and Armin Tschoepe 1965, *Sozialkunde der Bundesrepublik Deutschland*, Düsseldorf: Diederichs.

Clarke, Simon (ed.) 1991, *The State Debate*, Houndmills, Basingstoke, Hampshire: Macmillan.

Comité Central du Parti Communiste Français 1970 [1968], 'Pour une démocratie avancée, pour une France socialiste', *Les intellectuels et les luttes de classes*, edited by Antoine Casanova et al., pp. 157–161.

Dahn, Daniela 2010, *Wehe dem Sieger! Ohne Osten kein Westen*, Reinbek bei Hamburg: Rowohlt.

Dahrendorf, Ralf 1952, *Der Begriff des Gerechten im Denken von Karl Marx*, Hanover: JHW Dietz.

Demirović, Alex 1999, *Der nonkonformistische Intellektuelle. Die Entwicklung der Kritischen Theorie zur Frankfurter Schule*, Frankfurt am Main: Suhrkamp.

Demirović, Alex 2006, 'Theorie, Praxis und Demokratie. Zum Verhältnis von Wolfgang Abendroth zur Kritischen Theorie', *'Antagonistische Gesellschaft und Politische Demokratie'. Zur Aktualität von Wolfgang Abendroth*, edited Hans-Jürgen Urban et al., pp. 27–46.

Deppe, Frank 1968, *Zum Verhältnis von politischer Theorie und politischer Praxis bei Louis Auguste Blanqui. Eine Studie zur Entwicklung des Begriffs der sozialen Revolution im 19. Jahrhundert*, Frankfurt am Main: EVA.

Deppe, Frank 1970, *Verschwörung, Aufstand und Revolution. Auguste Blanqui und das Problem der sozialen Revolution im 19. Jahrhundert*, Frankfurt am Main: EVA.

Deppe, Frank 1971, *Das Bewußtsein der Arbeiter. Studien zur politischen Soziologie des Arbeiterbewußtseins*, with an appendix by Helga Deppe-Wolfinger, Cologne: Pahl-Rugenstein.

Deppe, Frank (ed.) 1977, *2. Juni 1967 und die Studentenbewegung heute*, Dortmund: Weltkreis Verlag.

Deppe, Frank 1979, *Autonomie und Integration. Materialien zur Gewerkschaftsanalyse*, Marburg: Verlag Arbeiterbewegung und Gesellschaftswissenschaft.

Deppe, Frank 1981, *Einheit und Spaltung der Arbeiterklasse. Überlegungen zu einer politischen Geschichte der Arbeiterbewegung*, Marburg: Verlag Arbeiterbewegung und Gesellschaftswissenschaften.

Deppe, Frank 1984a, *Ende oder Zukunft der Arbeiterbewegung? Gewerkschaftspolitik nach der Wende. Eine kritische Bestandsaufnahme*, Cologne: Pahl-Rugenstein.

Deppe, Frank 1984b, 'Intellektuelle, "Arbeiterklassenstandpunkt" und "strukturelle Hegemonie". Einige Gegenargumente', *Marxismus – Ideologie – Politik. Krise des Marxismus oder Krise des "Arguments"?*, edited by Hans Heinz Holz et al., pp. 97–117.

Deppe, Frank 1987, *Niccolò Machiavelli. Zur Kritik der reinen Politik*, Cologne: Pahl-Rugenstein.

Deppe, Frank 1999, *Politisches Denken im 20. Jahrhundert. Die Anfänge*, Hamburg: VSA.

Deppe, Frank 2003a, 'Organisierter Kapitalismus und Wirtschaftsdemokratie – Rudolf Hilferding und die Sozialdemokratie zwischen den Kriegen', *Politisches Denken im 20. Jahrhundert. Band 2: Politisches Denken zwischen den Weltkriegen*, Hamburg: VSA, pp. 277–322.

Deppe, Frank 2003b, *Politisches Denken im 20. Jahrhundert. Band 2: Politisches Denken zwischen den Weltkriegen*, Hamburg: VSA.

Deppe, Frank 2006a, 'Aktualität des "organischen Intellektuellen" der Arbeiterbewegung', *Antagonistische Gesellschaften und politische Demokratie*, edited by Hans-Jürgen Urban et al., pp. 47–66.

Deppe, Frank 2006b, *Politisches Denken im Kalten Krieg, Band 3, Teil 1: Die Konfrontation der Systeme*, Hamburg: VSA.

Deppe, Frank 2008, *Politisches Denken im Kalten Krieg, Band 3, Teil 2: Systemkonfrontation, Golden Age, antiimperialistische Befreiungsbewegungen*, Hamburg: VSA.

Deppe, Frank 2010, *Politisches Denken im Übergang ins 21. Jahrhundert. Rückfall in die Barbarei oder Geburt einer neuen Weltordnung?*, Hamburg: VSA.

Deppe, Frank 2012a, *Gewerkschaften in der Großen Transformation. Von den 1970er Jahren bis heute. Eine Einführung*, Cologne: PapyRossa.

Deppe, Frank 2012b, 'Leben im "Zeitalter der Extreme" – Lisa Abendroth (27.2.1917–4.2.2012)', *Sozialismus* 39/3, pp. 50–3.

Deppe, Frank 2014 [1987], *Niccolò Machiavelli. Zur Kritik der reinen Politik*, Cologne: PapyRossa.

Deppe, Frank 2018, 'Marx in Hessen – unter besonderer Berücksichtigung der "Marburger Schule"', *Z. Zeitschrift Marxistische Erneuerung* 115, pp. 150–67.

Deppe, Frank et al. 1969, *Kritik der Mitbestimmung. Partnerschaft oder Klassenkampf?*, Frankfurt am Main: Suhrkamp.

Deppe, Frank, David Salomon and Ingar Solty 2001, *Imperialismus*, Cologne: PapyRossa.

Deppe, Frank, Georg Fülberth and Jürgen Harrer (eds.) 1978 [1977], *Geschichte der deutschen Gewerkschaftsbewegung*, 2nd edition, Cologne: Pahl-Rugenstein.

Deppe, Frank, Georg Fülberth and Jürgen Harrer 1980, 'Kritik und Antikritik. Zur aktuellen Diskussion über die Geschichte der deutschen Gewerkschaftsbewegung', *Blätter für deutsche und internationale Politik* 25, pp. 83–102.

Deppe, Frank, Georg Fülberth and Rainer Rilling (eds.) 1996, *Antifaschismus*, Heilbronn: Distel-Verlag.

Deppe, Frank, Hellmuth Lange and Lothar Peter (eds.) 1970, *Die neue Arbeiterklasse. Technische Intelligenz und Gewerkschaften im organisierten Kapitalismus*, Frankfurt am Main: EVA.

Deppe, Frank, Willi Gerns and Heinz Jung (eds.) 1980, *Marxismus und Arbeiterbewegung. Josef Schleifstein zum 65. Geburtstag*, Frankfurt am Main: Verlag Marxistische Blätter.

Deppe, Frank and Werner Goldschmidt 2011, 'Zur Geschichte des politischen Denkens im 20. Jahrhundert', *Z. Zeitschrift Marxistische Erneuerung* 22, no. 87, pp. 80–118.

Diers, Andreas 2006, *Arbeiterbewegung, Demokratie, Staat. Wolfgang Abendroth: Leben und Werk, 1906–1948*, Hamburg: VSA.

Dörre, Klaus 1987, *Risikokapitalismus. Zur Kritik von Ulrich Becks 'Weg in eine andere Moderne'*, Marburg: Verlag Arbeiterbewegung und Gesellschaftswissenschaft.

Dörre, Klaus, Stephan Lessenich and Hartmut Rosa 2015 [2009], *Sociology, Capitalism, Critique*, translated by Jan-Peter Herrmann and Loren Balhorn, London: Verso.

Drury, Shadia B. 1999, *Leo Strauss and the American Right*, Basingstoke: Palgrave-Macmillan.

Drury, Shadia B. 2005, *The Political Ideas of Leo Strauss*, updated edition, Basingstoke: Palgrave-Macmillan.

Dutschke, Rudi 2003, *Jeder hat sein Leben lang ganz zu leben: Die Tagebücher 1963–1979*, Cologne: Kiepenheuer & Witsch.

Eicker-Wolf, Kai et al. 2001, 'Zwischen Keynesianismus und Institutionalismus. Geschichte und Programm der Forschungsgruppe Politische Ökonomie', *Politik und Wissenschaft. 50 Jahre Politikwissenschaft in Marburg*, edited by Wolfgang Hecker et al., pp. 285–90.

Engels, Friedrich 1987 [1883], 'Dialectics of Nature', *Marx and Engels Collected Works, Vol. 25*, London: Lawrence & Wishart, pp. 313–490.

Fachbeirat des Fachbereichs Gesellschaftswissenschaften 1979, untitled resolution, 19 April.

Fichter, Tilmann and Siegward Lönnendonker 2007 [1977], *Kleine Geschichte des SDS. Der Deutsche Sozialistische Studentenbund von Helmut Schmidt bis Rudi Dutschke*, 4th revised edition, Essen: Klartext.

Fischer-Lescano, Andreas, Joachim Perels and Thilo Scholle (eds.) 2012, *Der Staat der Klassengesellschaft. Rechts- und Sozialstaatlichkeit bei Wolfgang Abendroth*, Baden-Baden: Nomos.

Flechtheim, Ossip K., Wolfgang Rudzio, Fritz Vilmar and Manfred Wilke 1980, *Der Marsch der DKP durch die Institutionen. Sowjet-marxistische Einflußstrategien und Ideologien*, Frankfurt am Main: Fischer.

Frankfurter Rundschau 1979, various documents and reports on the *Gewerkschaftsgeschichte* controversy published on 2, 3, 4, 5 January.

Frankfurter Rundschau 1979, 'Wie lässt sich Geschichtsschreibung im DKP-Stil messen?', *Frankfurter Rundschau*, 11 April, p. 10 f.

Freier Zusammenschluss von StudentInnenschaften (fzs) 2006, 'Kontroverse um Helmut Schmidt in Marburg', www.fzs.de/news/32846.html.

von Freyberg, Jutta (ed.) 1973, *Protokoll des Kongresses 'Wissenschaft und Demokratie'. Veranstaltet vom Bund demokratischer Wissenschaftler, von der Bundesassistentenkonferenz, der Gewerkschaft Erziehung und Wissenschaft sowie dem Verband Deutscher Studentenschaften am 1. und 2. Juli in Marburg*, Cologne: Pahl-Rugenstein.

von Freyberg, Jutta, Georg Fülberth, Jürgen Harrer, Bärbel Hebel-Kunze, Heinz-Gerd Hofschen, Erich Ott and Gerhard Stuby 1975, *Geschichte der deutschen Sozialdemokratie 1863–1975. Mit einem Vorwort von Wolfgang Abendroth*, Cologne: Pahl-Rugenstein.

von Freyberg, Jutta 1989, *Geschichte der deutschen Sozialdemokratie von 1863 bis zur Gegenwart*, 3rd revised and expanded edition, Cologne: Pahl-Rugenstein.

Freyer, Hans 1931, *Revolution von rechts*, Jena: Diederichs.

Fülberth, Georg 1982, *Geschichte der Bundesrepublik in Quellen und Dokumenten*, Cologne: Pahl-Rugenstein.

Fülberth, Georg 1984, 'Geschichte der Arbeiterbewegung in "Das Argument"', *Marxismus – Ideologie – Politik*, edited by Hans Heinz Holz et al., pp. 118–26.

Fülberth, Georg 1991, *Sieben Anstrengungen, den vorläufigen Endsieg des Kapitalismus zu begreifen*, Hamburg: Konkret.

Fülberth, Georg 1993, *Eröffnungsbilanz des gesamtdeutschen Kapitalismus: Vom Spätsozialismus zur nationalen Restauration*, Hamburg: konkret.

Fülberth, Georg 1994, *Der große Versuch. Geschichte der kommunistischen Bewegung und der sozialistischen Staaten*, Cologne: PapyRossa.

Fülberth, Georg 1997, 'Mein Marburg. Bericht aus einem Städtchen mit zwei Realitäten', *Die Zeit* 40, 26 September.

Fülberth, Georg 1999a, *Berlin–Bonn–Berlin. Deutsche Geschichte seit 1945*, Cologne: PapyRossa.

Fülberth, Georg 1999b, 'Marxismus Emeritus. Die Vertreter des Historischen Materialismus an den deutschen Universitäten gehen in Rente', *Die Zeit* 30, 22 July.

Fülberth, Georg 2005, *G Strich – Kleine Geschichte des Kapitalismus*, 2nd revised edition, Cologne: PapyRossa.

Fülberth, Georg 2007, *Finis Germaniae. Deutsche Geschichte seit 1945*, Cologne: PapyRossa.

Fülberth, Georg 2010, *Sozialismus*, Cologne: PapyRossa.

Fülberth, Georg 2012, *Geschichte der BRD*, Cologne: PapyRossa.

Fülberth, Georg 2018 [2010], *Kapitalismus*, Cologne: PapyRossa.

Fülberth, Georg and Jürgen Harrer 1974, *Die deutsche Sozialdemokratie 1890–1933*, Darmstadt and Neuwied: Luchterhand.

Gehrke, Bernd and Gern-Rainer Horn (eds.) 2018, *1968 und die Arbeiter: Studien zum 'proletarischen Mai' in Europa*, Hamburg: VSA.

Gerns, Willi and Robert Steigerwald 1973, *Probleme der Strategie des antimonopolistischen Kampfes*, Frankfurt am Main: Verlag Marxistische Blätter.

Görtemaker, Manfred 1999, *Geschichte der Bundesrepublik Deutschland. Von der Gründung bis zu Gegenwart*, Munich: C.H. Beck.

Gorz, André 1967 [1964], *Strategy for Labor. A Radical Proposal*, translated by Martin A. Nicolaus and Victoria Ortiz, Boston: Beacon Press.

Gramsci, Antonio 1967, *Philosophie der Praxis. Eine Auswahl*, edited and translated by Christian Riechers with a foreword by Wolfgang Abendroth, Frankfurt am Main: S. Fischer.

Grebing, Helga 1979, '"Eine große wissenschaftliche und pädagogische Leistung"? Bemerkungen zu dem Buch von Deppe, Fülberth, Harrer (Hg.): Geschichte der deutschen Gewerkschaftsbewegung', *Gewerkschaftliche Monatshefte* 30 (4), pp. 204–22.

Greven, Michael, and Gerd van de Moetter 1981, 'Vita Constructa. Ein Versuch, die Wahrnehmung von Heinz Maus mit seinem Werk in Einklang zu bringen', *Die Traumhölle des Justemilieu. Erinnerungen und die Aufgaben der Kritischen Theorie*, edited by Michael Greven and Gerd van de Moetter, Frank am Main: EVA, pp. 7–41.

Habermas, Jürgen 1966, 'Partisanenprofessor im Lande der Mitläufer. Marburger Ordinarius wird am 2. Mai sechzig Jahre alt', *Die Zeit*, 26 April.

Habermas, Jürgen 1968, 'Die Scheinrevolution und ihre Kinder. Sechs Thesen über Taktik, Ziele und Situationsanalysen der oppositionellen Jugend', *Die Linke antwortet Habermas*, edited by Wolfgang Abendroth et al., pp. 1–15.

Habermas, Jürgen 1975 [1973], *Legitimation Crisis*, translated by Thomas McCarthy, London: Heinemann.

Habermas, Jürgen 1984 [1981], *The Theory of Communicative Action, Volume One: Reason and the Rationalization of Society*, translated by Hans Joas, Boston: Beacon.

Habermas, Jürgen 1990 'What Does Socialism Mean Today? The Rectifying Revolution and the Need for New Thinking on the Left', *New Left Review* (1) 183, pp. 3–21.

Habermas, Jürgen 1991 [1962], *The Structural Transformation of the Public Sphere. An Inquiry into a Category of Bourgeois Society*, translated by Thomas Burger, Cambridge, MA: MIT Press.

Habermas, Jürgen 1998, '"Meine Damen und Herren ..."', *Frankfurter Schule und Studentenbewegung. Von der Flaschenpost zum Molotowcocktail 1946–1995*, edited Wolfgang Kraushaar, Hamburg: Rogner & Bernhard, p. 254.

Hahn, Erich 1968, *Historischer Materialismus und marxistische Soziologie*, Berlin (GDR): Dietz.

Halberstadt, Heiner 2012, 'Ein Leben für eine freundliche Welt', *Sozialismus* 39 (3), pp. 53–5.

Harrer, Jürgen 1973, *Die mexikarische Revolution 1910–1917*, Cologne: Pahl-Rugenstein.

Haug, Wolfgang Fritz 1983, 'Krise oder Dialektik des Marxismus?', *Aktualisierung Marx, Argument Sonderband 100*, edited by Detlev Albers, Elmar Altvater and Wolfgang Fritz Haug, Berlin: Argument, pp. 8–34.

Haug, Wolfgang Fritz 1985–7, *Pluraler Marxismus*, 2 volumes, Hamburg: Argument.

Haug, Wolfgang Fritz 1989, *Gorbatschow: Versuch über den Zusammenhang seiner Gedanken*, Hamburg: Argument,

Hecker, Wolfgang 1999, 'Ideologiekritik, Gesellschaftslehre und Sozialökonomie', *Werner Hofmann. Gesellschaftslehre in praktischer Absicht*, edited by Herbert Claas et al., Marburg: BdWi-Verlag, pp. 107–23.

Hecker, Wolfgang, Joachim Klein and Hans Karl Rupp (eds.) 2001, *Politik und Wissenschaft. 50 Jahre Politikwissenschaft in Marburg, Band 1: Zur Geschichte des Instituts*, Münster: Lit.

Heigl, Richard 2008, *Oppositionspolitik. Wolfgang Abendroth und die Entstehung der Neuen Linken (1950–1968)*, Hamburg: Argument.

Heither, Dietrich and Adelheid Schulze 2015, *Die Morde von Mechterstädt 1920. Zur Geschichte rechtsradikaler Gewalt in Deutschland*, Berlin: Metropol.

Henning, Klaus 2006, *Politische Intellektuelle in den USA und der 'Neue Imperialismus'*, Cologne: Neuer ISP Verlag.

Hilferding, Rudolf 1982 [1924], 'Probleme der Zeit', *Zwischen den Stühlen oder die Unvereinbarkeit von Theorie und Praxis. Schriften Rudolf Hilferdings 1904–1940*, edited by Cora Stephan, Berlin and Bonn: Dietz, pp. 166–81.

Hitzer, Bettina and Thomas Welskopp (eds.) 2010, *Die Bielefelder Sozialgeschichte.*

Klassische Texte zu einem geschichtswissenschaftlichen Programm und seinen Kontroversen, Bielefeld: transcript.

Hochhuth, Ralf 2006 [1963], *The Deputy*, translated by Clara Winston and Richard Winston, New York: Grove.

Hofmann, Werner 1956, *Die Arbeitsverfassung der Sowjetunion*, Berlin: Duncker & Humblot.

Hofmann, Werner 1959, 'Zum Gesellschaftsbild der Nationalökonomie von heute', *Kölner Zeitschrift für Soziologie und Sozialpsychologie* 29, pp. 682–98.

Hofmann, Werner 1961, *Gesellschaftslehre als Ordnungsmacht. Die Werturteilsfrage – heute*, Berlin: Duncker & Humblot.

Hofmann, Werner 1969a, *Grundelemente der Wirtschaftsgesellschaft. Ein Leitfaden für Lehrende*, Reinbek bei Hamburg: Rowohlt.

Hofmann, Werner 1969b [1967], *Stalinismus und Antikommunismus. Zur Soziologie des Ost-West-Konflikts*, Frankfurt am Main: Suhrkamp.

Hofmann, Werner 1970a, *Abschied vom Bürgertum: Essays und Reden*, Frankfurt am Main: Suhrkamp.

Hofmann, Werner 1970b, 'Zur Soziologie der Studentenrevolte', *Abschied vom Bürgertum*, pp. 77–91.

Hofmann, Werner 1971a, 'Das Aufbegehren der Studenten', *Abschied vom Bürgertum*, pp. 41–48.

Hofmann, Werner 1971b, 'Das Elend der Nationalökonomie', *Abschied vom Bürgertum*, pp. 117–40.

Hofmann, Werner 1971c [1962], *Ideengeschichte der sozialen Bewegung*, Berlin and New York: de Gruyter.

Hofmann, Werner (ed.) 1971d [1964], *Sozialökonomische Studientexte, Band 1: Wert- und Preislehre*, 2nd edition, Berlin: Duncker & Humblot.

Hofmann, Werner (ed.) 1971e [1966], *Sozialökonomische Studientexte, Band 3: Theorie der Wirtschaftsentwicklung. Vom Merkantilismus bis zur Gegenwart*, Berlin: Duncker & Humblot.

Hofmann, Werner 1971f [1968], *Universität, Ideologie, Gesellschaft. Beiträge zur Wissenschaftssoziologie*, Frankfurt am Main: Suhrkamp.

Hofmann, Werner (ed.) 1986 [1965], *Sozialökonomische Studientexte, Band 2: Einkommenstheorie. Vom Merkantilismus bis zur Gegenwart*, Berlin: Duncker & Humblot.

Hofmann, Werner 1988, *Industriesoziologie für Arbeiter. Eine Einführung*, edited by Herbert Claas and Rainer Rilling. Afterword by Alfred Oppolzer, Heilbronn: Distel.

Hofmann, Werner and Heinz Maus (eds.) 1967, *Notstandsordnung und Gesellschaft. Zehn Vorträge*, Reinbek bei Hamburg: Rowohlt.

Hofmann-Göttig, Joachim 1999, 'Werner Hofmann – Wir, die wir ihn verehrt, bewundert, gefürchtet und kritisiert haben, werden ihn nicht vergessen', *Werner Hoffmann*, edited by Herbert Claas et al., pp. 27–38.

Holz, Hans Heinz 1984, 'Vom vermeintlichen Untergang und der wundersamen Rettung der Philosophie durch Wolfgang Fritz Haug', *Marxismus – Ideologie – Politik*, pp. 28–53.

Holz, Hans Heinz, Thomas Metscher, Josef Schleifstein and Robert Steigerwald (eds.) 1984, *Marxismus – Ideologie – Politik. Krise des Marxismus oder Krise des 'Arguments'?*, Frankfurt am Main: Verlag Marxistische Blätter.

Holzhey, Helmut 1994, *Ethischer Sozialismus. Zur politischen Philosophie des Neukantianismus*, Frankfurt am Main: Suhrkamp.

Holzner, Burkart and John Marx 1979, *The Knowledge System in Society*, Boston: Allyn & Bacon.

Honneth, Axel 2017, *The Idea of Socialism: Towards a Renewal*, translated by Joseph Ganahl, Cambridge: Polity.

Horkheimer, Max and Theodor W. Adorno 1997 [1944], *Dialectic of Enlightenment*, translated by John Cumming, London: Verso.

Huster, Ernst-Ulrich et al. 1972, *Determinanten der westdeutschen Restauration 1945–1949*, Frankfurt am Main. Suhrkamp.

Hüttig, Christoph and Lutz Raphael 1992, 'Der "Partisanenprofessor" und sein Erbe. Wolfgang Abendroth und die "wissenschaftliche Politik" der "Marburger Schule(n)" im Umfeld der westdeutschen Politikwissenschaft 1951–1975', *Sprache und Kultur in der Demokratie. Hans Gerd Schumann zum Gedenken*, edited by Dieter Emig, Christoph Hüttig and Lutz Raphael, Frankfurt am Main: Lang, pp. 23–70.

Institut für Marxistische Studien und Forschungen 1969, *Die Septemberstreiks. Darstellung, Analyse, Dokumente*, Frankfurt am Main: IMSF.

Institut für Marxistische Studien und Forschungen 1973, *Klassen- und Sozialstruktur der BRD 1950–1970. Theorie, Diskussion, Sozialstatistische Analyse, Teil I: Klassenstruktur und Klassentheorie. Theoretische Grundlagen und Diskussion*, edited by Heinz Jung, Christof Kievenheim and Margarete Tjaden-Steinhauer, Frankfurt am Main: IMSF.

Institut für Marxistische Studien und Forschungen 1974, *Klassen- und Sozialstruktur der BRD 1950–1970, Teil II: Sozialstatistische Analyse, Erster Halbband*, edited by Hans Burbaum et al., Frankfurt am Main: IMSF.

Institut für Marxistische Studien und Forschungen 1975, *Klassen- und Sozialstruktur der BRD 1950–1970*, edited by Heinz Jung with Christof Kievenheim and Dorlies Pollmann, Frankfurt am Main: IMSF.

Institut für Marxistische Studien und Forschungen 1988, *IMSF 1968–1988. Arbeitsgebiete, Bibliographie, Veranstaltungsübersicht*, Frankfurt am Main: IMSF.

Jäger, Lorenz 2014, 'Als Marx an der Uni war', *Frankfurter Allgemeine Zeitung*, 11 June.

Jay, Martin 1973, *The Dialectical Imagination. A History of the Frankfurt School and the Institute of Social Research, 1923–1950*, London: Heinemann.

Jung, Heinz 1994, 'Abendroth-Schule', *Historisch-Kritisches Wörterbuch des Marxismus*, Vol. 1, edited by Wolfgang Fritz Haug, Hamburg: Argument, pp. 21–9.

Jung, Heinz et al. (ed.) 1971, *BRD–DDR. Vergleich der Gesellschaftssysteme*, Cologne: Pahl-Rugenstein.

Kaestner, Jürgen 1984, *Personalbibliographie Heinz Maus (1911–1978). Ein Beitrag zur Geschichte der deutschen Soziologie*, Berlin: Wissenschaftlicher Autoren-Verlag.

Kammler, Jörg, 1968, 'Gegenstand und Methode der politischen Wissenschaft', *Einführung in die politische Wissenschaft*, edited by Wolfgang Abendroth and Kurt Lenk, Bern: Francke, pp. 9–24.

Kammler, Jörg, 1974, *Politische Theorie von Georg Lukács. Struktur und historischer Praxisbezug bis 1929*, Darmstadt and Neuwied: Luchterhand.

Kammler, Jörg, 2001, 'Abendroth-Schule und die "Einführung in die Politische Wissenschaft"', *Politik und Wissenschaft*, edited by Wolfgang Hecker et al., pp. 143–53.

Kammler, Jörg, Hartfried Krause, Dietfried Krause-Vilmar and Paul Oehlke 1979, 'Kampagne oder Kritik? Zur Diskussion über das Buch "Geschichte der deutschen Gewerkschaftsbewegung"', *Das Argument. Zeitschrift für Philosophie und Sozialwissenschaften* 21 (117), pp. 686–706.

Kirchheimer, Otto 1966, 'The Transformation of the Western Party Systems', *Political Parties and Political Development*, edited by Joseph LaPalombara and Myron Wiener, Princeton, NJ: Princeton University Press, pp. 117–200.

Kofler, Leo 1984, *Der Konservatismus – zwischen Dekadenz und Reaktion*, Hamburg: VSA.

Köhler, Otto 1989, *... und heute die ganze Welt: Die Geschichte der IG Farben und ihrer Väter*, Bremen: Rasch & Röhring.

Köhler, Otto 1996, *Hitler ging – sie blieben: Der deutsche Nachkrieg in 16 Exempeln*, Hamburg: konkret.

Kraushaar, Wolfgang (ed.) 1998, *Frankfurter Schule und Studentenbewegung. Von der Flaschenpost zum Molotowcocktail. Band 2: Dokumente*, Hamburg: Rogner & Bernhard.

Krysmanski, H.J. and Peter Marwedel (eds.) 1975, *Die Krise in der Soziologie. Ein kritischer Reader zum 17. Deutschen Soziologentag*, Cologne: Pahl-Rugenstein.

Kuda, Rudolf 1970, *Arbeiterkontrolle in Großbritannien. Theorie und Praxis*, Frankfurt am Main: Suhrkamp.

Kühnl, Reinhard 1966, *Die nationalsozialistische Linke 1925–1930*, Meisenheim am Glan: Hain.

Kühnl, Reinhard, Rainer Rilling and Christine Sager 1969, *Die NPD. Struktur, Ideologie und Funktion einer neofaschistischen Partei*, Frankfurt am Main: Suhrkamp.

Kühnl, Reinhard 1971, *Formen bürgerlicher Herrschaft. Liberalismus, Faschismus*, Reinbek bei Hamburg: Rowohlt.

Kühnl, Reinhard (ed.) 1975, *Der deutsche Faschismus in Quellen und Dokumenten*, Cologne: Pahl-Rugenstein.

Kühnl, Reinhard (ed.) 1987, *Streit ums Geschichtsbild. Die 'Historiker-Debatte'. Darstellung, Dokumentation, Kritik*, Cologne: Pahl-Rugenstein.

Kühnl, Reinhard 1988 [1983], *Der Faschismus. Ursachen, Herrschaftsstruktur, Aktualität. Eine Einführung*, Heilbronn: Distel-Verlag.

Kühnl, Reinhard 1990, *Gefahr von rechts. Vergangenheit und Gegenwart der extremen Rechten*, edited by Karen Schönwälder, Heilbronn: Distel-Verlag.

Kühnl, Reinhard 2001, 'Biographischer Nachtrag', *Politik und Wissenschaft*, edited by Wolfgang Hecker et al., pp. 216–20.

Kuratorium der Rosa-Luxemburg-Stiftung 2008, 'Nachruf auf Peter von Oertzen', *Utopie kreativ. Diskussion sozialistischer Alternativen* 211, pp. 466–7.

Kurz, Robert 1999, *Schwarzbuch Kapitalismus. Abgesang auf die Marktwirtschaft*, Frankfurt am Main: Eichborn.

Kuzin, Aleksandr Avramievich et al. (eds.) 1972, *Die gegenwärtige wissenschaftlich-technische Revolution: eine historische Untersuchung*, Berlin (GDR): Akademie-Verlag.

Lambrecht, Lars, Karl Hermann Tjaden and Margarete Tjaden-Steinhauer 1998, *Gesellschaft von Olduvai bis Uruk. Soziologische Exkursionen*, Vol. 1 of *Studien zu Subsistenz*, Kassel: Jenior and Pressler.

Lange, Hellmuth 1972, *Wissenschaftlich-technische Intelligenz. Neue Bourgeoisie oder neue Arbeiterklasse. Eine sozialwissenschaftliche Untersuchung zum Verhältnis von sozialer Differenzierung und politischem Bewußtsein*, Cologne: Pahl-Rugenstein.

Lehmann, Hans Georg 1970, *Die Agrarfrage in der Theorie und Praxis der deutschen und internationalen Sozialdemokratie*, Tübingen: JCB Mohr.

Lenk, Kurt 1986, 'In memoriam Wolfgang Abendroth – 2. Mai 1906–15. September 1985', *Kölner Zeitschrift für Soziologie und Sozialpsychologie* 38, pp. 195–7.

Leonhard, Wolfgang 1979 [1955], *Child of the Revolution*, translated by C.M. Woodhouse, London: Ink Links.

Lepenies, Wolf (ed.) 1981, *Geschichte der Soziologie. Studien zu ihrer kognitiven, sozialen und historischen Identität. Band 2, Teil 3: Theoriegruppen, Schulen und Institutionalisierungsprozesse*, Frankfurt am Main: Suhrkamp.

Lübbe, Hermann 1974 [1964], *Politische Philosophie in Deutschland. Studien zu ihrer Geschichte*, Munich: Deutscher Taschenbuch.

Luhmann, Niklas 1995 [1984], *Social Systems*, translated by John Bednartz, Jr with Dirk Baecker, Stanford, CA: Stanford University Press.

Lukács, Georg and Werner Hofmann 1991, *Ist der Sozialismus noch zu retten? Briefwechsel*, Budapest: Hungarian Academy of Social Sciences.

Luther, Wilhelm Nikolai 1976, 'Vom Mißbrauch der Politischen Wissenschaft. Marxistisch-Leninistisches an der Universität Marburg', *Die politische Meinung*, July–August, pp. 81–94.

Machtan, Lothar and Dietrich Milles 1980, *Die Klassensymbiose von Junkertum und Bourgeoisie: Zum Verhältnis von gesellschaftlicher und politischer Herrschaft in Preußen-Deutschland 1850–1878/79*, Frankfurt am Main: Ullstein.

Magri, Lucio 2011, *The Tailor of Ulm*, translated by Patrick Camiller, London: Verso.

Mallet, Serge 1972 [1963], *Die neue Arbeiterklasse*, translated by Thomas Hartmann, Neuwied and Berlin: Luchterhand.

Mallet, Serge 1975 [1963], *The New Working Class*, edited and translated by Dick Howard and Dean Savage, Nottingham: Spokesman.

Mandel, Ernest 1968 [1962], *Marxist Economic Theory*, Vol. 1 & 2, translated by Brian Pearce, New York and London: Monthly Review Press.

Marcuse, Herbert 1965, 'Industrialization and Capitalism', *New Left Review* I (30), pp. 3–17.

Marcuse, Herbert 2007 [1964], *One-Dimensional Man. Studies in the Ideology of Advanced Industrial Society*, London and New York: Routledge.

Marcuse, Herbert 2014 [1969], 'Revolutionary Subject and Self-Government', *The Collected Papers of Herbert Marcuse, Volume 6: Marxism, Revolution and Utopia*, edited by Douglas Kellner and Clayton Pierce, London and New York: Routledge.

Marx, Karl 1987 [1866], 'Marx to Engels, 7 July 1866', *Collected Works of Marx and Engels, Vol. 42*, London: Lawrence & Wishart, pp. 289–92.

Marx, Karl 1993 [1939], *Grundrisse. Foundations of the Critique of Political Economy (Rough Draft)*, translated by Martin Nicolaus, London: Penguin.

Maus, Heinz, 1956, 'Geschichte der Soziologie', *Handbuch der Soziologie*, edited by Werner Ziegenfuß, Stuttgart: F. Enke, pp. 1–120.

Maus, Heinz, 1959, 'Bericht über die Soziologie in Deutschland 1933 bis 1945', *Kölner Zeitschrift für Soziologie und Sozialpsychologie* 11, pp. 72–99.

Maus, Heinz, 1973 [1967], 'Zur Vorgeschichte der empirischen Sozialforschung', *Handbuch der empirischen Sozialforschung, Band 1: Geschichte und Grundprobleme*, edited by René König, 3rd edition, Stuttgart: Ferdinand Enke, pp. 21–56.

Maus, Heinz, 1981a, 'Bemerkungen zu Comte (Für Theodor W. Adorno zum 50. Geburtstag)', *Die Traumhölle des Justenmilieu*, pp. 349–66.

Maus, Heinz, 1981b, 'Comte oder Marx', *Die Traumhölle des Justenmilieu*, pp. 300–5.

Maus, Heinz, 1981c, *Die Traumhölle des Justemilieu. Erinnerungen und die Aufgaben der Kritischen Theorie*, edited by Michael Th. Greven and Gerd van de Moetter, Frankfurt am Main: Europäische Verlagsanstalt.

Maus, Heinz, 1981d, 'Marx um seine Wahrheit gebracht', *Die Traumhölle des Justemilieu*, pp. 306–15.

Maus, Heinz, 1981e, 'Umstrittener Marx', *Die Traumhölle des Justenmilieu*, pp. 367–83.

Maus, Heinz, 1998 [1956], *A Short History of Sociology*, Abingdon: Routledge.

Meyer, Gert 1999, 'Sozialismus – Stalinismus', *Werner Hofmann*, edited by Herbert Claas et al., pp. 153–76.

Mies, Thomas ad Karl Hermann Tjaden (eds.) 2009, *Gesellschaft, Herrschaft und Bewußtsein. Symbolische Gewalt und das Elend der Zivilisation. Studien zur Subsistenz, Familie, Politik*, Vol. 4, Kassel: Verlag Winfried Jenior.

Mittag, Jürgen and Georg Ismar (eds.) 2009, ¿'El pueblo unido'? Soziale Bewegungen und politischer Protest in der Geschichte Lateinamerikas, Münster: Westfälisches Dampfboot.

Mooser, Josef 1984, Arbeiterleben in Deutschland 1900–1970. Klassenlage, Kultur, Politik, Frankfurt am Main: Suhrkamp.

Mück, Josef Franz 2001, 'Der Beitrag von Wolfgang Abendroth zu Theorie und Praxis der politischen Bildung', Politik und Wissenschaft, edited by Wolfgang Hecker et al., pp. 153–62.

Münkler, Herfried 1982, Machiavelli. Die Begründung des politischen Denkens der Neuzeit aus der Krise der Republik Florenz, Frankfurt am Main: Fischer.

Nordmann, Jürgen 2005, Der lange Marsch zum Neoliberalismus: Vom roten Wien zum freien Markt – Popper und Hayek im Diskurs, Hamburg: VSA.

Oertzen, Peter von 1963, Betriebsräte in der Novemberrevolution. Eine politikwissenschaftliche Untersuchung über Ideengehalt und Struktur der betrieblichen und wirtschaftlichen Arbeiterräte in der deutschen Revolution 1918/19, Düsseldorf: Droste.

Opitz, Reinhard 1999, Liberalismus – Faschismus – Integration, Edition in drei Bänden, Band 2: Faschismus, Marburg: BdWi-Verlag.

Panitch, Leo 1976, Social Democracy and Industrial Militancy, Cambridge. Cambridge University Press.

Panitch, Leo and Sam Gindin 2012, The Making of Global Capitalism: The Political Economy of the American Empire, London: Verso.

Perels, Joachim 2006, 'Zur Aktualität der Sozialstaatsinterpretation von Wolfgang Abendroth', 'Antagonistische Gesellschaft und politische Demokratie'. Zur Aktualität von Wolfgang Abendroth, edited by Hans-Jürgen Urban, Michael Buckmiller and Frank Deppe, Hamburg: VSA, pp. 101–10.

Peter, Lothar 1972, Literarische Intelligenz und Klassenkampf. 'Die Aktion' 1911–1932, Cologne: Pahl-Rugenstein.

Peter, Lothar 1980, 'Überlegungen zur RGO-Politik am Ende der Weimarer Republik', Marxismus und Arbeiterbewegung, edited by Frank Deppe, Willi Gerns and Heinz Jung, pp. 40–55.

Peter, Lothar 1984, 'Die Ideologie des "Arguments" in der Krise. Anmerkungen zu W.F. Haug: Krise oder Dialektik des Marxismus?', Marxismus – Ideologie – Politik, edited by Hans Heinz Holz et al., pp. 54–73.

Peter, Lothar 2001, 'Warum und wie betreibt man Soziologiegeschichte?', Jahrbuch für Soziologiegeschichte 1997/98, edited by Carsten Klingemann et al., Opladen: Leske & Budrich, pp. 9–64.

Peter, Lothar 2003, 'Periode der Katastrophen und antagonistische Diskurse', Sozialismus 30 (12), pp. 27–31.

Peter, Lothar 2006, 'Der Kampf gegen das CPE. Neue Aspekte der Protestbewegung in Frankreich', Z. Zeitschrift marxistische Erneuerung 17/66, pp. 61–71.

Peter, Lothar 2007, 'Marburger und Frankfurter Schule im Vergleich', *Das Argument. Zeitschrift für Philosophie und Sozialwissenschaften* 49/269, pp. 98–111.

Peter, Lothar 2011, 'Soziologische Kapitalismuskritik "back in". Symposiumsbeitrag zu Klaus Dörre / Stephan Lessenich / Hartmut Rosa, 2009: Soziologie – Kapitalismus – Kritik. Eine Debatte unter Mitarbeit von Thomas Barth, Frankfurt am Main: Suhrkamp', *Soziologische Revue* 34, pp. 145–52.

Peter, Lothar 2012, 'Für einen Typ der "Intellektuellen von unten"', *Gegen den Neoliberalismus andenken. Linke Wissenspolitik und sozialistische Perspektiven. Für Rainer Rilling*, edited by Alex Demirović and Christina Kaindl, Hamburg: VSA, pp. 51–64.

Peter, Lothar 2019, 'Kapitalismuskritik und sozialistisches Engagement. Die sozialwissenschaftliche Marburger Schule (1951 bis Anfang der 2000er Jahre)', *Soziologische Denkschulen in der Bundesrepublik Deutschland*, edited by Joachim Fischer and Stephan Mobius, Wiesbaden: SpringerVS, pp. 39–123.

Plé, Bernhard 1990, *Wissenschaft und säkulare Mission. 'Amerikanische Sozialwissenschaft' im politischen Sendungsbewußtsein der USA und im geistigen Aufbau der Bundesrepublik Deutschland*, Stuttgart: Klett-Cotta.

Popitz, Heinrich 1953, *Der entfremdete Mensch. Zeitkritik und Geschichtsphilosophie des jungen Marx*, Basel: Verlag für Recht und Gesellschaft.

Raphael, Lutz, 1997, '"Annales"-Schule', *Handbuch der Geschichtsdidaktik*, edited by Klaus Bergmann et al., 5th revised edition, Seelze-Velber: Kallmeyer, pp. 184–97.

Recker, Marie-Luise 2009, *Geschichte der Bundesrepublik Deutschland*, 3rd revised and expanded edition, Munich: C.H. Beck.

Reich, Wilhelm 1980 [1933], *The Mass Psychology of Fascism*, edited by Mary Higgins and Chester M. Raphael, MD, New York: Farrar, Straus and Giroux.

Rilling, Rainer 1975, *Theorie und Soziologie der Wissenschaft. Zur Entwicklung in BRD und DDR*, Frankfurt am Main: Fischer.

Ringer, Fritz K. 1990 [1969], *The Decline of the German Mandarins. The German Academic Community, 1980–1933*, Hanover and London: Wesleyan University Press.

Römer, Peter 1986, *Recht und Demokratie bei Wolfgang Abendroth*, Marburg: Verlag für Arbeiterbewegung und Gesellschaftswissenschaft.

Römer, Peter 1989, *Im Namen des Grundgesetzes. Eine Streitschrift für die Demokratie*, Hamburg: VSA.

Römer, Peter 2001, 'Demokratie als inhaltliches Prinzip der gesamten Gesellschaft. Wolfgang Abendroths Beitrag zur Verteidigung demokratischer Positionen in der Bundesrepublik Deutschland', *Wolfgang Abendroth*, edited by Friedrich-Martin Balzer et al., pp. 49–72.

Rosa-Luxemburg-Club (ed.) 2013, *Marburg rauf und runter. Stadtspaziergänge durch Geschichte und Gegenwart*, Marburg: BdWi-Verlag.

Rosenbaum, Heidi 1973, *Familie als Gegenstruktur zur Gesellschaft. Zur Kritik grundlegender Ansätze der westdeutschen Familiensoziologie*, Stuttgart: F. Enke.

Rosenberg, Arthur 1939, *Democracy and Socialism. A Contribution to the Political History of the Last 150 Years*, translated by George Rosen, London: G. Bell & Sons.

Rupp, Hans Karl 2001, 'Die Berufung Wolfgang Abendroths nach Marburg.' Politische Wissenschaft als politische Erziehung', *Politik und Wissenschaft*, edited by Wolfgang Hecker et al., pp. 64–76.

Salomon, David 2012, 'Traditionalität und Aktualität (in) der Soziologie von Heinz Maus. Ein Versuch zur Kritischen Theorie', *'... wenn die Stunde es zuläßt.' Zur Traditionalität und Aktualität kritischer Theorie*, edited by Malte Völk et al., pp. 85–105.

Sanbonmatsu, John 2004, *The Post-Modern Prince: Critical Theory, Left Strategy and the Making of a New Political Subject*, New York: Monthly Review Press.

Schäfer, Gerhard 2006, 'Das Marburger Dreigestirn: Wolfgang Abendroth – Heinz Maus – Werner Hofmann. Zur Vorgeschichte kritischer Gesellschaftswissenschaft in Marburg', *Soziologie als Gesellschaftskritik. Wider den Verlust einer aktuellen Tradition. Festschrift für Lothar Peter*, edited by Stephan Moebius and Gerhard Schäfer, Hamburg: VSA, pp. 44–71.

Schildt, Axel and Detlef Siegfried 2009, *Deutsche Kulturgeschichte. Die Bundesrepublik – 1945 bis zur Gegenwart*, Munich: Hanser.

Schmidt, Eberhard 1970, *Die verhinderte Neuordnung 1945–1952: Zur Auseinandersetzung um die Demokratisierung der Wirtschaft in den westlichen Besatzungszonen und in der Bundesrepublik Deutschland*, Frankfurt am Main: EVA.

Schmidt, Ute and Tilman Fichter 1971, *Der erzwungene Kapitalismus: Klassenkämpfe in den Westzonen 1945–1948*, West Berlin: Klaus Wagenbach Verlag.

Schöler, Uli 2001, 'Wolfgang Abendroth – Fragen an einen politischen Lebensweg', *Wolfgang Abendroth*, edited by Friedrich-Martin Balzer et al., pp. 11–46.

Schumann, Michael, Frank Gerlach, Albert Gschlössl and Petra Millhofer 1971, *Am Beispiel der Septemberstreiks – Anfang der Rekonstruktion der Arbeiterklasse? Eine empirische Untersuchung*, Frankfurt am Main: EVA.

Schütrumpf, Jörn, Ingar Solty and Uwe Sonnenberg 2018, 'Wer weitergeht, wird erschossen! Warum die soziale Revolution 1918/19 scheiterte', *LuXemburg: Gesellschaftsanalyse und linke Praxis* 10 (3), pp. 8–15.

Sieg, Ulrich 1994, *Aufstieg und Niedergang des Marburger Neukantianismus. Die Geschichte einer philosophischen Schulgemeinschaft*, Würzburg: Königshausen und Neumann.

Söllner, Alfons 1992, 'Kronjurist des Dritten Reiches – Das Bild Carl Schmitts in den Schriften der Emigranten', *Jahrbuch für Antisemitismusforschung*, Vol. 1, pp. 191–216.

Solty, Ingar 2008, 'The Historic Significance of the New German Left Party', *Socialism and Democracy* 22 (1), pp. 134.

Solty, Ingar 2015, 'Post-Fascist Continuity and Post-Communist Discontinuity in German Cinema', *Socialism and Democracy* 29 (1), pp. 43–72.

Solty, Ingar 2019, 'Talking About Power: The Crisis of the German Left', *Jacobin*, 5 January.

Sorg, Richard 2014, 'Lothar Peter, Marx an die Uni. *Die "Marburger Schule" – Geschichte, Probleme, Akteure'*, *Das Argument* 56 (309), pp. 604–9.

Sperber, Jonathan 2013, *Karl Marx. A Nineteenth-Century Life*, New York and London: Liverlight.

Sperling, Urte and Margarete Tjaden-Steinhauer 2004, *Gesellschaft von Tikal bis irgendwo. Europäische Gewaltherrschaft, gesellschaftliche Umbrüche, Ungleichheitsgesellschaften neben der Spur. Studien zur Subsistenz, Familie, Politik*, Vol. 3, Kassel: Verlag Winfried Jenior.

Steffen, Michael 2002, *Geschichten vom Trüffelschwein. Politik und Organisation des Kommunistischen Bundes 1971 bis 1991*, Berlin: Assoziation A.

Steinhauer, Margarete 1966, *Die politische Soziologie Auguste Comtes und ihre Differenzen zur liberalen Gesellschaftstheorie Condorcets*, Meisenheim am Glan: Hain.

Stephan, Cora (ed.) 1982, *Zwischen den Stühlen oder über die Unvereinbarkeit von Theorie und Praxis. Schriften Rudolf Hilferdings 1904–1940*, Berlin: Dietz.

Theimer, Walter 1960 [1950], *Der Marxismus. Lehre, Wirkung, Kritik*, Bern and Munich: Francke.

Tjaden, Karl Hermann 1964, *Struktur und Funktion der 'KPD-Opposition' (KPO). Eine organisationssoziologische Untersuchung zur 'Rechts'-Opposition im deutschen Kommunismus zur Zeit der Weimarer Republik*, Meisenheim am Glan: Hain.

Tjaden, Karl Hermann 1971a, 'Einleitung: Die Entwicklung des Begriffs des Sozialsystems als Entfaltung soziologischer Ideologie', *Soziale Systeme*, pp. 13–52.

Tjaden, Karl Hermann 1971b, 'Nachwort: Ansätze einer gesellschaftswissenschaftlichen Systemtheorie', *Soziale Systeme*, pp. 439–59.

Tjaden, Karl Hermann 1971c, *Soziale Systeme. Materialien zur Dokumentation und Kritik soziologischer Ideologie*, Neuwied and Berlin: Luchterhand.

Tjaden, Karl Hermann 1972, *Soziales System und sozialer Wandel. Untersuchungen zur Geschichte und Bedeutung zweier Begriffe*, Stuttgart: F. Enke.

Tjaden, Karl Hermann 1990, *Mensch – Gesellschaftsformation – Biosphäre. Über die gesellschaftliche Dialektik des Verhältnisses von Mensch und Natur*, Marburg: Verlag für Arbeiterbewegung und Gesellschaftswissenschaften.

Tjaden, Karl Hermann and Lothar Peter 2006, 'Wolfgang Abendroth heute – kann man von ihm noch etwas lernen?', *Sozialismus* (6), pp. 33–9.

Tjaden-Steinhauer, Margarete and Karl Hermann Tjaden 2001, *Gesellschaft von Rom bis Ffm. Ungleichheitsverhältnisse in West-Europa und die iberischen Eigenweg. Studien zur Subsistenz, Familie, Politik, Vol. 2*, Kassel: Verlag Winfried Jenior.

Thompson, E.P. 1978, *The Poverty of Theory and Other Essays*, London: Merlin.

Thompson, E.P. 2013 [1963], *The Making of the English Working Class*, London: Penguin.

Urban, Hans-Jürgen, Michael Buckmiller and Frank Deppe (eds.) 2006, 'Antagonistische

Gesellschaft und politische Demokratie'. Zur Aktualität von Wolfgang Abendroth, Hamburg: VSA.

Urban, Hans-Jürgen 2009, 'Die Mosaik-Linke. Vom Aufbruch der Gewerkschaften zur Erneuerung der Bewegung', *Blätter für deutsche und internationale Politik* 54 (5), pp. 71–8.

Vetter, Ernst Günter 1979, 'Die Roten sind auf dem Marsch. Zur kommunistischen Infiltration der Gewerkschaften', *Frankfurter Allgemeine Zeitung*, 21 April, p. 13.

Vilmar, Fritz, Wolfgang Rudzio and Manfred Wilke 1981, *Was heißt hier kommunistische Unterwanderung? Eine notwendige Analyse – und wie die Linke darauf reagiert*, Frankfurt am Main, Berlin, Vienna: Ullstein.

Vilmar, Fritz 1977, 'Parteihochschule in der Universität Marburg? Die Unterwanderungstaktik der Deutschen Kommunistischen Partei', *Sozialwissenschaft und Arbeitnehmerinteresse*, pp. 123–7.

Völk, Malte et al. (eds.) 2012, '... wenn die Stunde es zuläßt'. Zur Traditionalität und Aktualität kritischer Theorie*, Münster: Westfälisches Dampfboot.

Vorstand der Sektion Marburg des Bundes demokratischer Wissenschaftler (BdWi) (ed.) 1977, *Sozialwissenschaft und Arbeitnehmerinteresse. Die Auseinandersetzungen um den Fachbereich Gesellschaftswissenschaften der Universität Marburg*, Cologne: Pahl-Rugenstein.

Walpen, Bernhard 2004, *Die offenen Feinde und ihre Gesellschaft: Eine hegemonietheoretische Studie zur Mont Pèlerin Society*, Hamburg: VSA.

Weipert, Axel 2015, *Die zweite Revolution: Rätebewegung in Berlin 1919/1920*, Berlin: be.bra.

Weiß, Gerhard 2015, 'Marx in Marburg', *Blätter für deutsche und internationale Politik* 60 (5), pp. 121–3.

Weiss, Peter 2010 [1965], *The Investigation. Oratorio in 11 Cantos*, translated by Alexander Gross, London and New York: Marion Boyars.

Wesel, Uwe 1990, 'Innerlich erröten', *Kursbuch* 100, pp. 42–53.

Westdeutscher Rundfunk 2012 [1987], *Ein deutsches Schicksal: Wolfgang Abendroth* (DVD).

Wetter, Gustav A. 1966 [1962], *Soviet Ideology Today. Dialectical and Historical Materialism*, translated by Peter Heath, London: Heinemann.

Wetter, Gustav A. 1973 [1952], *Dialectical Materialism: A Historical and Systematic Survey of Philosophy in the Soviet Union*, translated by Peter Heath, Westport, CT: Greenwood Press.

Wippermann, Wolfgang 2009, *Dämonisierung durch Vergleich. DDR und Drittes Reich*, Berlin: Rotbuch.

Wiggershaus, Rolf 1995 [1986], *The Frankfurt School: Its History, Theories, and Political Significance*, translated by Michael Robertson, Cambridge, MA: MIT Press.

Wirsching, Andreas 2006, *Abschied vom Provisorium. Geschichte der Bundesrepublik Deutschland 1982–1990*, Munich: Deutsche Verlagsanstalt.

Wolf, Dorothee, Sabine Reiner and Kai Wolf-Eicker (eds.) 1999, *Auf der Suche nach dem Kompaß. Politische Ökonomie als Bahnsteigkarte fürs 21. Jahrhundert*, Cologne: PapyRossa.

Index

www.ingramcontent.com/pod-product-compliance
Lightning Source LLC
Chambersburg PA
CBHW070930030426
42336CB00014BA/2607